From Gail Ray, D.D.S.

"With the ongo[ing ...] society, Bob Mallinckr[odt's book opens doors to] alternative thinking."

From Steven Moore, Ph.D.

"Over the past 30 years or so Robert Mallinckrodt has developed, fine tuned, and practiced a philosophy of life that rejects the commonly accepted notions that humans are inherently imperfect beings, who must constantly strive to be more acceptable to society and God. Rather, with "NOBODY'S IMPERFECT," Robert argues that people must accept their inherent perfection so that they can overcome the insecurities, self-doubts, and hostilities that plague our world scene. The book describes in detail how significant experiences in Robert's life led him to discover this truth, discard past teachings, and achieve peace of mind. In doing so he offers the reader the chance to follow his footsteps to a happier life."

From Berlyn Brixner

"The significance of Mallinckrodt's Perfection-Now book is that it redirects our thinking in ways that increase our self-esteem, our pleasure of living, and our accomplishments at work. "He contrasts the Perfection-Now Position with our age-old imperfection-heritage, which leads to antagonism, hatred, revenge and vandalism."

(Berlyn Brixner was a photographer of explosions and an optical engineer at the Los Alamos Laboratory, 1943-1978. Brixner was photographer of the first Atomic Bomb Test, which was at the Alamogordo Bombing Range. Afterwards, he invented some of the fastest high-speed cameras for explosion research.)

A PERSONAL NOTE

Regardless of anything whatsoever, you are a perfect part of a perfect world and universe!

At this moment, just as you are, you have perfection now; and you have soul perfection now!

There is nothing that you must accept, believe, think, say or do that will make you any more perfect than you are now.

Universal perfection means universal equality!

The Perfection-Now Position is not a religion. There is nothing for you to join or contribute to.

Nevertheless, a realization of this valid concept will bring various benefits:

You can stop feeling inadequate and guilty for being the human creature that you are!

Feelings of self-doubt will vanish.

Awareness of high self-esteem increases.

R.G.M.

NOBODY'S IMPERFECT

NEW THINKING

FROM THE

PERFECTION-NOW POSITION

✱✱✱✱✱✱✱✱✱

ROBERT GEORGE MALLINCKRODT

THE PERFECTION-NOW STORY
VOLUME I

A SILVER CREST BOOK

FOR HAZEL AND FOR SHIRLEY
AND FOR CARLA

Cover Painting "Progress ?" by Hazel Brixner Mallinckrodt

ISBN: 0-9631888-0-1
Library of Congress Catalog Card Number: 91-68407

Copyright © 1991 by Robert George Mallinckrodt

All rights reserved. No part of this book may be used or reproduced in any manner without written permission except in the case of brief critical articles and reviews. For information address Silver Crest Publishing, Rt. 10 Box 305, Glenwood, New Mexico 88039

PRINTED IN THE UNITED STATES OF AMERICA

NOBODY'S IMPERFECT V

VOLUME I

THE PERFECTION-NOW STORY

CONTENTS

***

ACKNOWLEDGMENTS	VII
FOR A QUICK UNDERSTANDING	VIII
CHAPTER I ENLIGHTENMENT AT LAST	1
CHAPTER II THE PERFECTION-NOW POSITION	11
MAKING IT CLEAR	12
SIGNIFICANT FEATURES	17
NO COP-OUT	39
NOT A RELIGION	43
NO UTOPIAN FANTASY	50
CHAPTER III SOUL PERFECTION NOW	55
MYSTICAL OCCURRENCE AT SANTA MONICA	59

CONTENTS

SOUL INTERCOURSE	72
A NONRELIGIOUS GOD OR "X" FACTOR	80
A COMMON SENSE APPROACH TO MYSTICAL NONSENSE	86
CHAPTER IV ALTERNATIVE TO CHAOS	109
INSTANT PERFECTION THE INCREDIBLE ALTERNATIVE	113
TUNING IN ON INTUITION	127
PERFECTION-NOW BABY	146
BYE-BYE DILEMMA	165
CHAPTER V LOVE, HATE AND SEX	185
KNOW YOURSELF. LOVE YOURSELF.	190
PROTECT YOURSELF AT ALL TIMES	199
LOVE ANYWAY	215
COMMON SENSE SEX	232

ACKNOWLEDGMENTS

This is about the last bit of writing that is needed to get this book ready for the printers to take over.

Somehow, just to say thank you to all the ones who have helped me seems inadequate.

From the Perfection-Now Position, enjoyment and appreciation have emerged as the dual purposes for our being here as we are. Two words, but in essence they are one thing. Love seems to be the only single word that really expresses what I feel, for all those who have been so helpful to me in this extended literary project.

I have felt love coming from all of them. And they need to know that I have love in my heart making the return trip back to all who gave love to me.

Perhaps the greatest enjoyment possible in this life, is to know and feel that someone loves you.

Above all, I am grateful to my wife, Hazel, who gave me the direction I needed to find what I was searching for. In addition, she gave me my daughter, Shirley, who has always been there for me, and I am so thankful for her help and that I have her. Also, I am grateful to her that she gave me three beautiful grandchildren: Robert, Marie Louise and JB.

Carla and Edward Bashista have been very good friends. Carla's special character and talents were vital in getting me through difficult times in getting this book ready for publication.

Special thanks to Edwina and Dick Manning.

Steven Moore's expert editorial and computer assistance have my greatest appreciation. Also, I am grateful to Vicki and Bob Moore and June and Jack Biggs for their thoughtful concern.

VIII   **NOBODY'S IMPERFECT**

FOR A QUICK UNDERSTANDING

I think I know how Galileo must have felt when he attempted to show that this world was not the stationary center of a revolving universe. The Roman inquisition made him recant and put him in jail for a while for his efforts.

I am trying to show that we have been mistaken in saying, "Nobody's perfect; everybody knows that we are living in an imperfect world."

I suggest that <u>NOBODY'S IMPERFECT</u>; that we are all perfect people, living within a perfect world and universe. <u>EXISTENCE IS PERFECTION</u>. We have <u>PERFECTION NOW</u>. We have <u>SOUL PERFECTION NOW</u>.

It should be obvious that we cannot change the world or human nature. But <u>we can change our thinking</u> on this subject. We have made a good-faith error in judging human nature imperfect because of our sometimes irrational behavior. <u>JUDGMENT IS NOT DETERMINED BY ABUSE</u>. For a quick understanding, we separate <u>what we are</u> from <u>how we function</u>. Our existence, that <u>which we are, what the universe is</u> -- is locked in, unchangeable and perfect now; regardless of how we perform.

Our thoughtless condoning of inherent imperfection (in ourselves and in the world) could be the hidden cause of much of our serious problems. By eliminating this <u>one misconception,</u> alternative directions for new thinking are revealed for our consideration. It is great relief to accept ourselves <u>exactly as we are</u>. We are pleased to realize that we do not have to become anything other than what we have always been. It is unnecessary to condemn and punish ourselves for acting and reacting like the human creatures that we are.

Having SOUL PERFECTION NOW, we need not be bothered with religious damnation and salvation. With universal perfection, we can investigate the vast unknown and the hereafter (whatever it may or may not be) without fear.

UNIVERSAL EQUALITY goes hand in hand with cosmic excellence. There are no degrees of absolute perfection.

Regardless of circumstances, SELF-ESTEEM IS INCREASED.

Knowing that we have perfection now, our primary purpose in being here as we are is to ENJOY and APPRECIATE the miraculous wonders of perfection that are available for us.

Under our imperfection heritage, there is no consistent basis for ethics and morality. The PERFECTION-NOW POSITION offers a valid foundation for good behavior. We avoid wrong-doing because of the distress it causes. And we choose goodness, because that is the way to fulfill our purpose of enjoyment and appreciation.

I am not worried about the Roman Inquisition; but my wife told me that religious bigots might want to stone me.

Nevertheless, I think we would all benefit from adjusting our thinking to correspond with the reality of PERFECTION NOW.

CHAPTER I

ENLIGHTENMENT AT LAST

Before dawn, nearly every Saturday morning I would load my fishing equipment into my car and head for the pier at Malibu.

I remember one such morning especially. I don't recall exactly, but it must have been warm enough to have my car windows open. It was still dark--about 5 am.

Shortly after leaving the driveway, I heard the most beautiful bird singing. As I continued to drive, the delightful melody stayed with me. I thought Topanga Canyon must have been invaded with thousands of these same birds that were singing so loud and clear. I had never heard such glorious music before.

The strange thing was that the same musical notes were repeated over and over again. The performance stayed with me for about 2 miles down Topanga Canyon Blvd. There is a spring where a little water comes out of a pipe set in the rock face of the canyon wall. And that is the place where the bird-song melody left me.

When I returned home that afternoon, I told Hazel about my strange bird-song experience. My wife said she hadn't heard anything unusual. I didn't think much about it until years later when I read that many have encountered that same mystical happening. I had to conclude that there were no visible birds--surely not that many that could repeat that same heavenly sound while I traveled 2 miles down the canyon road.

At that time my fishing enjoyment was much stronger than my interest in mystical bird singing. And the novel experience faded into the background of my mind. Going fishing was my protection, my way of coping with the pressures of running a small custom upholstering shop--and all the other complications of just living and managing in an alleged imperfect world.

I had been fascinated with everything required to catch a fish since I was eight years old. It all started when I had discovered a small fish in a puddle alongside the creek near our home in Oklahoma. Evidently, the puddle was the result of a minor flood that spilled over the bank and filled this small depression. Somehow, I scooped most of the water out of the puddle and caught my first fish.

And now I was going fishing every weekend on the live-bait boats at Malibu, Santa Monica and Paradise Cove. I thoroughly enjoyed everything connected with a fishing expedition; fishing poles, hooks, lines, sinkers, fishing reel, tackle box and getting up early on Saturday morning, loading it all into my car and heading down Topanga Canyon to the vast Pacific Ocean.

Usually I would meet old Doc. He was just as much of a fishing maniac as I was. We would walk to the end of the pier, park our equipment and, likely, be the first breakfast customers at the small restaurant there. Then we would buy our tickets, board the boat and head for the kelp beds up the coast beyond Paradise Cove.

It never occurred to me that one day my fishing trips would not continue to be as enjoyable as they had been for so many years. Two events made a difference. One involved a fellow fisherman, about my age (45 years) who, because of his somewhat boisterous character, was quite noticeable. We missed him for a couple of weeks and someone mentioned that he had suffered a heart attack and died.

The second happened a few weeks after that. I had gotten off the boat in the afternoon and, as usual, had to carry fishing poles, fish and heavy tackle box loaded with lead sinkers to my Pontiac parked on the highway. About half way there I suddenly realized I was very tired.

Immediately, I remembered our loudmouthed friend who had died a few weeks earlier. The situation sort of socked home to me that I was not a young man any more.

I didn't stop going fishing altogether, but the fishing magic gradually receded like the turning of high tide in the lagoons as they begin draining back into the ocean. The fun and excitement of a fishing excursion did not seem to satisfy me or shield me from complications the way it had before. And, like nearly everyone else, Hazel and I had our share of them.

Looking back, it seemed we had been struggling over one damn thing or another from the beginning of our marital togetherness. Eventually though, we had managed the material requirements for a supposedly good life. Our home was paid for. We had a suitable car. And I had my own business in Santa Monica. Moreover, we lived only 4 miles from the coast; and I could easily indulge my fascination with the ocean, boats and of course, fishing.

But with the pleasure of fishing becoming something of an additional burden, my other problems became more serious. Our home was not like it used to be. For a long time I had conducted my business from a shop in my garage. I added a small storage room and had plans to enlarge my shop area.

Topanga was in the unzoned area of Los Angeles County. There were no restrictions. But zoning finally came with restrictions and limitations. Future home industries were banned. I could continue operating my business as it was.

However, I could not enlarge my work area as I had planned. Because I needed more space, I was forced to pay rent in Santa Monica for a suitable place to work.

Our daughter was properly married and beginning her own marital hassle in Nevada. With Shirley gone, Hazel was campaigning for us to sell everything we had in California and move to a deserted, ghost town mining camp high in the Mogollon mountains of New Mexico. That's where she had been born and lived with her parents until she was fourteen. Having never been contented in California, my wife felt she could be happy if she could live again at the place of her birth.

I was satisfied with things the way they were. I couldn't see any way I could make a living in that ghost town, 80 miles away from the nearest city. It didn't make sense to me to give up all I had worked for and start all over again in an environment I knew nothing about.

In addition, there was the residue of a dwindling religious experience. Somehow, Hazel and I had pulled away from the fear of the world coming to an end with Jesus coming to kill off everyone except the most faithful, tithe-paying Seventh Day Adventist. Still, I was shocked when I heard one of our friends say, "Fuck Jesus."

On the other hand, the religious dogma of God-damnation and salvation--with its conditions and complications--had become too absurd to hang on to.

It was no comfort to me that most of our friends were also floundering in their own mental swampland of disturbances. With my long-standing fishing enjoyment becoming less effective, I decided to seriously consider just what was wrong with our civilized way of thinking that resulted, despite our best efforts, in so much cerebral confusion and emotional instability.

I felt it was imperative to start all over again in my thinking about the basic nature of man, and the difficulties involved in human experiences. By continuing my search along conventional directions, I was certain I would never find satisfactory answers to diminish the seemingly, ever-lingering cuss of the human dilemma.

For a new beginning, I attempted to detach from my consideration, all disturbing conclusions about humanity proposed by authorities in both science and religion. No belief at all appeared better than groping for understanding in an academic miasma where reason is too often ignored. A clean mental slate with no fixed determinations seemed preferable to looking for validity in psychological and ecclesiastical dogma that rationalizes unacceptable contradictions.

For examples, no one has ever explained how or why a perfect God could or would create imperfectly. And from the scientific school, reason was strained to accept that the innumerable miracles of living creatures, including man, could have accidentally evolved from a warm swamp millions of years ago.

I promised myself that, in this new inquiry, I would not go along with anything that did not easily correspond with my own common sense, reason and logic.

In fantasy, I tried to figure out what my conclusions might be if I had lived mostly alone on an island--so that my thinking would have been dependent on my own ideas, derived only from the evidence in the environment around me. I would have a special television allowing me to look at whatever was going on in the world--but preventing me from being brainwashed with any of the absurdities offered as an explanation for the confused debacle.

I suppose I had asked for it when I had contrived this mental house-cleaning experiment; but I was hardly expecting the startling awaking that occurred, shortly after a slight endeavor in my self-induced open-mindedness.

I had sort of hoped to discover exactly what aspects of humanity were actually imperfect and thus responsible for our belligerent attitudes and occasional periods of irrational behavior. Therefore, I was shocked when suddenly it became crystal clear to me that there was no imperfection! In the same jolting flash of awareness, I could see that the entirety of existence was absolutely perfect--just the way it was.

I remember saying to myself when the idea hit me, "My God, the whole thing is perfect." To me, the term "whole thing" meant absolutely everything existing in the universe.

On the ocean highway between Topanga Canyon and Santa Monica, there was a large portion of the Palisades that, for years, had been slipping towards the ocean. The macadamized pavement in front of this moving mass of earth was always rough and bumpy. No matter how many times it was repaved, the undulating bumps would come back. I noticed it every day as I drove to my shop in Santa Monica.

On occasions, when Hazel and Shirley were riding with me, I would point out this earth movement and say, "Some day this whole thing is going to slip clear out into the ocean". Once in a while there would be a few clods of dirt tumbled on to the edge of the highway. Whenever Hazel and Shirley would see that, they would kid me, saying, "Look, the whole thing is going into the ocean."

But one day the "whole thing" did slide down--and actually pushed a Volkswagen before it into the breakers. The small car was shoved like a large beach ball without being covered up; and the surprised man inside was not injured.

The certainty of this "perfection-now" conclusion was so forceful in my mind, that I felt it was incredible that we have thoughtlessly accepted the false assumption of inherent human imperfections in place of the cosmic excellence that has always existed as the factual quality of both physical and nonphysical reality.

After this exciting information settled down a little, I realized that this single, good-faith error in judgment was mainly responsible for much of our man-caused turmoil. Our civilized thinking and performing has been contaminated by this one misconception about the cosmic makeup of human nature.

Nevertheless, it was comforting to know that being incorrect in our assumptions regarding ourselves was not as vital a problem as being innately imperfect in our original nature.

Hazel and I were blaming each other for our dissatisfactions. My wife resented my fascination with fishing. And she thought it was my fault that she had to live all these years in California where she was homesick for her mountain and blue sky country of New Mexico.

And of course, I blamed much of my upset feelings on Hazel. I thought she should accept me the way I was and stop being so resentful. If she would only change her attitude, I felt I could have more enjoyment out of my life. At the same time, Hazel thought; if only I would go along with her plans, her living experience would be better.

For a while I had considered that desires might be the imperfection flaw in human nature. I wondered if my longing for pleasure and happiness was what was imperfect with me. I had even tried to get rid of my search for enjoyment. But it was a frustrating mental struggle. I could not overcome my fascination with fishing or any other desires, even though lately, fishing was not as important as it used to be.

Having "perfection now" made a difference. It finally dawned on me that we could not depend on another person or circumstances for a satisfactory state of mind. Realizing for the first time that it was unnecessary for me to <u>become</u> anything other than what I had always been, much of the frustration of my own dilemma was dispersed in the pleasant awareness of this welcome enlightenment.

Several weeks later another episode occurred which was more fascinating than the first "Nobody's Imperfect" revealing incident. This was something of a mystical, direct-knowing experience, lasting about 35 or 40 minutes. A part of my inner self that I had hardly known existed, gradually emerged to full consciousness; and to the utter amazement of my normal surface mentality.

What happened was that my so-called subconscious became fully conscious in a positive, unmistakable manner. Here, thoroughly exposed for me to experience and evaluate, was the actual source of that first <u>Perfection-Now</u> conclusion. All of my intuitive prompting and instinctual tendencies must have originated in this previously, almost unknown dimension of my being.

But it was nothing like the lost, impure culprit I had figured occupied the mystical cavern of my inner self. In place of an irrational monster, it was evident that there was nothing about the subconscious that could be imperfect, incomplete or disordered because of an inherent lack of cosmic excellence.

In comparing the two, I could see that our familiar surface mentality is only a small, **but wholly sufficient** segment of our personal and indestructible cosmic consciousness which, seemingly to us, functions in a secondary, mostly hidden position during this material phase of our eternal existence.

And it is only our misdirected, surface-mind consciousness that is disturbed from the tainted intellectual victuals force fed to us as an essential part of our civilized training.

Before my soul awareness experience, I had the general fear of dying. I mentioned the palisades crumbling on to the highway because I had thought that someday it might tumble down on my vehicle; and that might be the end of me. But after knowing that my soul was perfect now, and would continue on regardless of what might happen to my body, the disturbing fear of death vanished.

The second occurrence (considered thoroughly in the chapter, "Soul Perfection Now") appeared to confirm my previous idea of unqualified perfection for all existence. But soon after these two mind-boggling happenings took place, I realized that I was, of course, exactly the same factual person that I had been before; except that now I had something additional, a seemingly unknown fact, a dimension of reality wholly unique and exciting to consider.

Nonetheless, this new thinking would have to prove itself to me. A lot of important details would have to be clearly resolved before I would wholeheartedly take it on as a vital factor in my quest for understanding.

But I did continue with my unbiased open-mindedness. And I find it just as essential and comforting now, fifteen years later, as it was when I first tried it out.

If we can cope with the physical requirements, and extract some pleasure from our experiences, I do not see any need to bind ourselves to one inflexible determination, which, perhaps for good reasons, must remain in the little uncertain realm of philosophical speculation.

Yet this sensible reservation does not restrict us from forming solid opinions. Still, there is nothing of an intellectual nature that must forever be regarded as absolute; even though we may desire to use that word occasionally.

The finest Rolls-Royce would be worthless to us if we chained it to a tree, or expected it to function with water instead of gasoline for its motivating power. We can all agree to this obvious fact.

But for a long time we have been expecting our mental and emotional equipment to work properly under just such impossible conditions. The inherent nature of our thinking and feeling ability seems to be in an almost continuous state of selectivity. In shackling any part of our surface intellect to incorrect basic assumptions, our mental machinery is no more effectual for finding satisfactory understanding and happiness than a motor vehicle would be mobile while tied to a post.

It is not too difficult to change your location to a better

viewpoint if you want to see what the world looks like from a different level than the one you are now clinging to.

But no bird can roost on two branches at the same time. So, if you might be curious as to how I resolved this new concept about the basic natures of all men, women, and children (as well as all horses and horse's asses), release your clutching claws from the insecure limb on which you have been stranded and fly along with me. Together, we will observe and experience a somewhat different and more satisfying world from the perfection-now position.

CHAPTER II

THE PERFECTION-NOW POSITION

The position we take for this novel consideration is simply that of an inquisitive and unbiased observer. It allows us to look into vital areas of information that have been well hidden by our conditioned adherence to the general imperfection hypothesis. Our unique observation post does not require full or even partial acceptance of the proposed, basic perfection-now concept itself.

Neither is there ever any requirement to go along with relative implications and applications appearing as we proceed. Rather, we experience a delightful sense of mental freedom for this revealing exploration into new areas of thinking. For, if we eventually find our cosmic make-up to be the essence of perfection <u>now</u>, just as we are, then whatever we believe, all that we think and even that which we do, are revealed as only selective or responsive <u>functions of</u> our existence.

But these mental and physical activities have no ability to alter or even disturb the primary, innate nature of our total being. Already having <u>perfection now</u>, we are always the recipients and benefactors of that existing universal excellence; irrespective of our lack of awareness of such a desirable condition; or regardless of our perhaps inadequate performance.

But before we make a full-power climb into the uncontaminated atmosphere of truthful knowing on this free flight into unexplored territory, it would be well to come to some essential understanding regarding this unusual platform from which we will begin our investigation.

MAKING IT CLEAR

Back in the early days of color motion pictures there was a period of experimentation with three-dimensional films. I attended one of these exhibitions and was handed a pair of eyeglasses which were an essential part of the procedure. Sure enough, with those spectacles on, you soon felt as though you were right there in the jungle. People screamed and scooted down in their seats to avoid the flying spears that the natives were throwing in our direction.

Since I embarked on this somewhat spectacular speculation, I have often wished I could provide others with a simple device which could help them to grasp this unique concept of reality. In some of my very early conversations I began to suspect that I was not communicating my thoughts too clearly, when one of my friends said, "Well Bob, if I believed as you do, I would rob a bank tomorrow. Then I'd have a ball for the rest of my life and say, 'To hell with everything'."

Sometime later, when another of my associates responded in almost the same larcenous language, I figured I had better be more cautious with my talking and carefully record this information, before I might be accused of conspiring to convert people into a "don't-give-a-damn"-bank-robbing culture.

Fortunately, certain aspects involved in the peculiar nature of the perfection-now idea releases me (or anyone else) from any compulsion or responsibility to persuade others to accept or even consider the perfection-now concept. From the beginning I could see how _relatively_ unimportant (in an overall sense) our speculative thoughts and beliefs were, in relation to the factual existence of cosmic perfection ingrained into every atom and aspect of everything and everybody.

And yet, from an individual concern of personal involvement, the contents and validity of what we believed were vital to our mental satisfaction as well as being important to the welfare of people in general. This responsibility angle will be looked into more thoroughly later on. But regardless of obligation one way or the other, I am convinced there is much to be gained in a sensible examination of this new alternative, labeled, The Perfection-Now Position.

There has been too much misunderstanding and lack of communication already; and I surely do not wish to add to the confusion. In this writing endeavor, I hope to present that which I feel is valid in a simple way, that will leave no doubt as to exactly what I mean to say. Perhaps the banks will be grateful for all the trouble I might be saving them from.

And now it is time to get on with making it clear just what I mean by <u>perfection-now</u>. Most of us likely have never felt it necessary to consider what all is involved when we casually refer to our assumed, but seemingly self-evident state of basic imperfection. Such could have been the case when the late President Johnson attempted to excuse his failure to resolve the Vietnam disaster.

In a televised comment he used the familiar statement, which until now, no one has ever seriously questioned: "Of course, nobody's perfect. Everyone knows that we are all living in an imperfect world." President Nixon may have been of the same mind when he mentioned that likely there would never be a perfect way to control prices and wages.

Usually, our customary idea of inherent imperfection is a vague implication of some primary fault or incompleteness in human nature. But for most of us it would be difficult to define exactly what there was about ourselves that could correctly be classified as imperfect.

Dictionary definitions of perfectionism <u>do not</u> apply to the perfection-now term we are using here. Although I tend to be particular in some matters, I certainly do not consider myself a perfectionist. A perfectionist shares the general false assumption that we are all basically imperfect to start with; but believes that his qualified plan for ultimate perfection may eventually be attained.

Some "scientific" speculation that I happened to hear about suggested that the perfectibility of mankind could (under certain conditions) be accomplished in the future. Of course, this utopian attainment would require strict regimentation, treating everybody as if they were psychotic patients in a global mental hospital. An enforced program of rewards and punishments would be "scientifically" employed, along with drugs and other repulsive measures, that would deprive individuals of their dignity, privacy and freedom. Also, it would mean that we would have to surrender our cherished right of self-determination, allowing only a few alleged "experts" to decide just what a "perfect" existence would or should be.

To a large degree, this is almost the same program that religionists have been struggling unsuccessfully to put across for thousands of disastrous years. They have succeeded only in convincing most of us that we are all imperfect, near idiots, assigned to this great mental sanitarium in the sky; and just waiting for the disgusted Chief Cosmic Director to say, "To hell with all of you."

If the scientific "in" experts are no more productive than their "somewhat out" religious predecessors have been, we need not worry too much that such an obnoxious plan will ever go beyond minor experimentation. Nevertheless, it is a little chilling to hear that such disordered thinking is even discussed by those having some authority and power.

Although psychiatrists and psychologists readily admit that they do not know what causes mental abnormalities, there is an implied indication that irrational hostilities are inherent in the unconscious or subconscious areas of our humanness. These allegedly imperfect instinctual tendencies are incorrectly thought to be a genetic, evolutionary holdover from our bloody, "fang and claw" animalistic heritage. While some may play with the idea of modifying Homo sapiens to eventually breed up to a fair degree of qualified perfection, it is fairly clear that such an endeavor would be impossible to expedite. Hitler demonstrated that point rather effectively and disastrously.

But that's enough for now concerning our lack of comprehension of the negative imperfection postulate. It's time to get down to the real meat of the positive side of our subject. Perfection-now thinking means the total rejection of all conditional and qualified ideas of <u>attaining</u> ultimate perfection regarding any aspect of <u>existence</u>.

As an alternative, we consider everything existing as being the ultimate of perfection <u>now</u>. By everything, we mean the absolute totality of existence. Nothing whatsoever is excluded. All relative aspects of goodness <u>and</u> <u>evil</u> <u>are</u> <u>included</u>. Happiness and sorrow, good health and sickness are also there. All action, reaction, good luck and misfortune have their essential part. Truth and falsehood, fact and fancy, reality and illusion--all have perfection as an integral portion of their nature.

The full scope of our personal existence, whatever we were before this life, that which we are now, and our future existence beyond this living experience (whatever it may or may not be) has unconditional cosmic perfection as a primary characteristic of its unique composition. All effort, forces, instinctual tendencies and intuitive promptings as well as all believing, thinking and speculating are also classified as perfection, <u>regardless</u> <u>of</u> <u>any</u> <u>disagreeable</u> <u>reaction</u> <u>involved</u>.

In fact, the reactionary adversity emerging is, in itself, a perfect and essential, though sometimes painful, indicator of an incorrect determination or impractical arrangement. There are no qualifications about what is considered to be perfect--a simple everything and everybody! Existence is perfection. Everybody's perfect. <u>Nobody's</u> <u>imperfect</u>. We all have <u>perfection</u> <u>now</u>.

The philosophical concept of universal excellence is unique in the realm of ideas concerning the quality and innate make-up of our existence. As almost all previous thinking about perfection has implied an ultimate but unlikely attainment, it is somewhat startling to consider even the most remote possibility that nothing at all need be accomplished with respect to <u>that</u> <u>which</u> <u>we</u> <u>are</u>. This welcome awareness does not factually change us in the least, but it makes a <u>big difference</u> in our future thinking, believing and behavior.

It was this one single factor of difference, applying in some manner to almost every aspect of our physical adventure, that struck me with such overwhelming force back in my old rat-race days of 1960. In that one clear moment of intensified, intuitive thinking, I realized that my own problem was simply one of intelligently adjusting my mistaken ideas regarding the absolute and unalterable nature of all existence.

At the same time, I found I could gladly quit the impossible struggle to somehow improve, change or even control my <u>natural</u> <u>human</u> <u>tendencies</u> <u>and</u> <u>inclinations</u>. I could stop feeling inadequate and guilty for acting and reacting, thinking and feeling like the human creature that I was.

There was also an emerging sense of a new concept of responsibility accompanying this beginning comprehension of cosmic security and freedom. I fully realized that it was most essential to proceed carefully and slowly in discovering and assimilating whatever potential benefits might develop from following this novel approach to a better understanding of our true nature. A gradual modification of my thinking along various alternative directions appeared to be within the scope of my ability to manage.

With only a very immature grasp of the significance involved in this new look at reality, my wife, Hazel and I, sold our home and business in California and moved to a small, almost deserted mining camp community high in the Mogollon mountains of New Mexico. Our little ghost town was completely surrounded by the extensive Gila National Forest. Here I felt that we had a better chance to discover and soak up the goodness that we surmised was waiting for us.

SIGNIFICANT FEATURES

As this whole book is serving as the introduction to the perfection-now concept, it seems appropriate here to provide a brief preview of some of the most outstanding features that will be presented in greater depth and detail in following chapters.

One of the most practical and useful features that has proven itself to me through many years, is the subtle way that an awareness of the one valid fact of total perfection functions efficiently as a simple solution for almost any problem in the complex field of human relations.

And speaking of problems, it is general knowledge that about one out of every three marriages ends in divorce or estranged separation. Likely a large percentage of the other two are sweating it out, struggling to endure an unhappy debacle of inconvenient togetherness. Invariably sex is adversely affected in the traditional male and female hassle. And with all the belligerency erupting from the matrimonial mating madness, sex has emerged as the most complex problem in the world today.

Perhaps it would be more correct to say that a lack of natural sexual satisfaction is the foremost concern of those who are embroiled in the disenchantment phase of the imperfection-conditioned mating game. Satisfactory sexual involvement gets turned off when antagonism gets turned on. And from all that I have observed, the main, but well disguised, cause of most sex-killing bitterness can be laid squarely on our careless condoning of the imperfection postulate.

For a while, most young lovers are quite convinced that if God had made anything better than sex, likely He kept it for Himself. But instead of continuing to enjoy the full potential pleasures available, we have become largely a frustrated, sexless culture, vicariously bowing at the illusionary Playboy or Playgirl love-making altar.

The extensive fantasy togetherness that the professional sex authors and photographers accomplish for us has damned well turned us into a well-informed bunch of liberated, but lonely masturbators. One psychiatrist mentioned that he was very encouraged by the fact that lately, so many of his disturbed clients are now quite willing to discuss their experiments in masturbation.

But I do not wish to be critical of professional sex advisers. Under the prevailing circumstances, no doubt they are performing as best they can. Any worthwhile information you can glean from their offerings can be used more effectively however, if you approach the whole sorry debacle of male and female togetherness from the perfection-now position.

Of course, there are relative factors involved in everything. Most of us know that the natural enjoyment possible in various other activities <u>besides</u> <u>sex</u> is certainly increased to the degree that we are making out satisfactorily in bed. It is also no secret that sexual enjoyment is enhanced when the greater portion of our mental, emotional and social as well as our occupational and financial endeavors are managed with less turbulence and more tranquility.

The ultimate potential delight available in sexual fulfillment can only emerge as a spontaneous culmination of a happy and grateful attitude toward every other aspect of our living experiences. But the sorry fact is that most people are not very happy about anything--and the professionals are getting rich because of it. For many, sex problems are at the top of the list, but often there are other complications preventing the happiness we desire.

It is essential to go to the very foundation of our heritage to find the cause of our difficulties. The most discouraging fact in the world today is that established professionals, both clerical and secular, do not have acceptable answers to the "nitty-gritty" question of just what is really wrong with our so-called "civilized" society. How come there is such a wholesale lack of integrity in both high and low stations? An early 1974 poll showed that public confidence in the Congress as well as the somewhat overly Watergated Presidency to be at an all-time low. Nowhere will you find any practical information that might serve as a solution, or even a deterrent to the personal, social and legislative deterioration that appears to be forever snow-balling towards catastrophic proportions.

During this same time period, Mike Mansfield asked for and got prime television time to respond to President Nixon's 1974 somewhat self-serving State of The Union address. In the question and answer period following Senator Mansfield's initial remarks, he was seemingly disturbed when a reporter wanted to know what he could say regarding the fact that many democrats were apparently just as involved and guilty with their indiscretions as the republican administration appeared to be. The able Senator eased himself out of his uncomfortable position by replying something like, "Well, if you can show me one perfect individual or party, then we could expect to have more perfect performances." This reference to our alleged, basically imperfect state of being served to stop the adverse inquiry, but it was not a satisfactory answer to the question.

Neither was he willing to excuse the president on the same grounds. The implications were that Nixon's imperfections were so much greater that he should be eliminated by impeachment so that a somewhat less imperfect official could sit in the affluent political saddle.

The point I am trying to sock home is that our documented, authenticated and even "hallowed" imperfection-oriented culture is so messed up with inadequate, runaround answers, glaring injustices and inconsistencies, that it is almost impossible for anyone--even with the best of intentions, but adhering to the accepted programs of tradition--to come up with effective solutions to the serious problems adversely affecting everyone of us in some measure. It doesn't matter whether your personal hangup is sex, impeachment or the high price of beans and gas, under imperfection intellectualism with its deplorable rationalizations, we are not likely to resolve reactionary problems emerging directly from and because of that disordered imperfection-based establishment.

Disturbed psychiatrists cannot even resolve their own personal frustrations. The expensive, professional programs prescribed for their wealthy clients have no real ability to smooth out their own turbulent perplexities. According to several of the good doctors who occasionally appear on the Merv Griffin Show, psychiatrists have an occupational hazard of a higher incidence of coronaries and more suicides than any other specialists in the medical profession. Of course, some of this is surely due to the additional pressure of their client's distress commingling with their own problems. But you would think that a good mechanic should be able to keep his personal vehicle in adequate running order. If he is incapable of properly maintaining his own car, it is a reasonable deduction that he will not do any better with the mental motors we depend on in our vehicles--regardless of the high fees demanded for such poor services.

If we cannot trust the recognized authorities in cardinal matters of the head, the heart, the soul and sexual feelings, then where do we go to find the paramount information our

NOBODY'S IMPERFECT

instinctual natures apparently insist that we discover? How in this confused culture can we determine what is valid--and what is actually academic excrement cleverly disguised as either sacred, scientific or legalized authenticity?

How can we ever really know what our primary purpose is on this somewhat expendable, nonphysical soul-venture into a factual involvement with material reality? And just what can you and I accept regarding our personal responsibility in view of tragic injustices perpetrated and condoned in the bloody name of justified revolutionary violence or justified retaliation and punishment?

In early 1974, the fate of Patricia Hearst, the kidnapped granddaughter of the late publisher, William Randolph Hearst, was bartered in bizarre negotiations by an organization claiming to have loving compassion for the poor people of California. Demanding millions of dollars to alleviate the suffering of these unfortunates, their militant position was implied as being: Rectify this injustice--or we will kill an innocent young lady in the name of justice.

This was a notorious example of our disordered use of imperfection-based rationalization. The whole nation could easily see the fanatical, extreme unreasonableness in that potential tragedy. Yet we are thoughtlessly teaching holy versions of this justified injustice to small children on television and in Sunday School classes. Future Supreme Court Judges get the same indoctrination in advanced law schools.

A few months later in the middle of May 1974, the world was shocked at the insane slaughter of innocent Israeli school children by fanatical Palestinian guerrillas. This episode was followed by revengeful destruction by Israeli raiders on Lebanese villages giving refuge to the guerrillas. While one might attempt to excuse the reactionary violence erupting under the terrible duress existing in this unfortunate situation, it is impossible to justify any of the tragic occurrences on either side.

Injustice is never justified.

Fully aware of the gross inconsistencies and unresolved contradictions prevailing in our imperfection-based culture, it is no wonder that harassed psychiatrists are tempted to terminate their own frustrations in suicide. And it is not difficult to understand why some serious thinkers tend to consider this world as the cosmic insane asylum where ancient cosmonauts dumped imperfect human idiots--unfit to live in more peaceful and rational areas of the universe.

But we must return to the question of just where do we go to search out the necessary information our instinctual natures tend to indicate is available for us? As mentioned earlier, this was my initial problem. Fortunately, in simply rejecting the whole structure of unsatisfactory scientific and ecclesiastical conclusions regarding the origin, nature and destiny of man, I accidentally found that the needed discernment we all seem to require is readily available to each individual, <u>wholly within</u> the instinctual make-up of his own perfect and fully adequate nature.

While it is something of a continuation of the principal problem-solving aspect we have been considering, this last statement brings up a second important feature which is examined in some depth under the subject title, "Tuning In On Intuition." In this particular area it is almost imperative that we approach the subject with a completely unbiased and uncluttered mind, because this unhampered attitude is the master key which unlocks the somewhat mystical doors of your own, fully adequate, intuitive awareness.

As previously related, I discovered this available source of valid knowledge through a somewhat desperate personal experiment. Looking back on that experience, I can presently see that it was only necessary for me to clear out the worthless intellectual rubbish from my mind. As soon as this was accomplished, proper answers that I desired began to filter through in startling clarity--apparently, after I had gropingly managed the essential mental attitude, to recognize and evaluate the material with normal reason and logic, and a fair measure of common sense.

Now I realize that the cleaning-out process is easily accomplished by a simple, determined suggestion to your mind that you are discarding everything of a doubtful nature pertaining to some particular phase of your inquiry. At the same time you are indicating to your instinctual nature that you seriously desire suitable information as an alternative to the ineffectual debris you are eliminating.

In my own initial experiment, I was pleasantly surprised at the beneficial reaction which happened in my unhappy perplexities from this mental clean-out alone. And I found that it was not at all difficult to get rid of the sorry stuff, because the damnable crap you are mentally shoveling out the door, has been bugging the unholy hell out of you for far too long.

In fact, it's a great relief to rid yourself of something that is useless and bothersome. So why put up with and hang on to such nonsense? If some pesty person is continually hanging around making you miserable, and you decide you have had enough of that obnoxious individual, you can simply tell him to get out!

The same procedure seems to work for any irksome ideas which are occupying the living room of your mind. You just tell them to go too. That's all there is to it; it's actually that simple! And sometime later on it is equally simple to recognize acceptable indications when they appear in the ordinary, everyday thinking which you are always using for everything else anyway.

No concentration, no meditation, and no boring daily procedures are needed. In fact, any attempt to speed up the normal function of your intuitive awareness will only impede the subtle communication which will become known to you at a time and place determined by your instinctual nature. Any effort expended to get quick results is almost a sure way of preventing the valid answers you desire.

If the completely open-mind approach is the first essential factor, a no-effort, no-concern attitude regarding the outcome would be the second most important aspect in this delicate, but utterly simple way to discover whatever you want to know from your own personal, built-in, cosmic storehouse of knowledge and wisdom.

If the information you need can easily be found in the dictionary or some other available source, such as the library, you just might get the idea to consult these handy references. But of course we are mainly concerned here with troublesome areas for which traditional authorities have not yet provided practical solutions and satisfactory answers.

During the interval, after you have sort of put in your request for something specific, and the time when the order is filled in the normal course of your natural thinking process, I am convinced that the best thing you can do is simply enjoy yourself at any endeavor that is attractive and easily available to you. So have a good time if you can manage it, and learn whatever you require at the same time.

It may be just a coincidence, but a small incident just occurred which interrupted my writing at this point. A few weeks ago Hazel got a new Maytag washing machine. She has a congenital distrust of any mechanical equipment larger than a needle and thread, and had delayed trying it out until this morning. She seemed a little upset. "Where's that instruction manual?" she asked me. "You had it. What did you do with it? I can't find it anywhere."

I knew that I had not put it away among my things, but I went through the motion of looking, on the bare chance that I could be mistaken. Finally I had to give up, and as I was retyping the last couple of paragraphs, it occurred to me that we ought to be able to find that instruction book. So I simply registered my request for a little assistance in this matter and went on with my work.

A little later I checked in on Hazel to see how she was making out and found everything OK. "Well I guess you are vindicated about that operating pamphlet," she told me. "I found it right where I had put it in my desk." Then I related how I had given up looking and enlisted the help of our intuitive awareness. Evidently Hazel had gotten the idea to look in the right place about that same time.

But it is senseless to make a big deal out of this, because it is only a more thorough application of the quite ordinary mental function most of us use all the time for a lot of uncomplicated tasks such as the occasional notions we get to look in the dictionary for better understanding. All common-sense determinations we usually employ on many other successful projects come directly from this inner source. We are inclined to take the miracle of ordinary intuitive perception too much for granted, hardly realizing or appreciating the cosmic perfection inherent in our marvelous ability to judge and select.

It is a crying shame that our leaders and specialists are often shackled in their responsible endeavors to incorrect fundamental assumptions which distrub, degrade, and eventually, tend to atrophy our most essential and valuable instinctual nature. While I now feel certain that various irksome aspects of our traditional thinking are nothing more than dressed up, neatly documented bull statements (and it's high time to drag it all out, label it for what it actually is and then bury the stinking stuff), I have great respect and admiration for the wealth of facts that so many dedicated men and women have already discovered and made available to us.

But it is most incredible that with all the tremendous increase in knowledge in the physical realm, we are still plagued with unnecessary mental and emotional distress directly caused by religious and scientific garbage, force-fed to trusting minds by those who are actually in the business of assisting people in their difficulties.

Not too long ago there was quite a hullaboo over The Exorcist. If I should ever compile an imperfection crap-list, I would put the deranged concept of a real, personified devil, occupying the mental recesses of susceptible individuals, at the very top. The clamoring phenomenon occurring with the presentation of this motion picture demonstrates clearly how thoroughly we have been conditioned to eat garbage--even when we have been forewarned that it is likely to make us puke before we have half finished the abominable meal. However, it also shows that many are starving for even a measure of comprehension regarding that delicate and mostly unknown area of the ego, subconscious or unconscious, which for simplicity's sake, we will call the soul.

For a large segment of my life, I was as much in the spine-chilling, spooky darkness regarding this hellish subject of demonology as, obviously, so many are today. But after many years of considering everything from the perfection-now position, I have found that it is now easy to look clearly (and at last without fear) at the unwholesome, ungodly serving of demonology and evaluate it for exactly what it is.

In the first place, it is essential to realize the important difference between an <u>idea</u> <u>or</u> <u>concept</u> <u>about</u> something, and the factual thing itself--assuming there actually is something real to think about. It is elementary knowledge that awareness of both real objects or beings, as well as fantasy mental creations, are communicated to our surface perception through the use of thoughts or concepts. For instance, we all have a clear idea of the very real house in which we live established firmly in our minds. At the same time, we might easily create for ourselves a potential dream house that could be more desirable than the factual one we already possess. But even if some day that ideal dream castle became a real one of wood and stone, it could never actually occupy the thought space in our mental or soul make-up.

The significant point here is that, regardless of fact or

fancy, in either case, only ideas about things are capable of entering the thinking area of our beings. It is also essential to realize that this adaptable thought receiving station is uniquely ours, to use intelligently or misuse irrationally--if we allow ourselves to be conned into seriously taking on scatological suggestions as the real thing, rather than the absurd thinking they are.

Once we are able to recognize the full significance of the perfection-now factor existing inherently in everything and everybody, it becomes clearly evident that the whole paranoid myth of demonology has been contrived to coerce subjects into a seemingly hopeless state where they can easily be persuaded to contribute their devotion, services and their money. Actually they are being mentally blackmailed--and give because they are usually scared to death of what might happen if they did not.

The most diabolical aspect of the revolting demon business is that the whole concoction of satanic insanity has been ladled out as holy nourishment by ecclesiastical officials who are later persuaded to exhort the fabricated, fantasy demons from our supposedly devil-possessed minds. The process is somewhat as if a medical doctor deliberately prescribed a potion that would eventually make us violently ill to insure that we would come back to him to be cured from the trouble that he had caused in the first place.

Actually nothing in this universe can really take over our thinking for us. Evil, deranged thoughts cannot possess us. But it is no big mystery that we are fully capable of possessing devilish conclusions just as easily as we can select the most loving, forgiving and saintly attitude when our mental motivations are directed in that pleasing direction.

Of course, when someone is hysterically bogged down in the very real miseries of seeming demon degradation, it is not too difficult for the victim to go along with a corresponding additional deception apparently supporting the false idea he had been following in the first place. So the religious exhorter keeps the damnable delusion energized and authoritatively commands the nonexisting demon to stop troubling the individual.

Since the initial suggestion of demon possession originated from this same ecclesiastical source, the gullible subject can usually respond to the counter-suggestion that the devil is actually releasing him. But in fact, the subject himself does the releasing. The firm suggestion that the devil is not to bother him anymore replaces the previous suggestion of his personal involvement with demon possession.

It is incredible that we still allow ourselves to get embroiled in such disordered false conclusions. However, our credulity is understandable when observing how we are mentally conditioned, through many formative years of repetitious suggestions, to surrender our natural, intuitive awareness of common sense and reasonableness. At the same time, we acquire a pitiful dependency on authorities, who, as in the case of exorcism, are themselves victims of invalid suggestions and ensnared to some extent in the same deranged mental nightmare. If we paid proper attention to our normal intuitive awareness, the disagreeable reaction, clearly evident in any association with the revolting dogma of satanic demons, would be sufficient, in itself, to readily turn us away from accepting such unreasonableness.

In view of our imperfection-based heritage, it is no wonder that we have lost confidence in the reliable promptings of our instinctual nature. From the perfection-now position, we can find our way back into a more trusting association with the marvelous functioning of our own inner knowing--which begins to perform adequately and naturally as soon as we realize that our personal mental make-up is ours alone to manage intelligently for our own well-being.

Having the extensive freedom to grossly misuse our intellectual abilities, as the exorcising devil debacle clearly demonstrates that we occasionally do, is not in itself a valid indication of an inherent imperfection in our nature. Clearing up this point and others relative to the subject will be accomplished in following chapters. A perfection-now consideration of various aspects of the perplexing problem of good and evil will help us to resolve those troublesome areas that occasionally cause some to blow their minds in extreme cases of provocation.

But the most significant fact we wish to spotlight here is that correct, problem-solving ideas are quite willing to enter our surface comprehension when we have made room for them and are prepared to recognize these cosmic gems of knowledge when they make themselves known.

As an example, shortly after this perfection-now business started, it seemed imperative that I discover a simple and reliable method to determine truth. Of course, I realized that this question is one of the many unresolved problems that have driven philosophers nuts for centuries. Striving in the restricted, runaround pollution of insipid imperfection deceptions, a satisfactory answer for this basic question has never been forthcoming. I was particularly concerned with the subject because it seemed essential to understand the nature and essence of truth if I ever were to arrive at a valid, truthful conclusion regarding the perfection-now concept itself.

Following the procedure I have suggested, in about two weeks the simple answer came to me in the very familiar word: application. Truth <u>applies</u> universally and eternally. This reasonable statement harmonizes exactly with the perfection-now position. And it was quite apparent why this almost obvious fact of truth could not be included in the somewhat inadequate theories of truth which traditional philosophy has settled for as a substitute for the real thing.

The correspondence and coherence theories imply a degree of application, but, considered from the imperfection postulate, they also allow inconsistencies and contradictions to the sorry extent that the agnostic theory that man is incapable of knowing anything beyond that which is clearly evident in material phenomena, makes a lot of sense--at least as long as he continues to suck on the imperfection tit.

To illustrate, religionists have never been able to offer an acceptable explanation of how a supposedly perfect and all-wise God-Creator either created imperfectly or allowed imperfection to evolve in His creation. Since the underlying, main structure of nearly all Western religious thinking requires these two postulates, (1) a perfect God or Creative Force and (2) an imperfect physical creation, it is understandable why there are so many unresolved problems emerging for anyone attempting to find reasonable answers while adhering to irrational assumptions.

The third main theory regarding truth, pragmatism, has a lot of common-sense involvement to support it, but it is also inconclusive because of its tendency to encourage rationalization.

No man can walk in two directions at the same time, and it is impossible to cook up palatable mind food out of sanctified religious feces. And then when secular authorities also impose equally absurd fundamentals--such as our alleged evolutionary, bestial heritage--from which we are expected to understand ourselves and get along peacefully with one another, our well informed instinctual natures refuse to condone the required irrational implications and we find ourselves unhappily stuck on a very insecure limb with no clear way to get to a more solid location.

Taking on the perfection-now position, we are able to employ the full, innate, natural excellence of our instinctual knowing to obtain any vital information we seriously desire to have. All that is presently valid and worthwhile--and of course there is much in all fields of endeavor to consider--originated in and emanated from the subtle source of our intuitive awareness despite the difficulties we have had to endure. If we are to discover and enjoy them, future correct conclusions and benefits will have to pass the excellent discernment of our personal instinctual natures.

A third significant feature, also uniquely related to the principal problem solving aspect of the perfection-now position, emerged as one of the most delightful developments occurring in my continuous program to test and relate this new thinking to the various, everyday requirements of our experiences. This was a very simple and satisfying resolution to the perplexing question of <u>why</u> we are here as we find ourselves to be. What is the real meaning of our brief and expendable performance on this planet? Just exactly what is the primary purpose in our being here at all?

The emerging results of this inquiry turned out to be the pleasing and most natural conclusion that we are here, mainly, to fulfill our principal purpose of enjoyment and appreciation of the wonder and excellence of all existence.

Other aspects of our make-up, such as our quite apparent (but scientifically questioned) free will power of personal determination, our spontaneous feelings of love and concern, and our inner desire to have and understand a meaningful motivation for our endeavors, are also involved in this consideration.

In contrast, our imperfection thinking, both religious and secular, has not been able to provide a consistently logical explanation regarding our primary purpose which, obviously, is most essential to know if we are to successfully manage the many secondary aims and endeavors that occupy most of our time and interest.

As an example of what I mean, the time, money and effort I am investing in this extensive writing project is, foremost of all, in my estimation, a joyful and rewarding occupation in itself. Of course, there is the possibility that eventually I will be adequately paid for my literary labors. But regardless of whatever occurs along that line, I am happily doing what I enjoy doing most at this time. If others appreciate the work I have put together and some essential bread should come my way, this becomes extra icing on the cake I already have.

In some respects, a logical understanding of our main purpose for this life ties together the various essential factors needed to establish an acceptable validity to the perfection-now position. Therefore, the important chapter, Excellence With A Purpose in Volume II, is best considered after we have looked into other equally basic questions.

There is one more feature that almost demands a special introduction. It, too, is an essential part of the overall problem-resolving aspect existing inherently in the perfection-now position. This surprising feature might be the practical and peaceful means that eventually allows desirable adjustments to develop--first in our hearts and minds, and later in our behavior and humane consideration for others.

From observed facts of my own experiences during the last fifteen perfection-now years, there is a positive indication (at least to me) that eventually there could be an abolishment of condemnation and punishment from our personal, social, legislative and even future religious thought structure.

The perfection-now position on condemnation and punishment is unique in the almost imperceptible manner it has gradually developed since I first became involved in this novel approach to understand and resolve my own troubles. The potentiality for the total abolishment of condemning and punishing tendencies from my surface thinking has emerged without any deliberate personal effort from me in that direction. From the beginning I have noticed slight feelings along this line, but it has been only relatively lately that I have realized the important significance of this evolvement which has come into view seemingly under its own subtle power and persistence.

Now the amazing thing (again to me) that has taken

place in my long association with the perfection-now position is that somehow I have shed just about all of my old antagonistic feelings toward my fellow Homo sapiens. If some damnable ideas had assholes and shoulder blades, I occasionally would still like to kick the former up into the latter. But the little amount of disgust and contempt I still feel is wholly directed at wrong thinking. And I immediately excuse the thinker because, to some extent, we are all like trained circus animals. We cannot be blamed and should not be punished for believing and performing exactly as we have been conditioned to function under the imperfection-oriented nightmare.

After more than a decade and a half of perfection-now exposure, a whole new set of reactions have developed to replace the vindictive frustrations that previously had dominated my mental and emotional tendencies. I cannot recall ever doing anything to accomplish this desirable state of mind. These happier, more tolerant feelings managed the beneficial switch somehow on their own volition. If I had any part at all, it was simply a continuation of my initial experiment to provide the open-minded freedom for my innate make-up to function more naturally, while observing from time to time what was taking place.

To show what I mean, a few years back I received a message early in the morning that a cabin I had built had burned through the night and was completely destroyed. In addition, a mobile home we had occupied while constructing the small house, had also been consumed in the blaze.

There was no insurance on the trailer-house or the cabin. It was a total loss. The weekend vacation property was in a beautiful, mountain-forest area about thirty five miles from where we live, and I hurried there to see what had happened.

The evidence was plain to see. Apparently some Wetbacks had camped for the night in the partially enclosed back porch. An old washtub with holes and cracks in the bottom had been employed to hold a warming fire. They had used a thin layer of dirt to stop up the cracks, and this makeshift heater was placed right on the dry, rough boards of the porch floor.

Their insulation job must have been insufficient, and some burning embers evidently leaked out and ignited the floor while the campers were sleeping. Fortunately, there was no wind, and the fire did not spread into the adjacent forest. Because of the isolated location, none of the very few neighbors were aware of what was going on. Likely, the surprised Wetbacks were afraid to inform anyone and didn't bother to hang around to talk about the incident.

But the important thing about this whole destructive business was the unexpected tranquility I experienced after arriving at the slightly, still-burning scene, and realized the substantial loss we had to face. I remember one particular thought that seemed a little strange under the circumstances. The cleared property, without the mobile home or cabin, once again seemed to reveal the natural beauty and charm that had attracted us at first.

Later there had been some irritation, striving and trouble associated with the building of the cabin and our living there for a while in the mobile home. All of these unpleasant involvements happily appeared to have been dispersed with the total consummation brought about by the fire. I could hardly believe it, but I found it almost impossible to feel any anger or resentment toward the ones who were responsible for the careless vandalism. Neither could I manage to work up much anguish about the monetary loss involved. Our main house on Silver Creek was intact, and there were no real problems to bother us.

When I returned home and told Hazel all about it, she too, seemed to experience little distress over the tragedy. In some respects, we both felt relieved that our active involvement with that particular episode was effectively settled for us. Later we sold the lots, and the increased land values compensated us a little to offset the financial forfeiture caused by the fire.

The significant point demonstrated clearly here is that the initial misfortune suffered by us and the Wetbacks was ample in itself, without any further involvement in a vindictive and likely futile manhunt to find and punish the weary perpetrators. Strangely enough there were some beneficial aspects, and Hazel and I were far better off by not getting ourselves into a frustrating state of resentment against all Wetbacks, or even the unknown persons who actually caused the firey destruction.

Our less belligerent reactions were so unexpected in this occurrence that later I began to wonder, why wouldn't the same sensible attitude be proper in various other difficulties where you know very well who is responsible for the trouble? In any crime or offence against us or our property, the first distress or loss is only increased by our usual condemnation and punishment attitude.

Awhile back we mentioned how a feeling of revulsion occurs as a natural indication that would normally turn us away from serious involvement in the revolting dogma of demonology. There is something of the same distasteful consequences seemingly involved in our established programs of "legalized and justified" condemnation and punishment.

Much like the sickening devil deal, our acquired acceptance of this unjust, inhumane practice originated thousands of years ago and has become an almost unyielding blight of our terribly inadequate civil and religious heritage.

To some extent, we have all inherited the insane rationalization that you can beat someone to death with a club and teach him about the finer things of life at the same time. This alleged, God-sanctioned aspect of the imperfection assumption has been contaminating our deranged culture like a malignant cancerous development.

While this may sound somewhat exaggerated, just a little clear thinking on the disastrous facts dominating the subject matter of national and local news will show that it is a valid representation of the paranoid unreasonableness constantly employed in our disordered, comdemning and punishing relations with one another. Because most of us fortunately stop short of actually killing each other doesn't sweeten our extensive, personal practice of psychotic comdemnation and punishment.

Unjust, destructive violence is often rationalized as a noble, justified effort to improve our supposedly imperfect world, such as the Biblical myth of God destroying the world with a flood. Fanatically following such absurd examples of irrational thinking, some resort to extremes of criminal behavior in a futile attempt to secure peace and goodness for the world. In disordered rationalization, these desperate involvements with violence are even performed with a personal attitude of righteous accomplishment. Throughout 1974, the extended, tragic story of Patricia Hearst commanded national attention, almost on a par with the wearisome Watergate hassle.

During that time, it was hard to believe that someone with such social and financial advantages would willingly join in with a radical group holding such inconsistent aims as providing help to the poor, while participating in criminal practices to accomplish their bizarre endeavors.

But to some extent, we have all been mentally conditioned by our inquisitional heritage where we might become deranged victims of such conclusions. It is rationalized that if it might help some, or if it's sacred, patriotic or legal--it's OK to commit inhumane and criminal acts against the minds, bodies and property of certain Homo sapiens. There is a ridiculous conjecture that such obscene activity will be beneficial to society.

Frustrated extremists can easily switch this deranged thinking to accomodate their fanatical depredations. For too long a time we have killed the killer--thinking that such a grisly program will prevent killing. We engage our nation in warfare, creating chaos and destruction upon others in a damn-fool attempt to provide security and peace for ourselves.

Our imperfection-based way of thinking is so screwed up, that we have come to the precarious place where some sick, pathogenic nut might push the atomic button, which could result in the utter destruction of most everything that is right, good and beautiful on our earthly spaceship.

Consider the frantic (May, 1974) impeachment hysteria. Irrespective of guilt or innocence (which may never be fully and properly determined), I could not help but observe, while it was occurring, how a large portion of the population was clamoring to take a punishing impeachment swat at President Nixon's political hide.

Our demoralizing condemnation and punishment madness came dangerously close to immobilizing much that is good, right and essential in our national government. While we were all condemning those in high places for relatively minor, letter-of-the-law, technical offences, no one was paying any attention to the inflationary insanity that is still eating away at the foundational structure of our vital economic system.

Before the Watergate debacle, we all thought everything would be rosey if we could extricate ourselves from active participation in the Vietnam horrors. Then we hoped that the fickle Gods of inflation, energy shortages and all political hanky-panky would be appeased if the great, presidential high priest himself were sacrificed on the hypocritical punishing altar of impeachment.

But history indicates clearly that extreme punishment can never be effectual in cooling insidious fires of strife and contention forever threatening our national security, wholly from within the sorry attitudes of crackpots still operating inside our armed fortress.

Surely it must be evident by now that our archaic crime and punishment thinking is worse than just inadequate. It is terribly expensive. It cost the taxpayers more than six million dollars to delve into the Watergate falderall.

Most vindictive feelings are futile and harmful to the punishers as well as the victims of such inquisitional irrationality.

And on a personal basis, our condemning and punishing activities have done more to eliminate happiness and sexual pleasure than any other single factor, except the imperfection assumption itself.

The perfection-now position suggests a needed alternative to reverse this condemning and punishing insanity--allowing a more natural and humane consideration of mistakes which, to some extent, are an unavoidable part of human experiences. We are considering only a basic change of attitude.

We are certainly not suggesting any curtailment of a proper use of essential forces to fully protect ourselves, our property and our nation. And yet, it appears possible that the vital, self-preservation requirements can be managed on a more understanding attitude of forgiveness and assistance, rather than the Dark Ages condemning and punishing which deters us from fulfilling our primary purpose of enjoyment and appreciation.

While the potential for noticeable improvement in notorious aspects may take many years of gradual development, there is nothing to prevent immediate, beneficial adjustments when the perfection-now position is applied on an individual basis.

NO COP-OUT

"How do I know for sure you haven't concocted all this perfection-now bull just to con me into thinking you are the perfect man, instead of the jackass idiot I know damn well you are? You used to pull that Dale Carnegie stuff on me, and now it's all this perfection hokum.

"You still haven't given me any sensible explanation that will relate your wild perfection idea to the millions of children who are starving to death. How can you talk about universal perfection with all the horrible destruction and insane killing going on?"

This challenge came out during one of our early discussions when Hazel was a little fed up with the perfection-now concept. My wife has an uncanny sense of perception. Our daughter, Shirley, used to say, "Boy, you can't fool Mama. She's got a mind like a super detective."

Perhaps there were some grounds for Hazel's first suspicion. Although I didn't agree with her rather derogatory opinion of almost all dirty old men in general and me in particular, I had at times performed idiotically and occasionally reacted like a damn-fool, stubborn jackass. Yes, I guess I would have done almost anything to get Hazel to recognize the real loveable me under all that crusty male facade I had taken on during a lot of gut-struggling years.

But for that part about relating the great amount of injustice and deranged behavior with the concept that <u>existence</u> <u>is</u> <u>perfection</u>, it was eight years before I was able to come up with an intelligent verbal answer that was acceptable for Hazel's discerning scrutiny. Like several other important answers that eventually came to the surface, I tried to boil this one down to its essence with as few words as possible: <u>Judgment</u> <u>is</u> <u>not</u> <u>determined</u> <u>by</u> <u>abuse</u>.

For thousands of years we have been beating the hell

out of one another. Looking at the awful destruction he had managed, someone said, "Look at how imperfect it all is. Nobody's perfect. Everyone knows we are all living in an imperfect world." And the whole world has been stewing in that contrived imperfection concoction ever since. And I reminded Hazel of something she has often said, "It doesn't have to be this way."

In some insidious measure, we are all involved in an imperfection con-game. With perhaps a few exceptions, no matter where you look--in business, politics, religion or whatever--our whole culture is contaminated with a screw or get-screwed attitude. It's about par for the course that the unique perfection-now position would be suspect too.

But as I see it, feel it and think I know it, the perfection-now concept is not another contrivance to justify further injustice or wrongdoing. Instead, profound implications offer a completely new alternative basis for more natural and satisfactory standards of ethics and morality. With a perfection-now attitude we tend to do the right and good things because of the pleasure and benefits they provide. And we are inclined to avoid doing what's wrong simply because of the distress and trouble it causes.

However, under the prevailing circumstances, I don't expect anyone to take on my conclusions on the strength of a few remarks made about the situation so far. And this brings me back to the statements of my two friends who, if they believed as I did, would rob a bank. I realize now that they couldn't possibly know what I believed from the inadequate verbalizing I was attempting to communicate at that time. One reason for this book is to make it certain that my ideas on the perfection-now position will not be mistaken for something other than what I precisely mean them to be.

But just in case someone might be misusing their reasoning ability to consider the perfection-now concept as a wide-open license to do anything they fancy, and to hell with the consequences, I will try and clear up that aspect right here and now. I think that in the case of my two friends who were both somewhat religiously oriented, that their handy bank-robbing response was mostly an expression of the old bogyman belief that it takes an ecclesiastical threat of eternal torment in hell to deter good people from yielding to their evil, carnal instincts, and indulging themselves in a greedy life of wickedness and crime.

But it is easy to see how someone could rationalize their thinking that if it's all perfection anyway--so what's the difference? Evidently, one fecal aspect of our deranged imperfection-conditioning is a "get-something-for-nothing-if-you-can" idea, which appeals to some as the first attractive difference in thinking that hits them.

It is hard to believe that after the atrocities performed in Hitler's insane attempt to exterminate the whole Jewish race, similar madness was erupting in Cyprus only a little more than thirty years later (September, 1974). Over 200,000 Cypriots were blasted from their homes, businesses and occupations. And there was grisly evidence of mass murders.

If I thought that my efforts in introducing the perfection-now concept would tend in the least manner to increase this destructive insanity, I wouldn't write another word. But the clear facts, as I see them, are that the imperfection assumption--condoned the world over--is the one fundamental false idea which is primarily responsible for most of the irrational behavior in the world.

Starting with the imperfection postulate, it is impossible to construct a proper structure of morality and ethics. We all need desperately a powerful, new basis for effectual thinking that will bring men and women back to a rational understanding of themselves, their world and their problems. New directions of mental exploration leading to just and considerate behavior in resolving problems are clearly indicated in the perfection-now position.

However, I am well aware of our brainwashed tendency to rationalize something new into a convenient excuse to justify additional injustice. So here is a little special message for any one who may still be considering the bank-robbing possibilities, or any other damn-fool ideas of crime and destruction.

Yes, after fifteen years of careful consideration, I thoroughly believe that, without exceptions, everything existing is innately perfect. You, the bank, the money, and even your ill-considered inclination to rationalize some justification for taking on a life of luxury and ease at someone else's expense, are all equally endowed with a full measure of cosmic perfection. But don't forget that the same perfection is also inherent in the <u>appropriate</u> <u>reaction</u> that will surely occur if you ignore your common sense and attempt such a foolish endeavor.

If you are at all observant, you should know that most banks today have perfect little cameras working all the time, taking a perfect picture every thirty seconds. If there is the slightest indication of trouble, the sequence is speeded up.

Should the perfect bank guard not kill you with a perfect bullet from his perfect pistol, cutting a perfect hole in your perfect guts and spilling your perfect blood all over the perfect sidewalk, chances are you would be caught later by a perfect cop and have a long time to sit on your perfect ass in a perfectly dreary cell, wishing to hell and back that you had used a little more of your apparently atrophied--but still perfect common sense.

But this has been said many times before. Patricia Hearst got her picture taken inside a bank holding a deadly weapon while her alleged associates in the Symbionese Liberation Army collected the loot. Later, it is possible that some of these same "liberators" ended their futile militant adventures in a fiery death shoot-out with the Los Angeles Police.

From the expanded-scope-potential of the perfection-now position, we can expect that death and the hereafter (whatever it turns out to be) are exactly the same perfection phenomena for everyone--despite variations of circumstances causing the profound, but inescapable transition.

The inevitable termination of our physical experiences also ends the reaction and consequences of those tumultuous material adventures. But this sensible arrangement of cosmic excellence functioning in an extended, overall perfection existence does not eliminate the very obvious fact that we invariably suffer here and now, the consequences of our own stupid mistakes, in addition to the misery inflicted upon us by the deranged behavior of our contemporaries.

Our primary purpose in this earthy experience is simply to enjoy and appreciate the universal perfection provided for us in every aspect of our adventures. We are equipped with sufficient abilities and ample intelligence to indicate the proper use of the forces we are able to command. Even with the most extreme misuse of our talents, we are always powerless to alter the existing perfection.

But the potential benefits and pleasures available to us are never forced upon us. In choosing to involve ourselves with programs of deceit and contention, we cannot at the same time expect to enjoy the beauty, serenity and profound contemplation of natural existence occurring when we feast our eyes on a host of heavenly blue morning-glories.

NOT A RELIGION

The perfection-now position is not a religion. It is basically only an alternative estimation regarding a single feature of the unalterable, innate nature of man and his cosmic environment. The more precise concept, <u>existence is perfection</u>, expands the scope of our consideration to include every aspect of anything, known or unknown, existing in the universe. Placing this complementary mantle of absolute cosmic excellence on the infinite expanse of reality involves us in incompatible controversies with traditional thinking, in our search to establish a measure of validity for our position. Almost obvious implications and applications emerging from this bold assertion places many of our conclusions in discord with fundamental precepts of most religions--as we generally understand the meaning of that term.

However, it is not my intention to present these alternative proposals with an adversary attitude. My personal conviction of the overriding perfection existing in all that we are considering--the good and bad, the true and false, reality and illusion--removes any feelings of antagonism which I have found are undesirable products of our imperfection conditioning. My contention is not against people--only disturbing ideas which are responsible for the despair and turmoil in the world.

But despite all the trouble, I am not too concerned with what anyone else believes. If I am correct in this new approach, it doesn't matter a great deal because the inherent excellence of our natures will manage and adapt--regardless of any difficulties. Irrespective of conflicting differences of opinion, the eternal end-results will be the same for everyone, anyway.

But no one needs ever to limit themselves to just one inflexible attitude. While to some extent and for the reasons I have just given, I am not too concerned whether anyone else adjusts their thinking to agree with conclusions I have determined are valid, I have an area of caring and serious concern for the unnecessary distress people cause themselves and others by carelessly taking on incorrect proposals which eventually lead to rotten consequences. The whole tragic Patty Hearst debacle provides a clear illustration of what I mean.

Not so clear, however, are the somewhat hidden, demented implications infesting religious doctrine that, in the past, compelled Christian soldiers of the cross to kill off the heathen and heretics. These militant evangelists performed their insane atrocities in paranoid fear that God might destroy the whole world if the imperfections of the pagans were not eliminated from the scene.

Hitler also rationalized that the world would be more perfect if the supposedly inferior Jewish race could be exterminated. At this late date here in America, we might think that we have progressed beyond falling for such thinking and inhumane bahavior. But the same false assumptions which led Hitler to run amuck and motivated the Christian crusaders to slaughter their irreligious contemporaries are still contaminating our thinking and behavior today.

Because of our anal imperfection thought structure, women find it difficult to endure the chauvinistic attitude that a lot of men easily slide into. And on the other horn of the imperfection-mating dilemma, men are frustrated by their inability to cope with women and their sexual attractiveness commingling with incomprehensible periods of female bitchiness. Each disgusted partner eventually concludes that their genetically imperfect mates are hopeless, and begins to shop around for a less imperfect specimen.

Much that is naturally right, good and desirable in the perfection-now position is the alternative counterpart of that which is unnatural, wrong and repulsive in religion. For instance, in the third chapter we consider the delightful conjecture that, without qualifications, we all have soul-perfection now. Almost all religious doctrine places our souls in a condemned, God-damned, lost and most imperfect condition.

The perfection-now position easily postulates a Universal Creative Force coexisting in and with a living creation, equally alike in cosmic perfection. Because of the alleged imperfections of our nature, religion adamantly limits absolute perfection to an unacceptable, personified deity existing separated and apart from His less than excellent, unworthy creatures.

Religious imperfections serve as a punishing, measuring device with man and his evil instinctual tendencies at the lowest point of the degrading scale. The fecal idea of original sin, the fall of man and subsequent "divine" plans for a conditional salvation is at the disordered center of the complex religious structure.

The nonreligious perfection-now concept implies that all these absurd assumptions are groundless--serving only as an impediment, effectively preventing us from fulfilling our simple purpose of earthly enjoyment and appreciation.

Religionists attempt to regulate our work, our rest and our finances. In addition, they put restrictions on what we should eat and what our desires ought to be. Perfection-now alternatives suggest the uttermost latitude of personal freedom and noninterference in all these matters as an essential requisite to our physical well-being and happiness.

If we are at all serious in our profession, religious affiliation burdens us with a grave responsibility to help save humanity from its doomsday destiny which a supposedly perfect God of love is scheduled to wrathfully execute on the allegedly imperfect creatures of His creation.

The perfection-now position cannot accept that a Universal Creative Force of absolute perfection could or would ever create imperfectly or allow any aspect of factual imperfection to exist even for a moment in His creation. If valid, this conclusion immediately places everybody, without exceptions or qualifications, on an absolute equality basis of cosmic excellence requiring no assistance or salvation as far as their eternal destiny is concerned.

This unneeded "saving" obligation imposed on us by invalid regligious doctrines becomes the contrived requisite for ecclesiastical organizations set up to expedite this con-game of deified damnation and salvation. In contrast, at least as I see it, the perfection-now position functions best as an independent, individual consideration.

Notwithstanding the many natural benefits emerging with an awareness of the perfection-now concept, don't expect this new direction of thinking to act as a magic cure-all for all your troubles. If you are really sick, the best thing you can do is go to a good doctor and follow his advice. Any references made in this book concerning our general well-being, our general health or our disturbed state of mind are suggestions offered only in that broad area where it is still possible, legal and proper to help ourselves without neglecting serious conditions which clearly require professional assistance.

Despite incorrect fundamentals which we are attempting to expose, we recognize that a great many competent religionists and psychiatrists do perform worthwhile services. In our exposure of both religious and secular irregularities, it is well to consider that the unqualified excellence of our existing make-up is functioning at all times for everyone, and in all extenuating circumstances.

The human phenomenon, a miraculous combination of both physical and nonphysical composition, has an enormous faculty for adaptation. And in spite of extreme difficulties encountered, because of our wholesale condoning of the imperfection assumption, the cosmic excellence ingrained in every facet of existence will always make it possible for a large majority of the people to perform adequately--regardless of adverse contingencies.

There are several good reasons why I am determined (if I can manage it) to keep the perfection-now position out of the decadent catagory of religious classsification. Some of these reasons will become obvious as we go along. But I think that the main basis for avoiding the contamination of religionism has to do with a serious fault existing in our educational programs, which is largely responsible for the deplorable lack of common-sense morality in the world today. Our sick culture has an imperative need for an alternative, nonreligious basis, from which students <u>and instructors</u> can freely consider vital questions of our existence.

Although the cherished separation of church and state is an accomplished fact, guaranteed by the constitution of our country, we do not yet have <u>freedom of education</u> in vital areas that organized religions claim as their exclusive domain.

Acceptable answers regarding who we are, what we are, and <u>why</u> we are here <u>as we are</u>, are not available in either public or church schools. Satisfactory grounds for integrity and humane considerations for others are nonexistent. While at this time it appears as an extreme speculation, I feel that the perfection-now factor could serve as an acceptable way to correct this present intellectual vacuum which is quite an obvious imcompleteness in our educational structure.

There is nothing implied or intended in the perfection-now position to suggest that we have no further need to continually improve our skills and understanding. Learning seems to be a never-ending requisite of our living experiences. But from our new approach we can relax any effort to actually become anything innately different than whatever we basically are now.

Nothing inherent in our <u>natural</u> make-up must be overcome, put down, eradicated or even controlled. <u>For sure, this statement must not be misjudged out of its specific context</u>. Relieved of any <u>unnatural burden</u> concerning our well-being in the hereafter, the free-flowing, natural function of our instinctual natures in our learning process is obviously essential to a well-ordered regulation of our mental and emotional reactions, as well as a common-sense indicator to control our behavior.

When the vital workings of our intuitive awareness is

better understood and appreciated, we may let up some on the boring, unnecessary struggle to mentally absorb vast amounts of relatively unimportant falderal--allowing more essential time for unburdened minds to recognize and ponder pertinent enlightenment from the instinctual areas of our personal, inner source of cosmic knowing.

Some novel educational experiments indicate that a few aware educators are exploring possibilities in this more natural and enjoyable approach to learning. Unfortunately, in principal, it does not correspond with some of our established, psychological fundamentals. Incorrect conclusions regarding our basic humanness condition us to ignore vital intuitive promptings of our inner nature.

Present educational programs require us to accept irrational determinations of "authorities," even when such information is in distressful contradiction with our natural instinctual judgments of reason and common sense. In conforming, we are compelled to rationalize that intuitive reason and human logic cannot be trusted and must often be disregarded.

This is the beginning of confusion and frustration. It is really awful to be saddled with the belief that our instinctual natures are imperfect, and are the source of most of the hostility in the world. Religious thinking is mainly the cause of this dilemma. But psychology, based on the unacceptable dogma of accidental evolution, must bear some of the responsibility.

From the perfection-now position we easily see there is nothing about our human make-up that is causing our distress. Instead, it is clear that it is our unnatural, false conditioning regarding our unalterable nature that is basically responsible for the general human dilemma.

Reason and logical understanding are restored to their proper usefulness when we are liberated from the incorrect conviction of inherent imperfection running wild in the unconscious areas of our being. Our problems are substantially diminished when we become aware that they are certainly not caused by our alleged imperfect natures--but are, in fact, difficulties that can easily be resolved through modified and proper, nonreligious educational procedures.

NO UTOPIAN FANTASY

I think it is important to establish that the perfection-now position _is_ _not_ an impractical, crackpot utopian contrivance concocted to persuade you to support another futile, "save-the-world" movement. As far as I am concerned, the world doesn't need saving. The very essence of this simple concept that <u>existence</u> <u>is</u> <u>perfection</u>, that we already have <u>perfection now</u>, that <u>nobody's</u> <u>imperfect,</u> indicates clearly that there are no exalted goals to reach, no idealistic accomplishments to attain to.

And I am convinced there is nothing vital in our natural make-up which we don't already have, and for which we must strive to get. The most that anyone can do about the perfection-now position is make a slight cerebral adjustment which would allow a fair assessment of its potential value and possible validity. There are no promised rewards for implicit believing, and there are no dire punishments threatened if you choose to ignore the subject altogether. If the perfection-now idea is valid, you are always a beneficiary of that cosmic fact--irrespective of your state of mind.

But suppose we do choose to consider the perfection-now position as an alternative approach to look at ourselves and the world. There is nothing in this mental exploration that would prevent us from accomplishing anything that our personal needs and desires suggest that we attempt to do. When any and every direction open for our exploration is impregnated with cosmic perfection, it is actually difficult to sit still too long while depending entirely on the hard-working efforts of others for all the material requirements of our worldly adventures.

It wasn't long after the perfection-now idea began to develop in my thinking before I noticed a profound change in my somewhat obnoxious attitude toward hard physical labor. I had always considered myself fortunate to have a trade (furniture upholstering) which allowed me to work inside and out of the hot sun. Also, the tools I used were relatively light in comparison to the heavy implements required in more rugged, general construction work.

But twenty-five years of the furniture business finally seemed enough of a supposedly good thing. I was surprised to find that I had a strong, compelling desire to do hard work, outside in the sun. And especially, I felt I wanted to take on something gut simple, like digging in the dirt with a shovel.

Be careful of what you want--you are liable to get it. Hazel had always wanted to be a lookout for the Forest Service; and with my newly acquired longing to dig in the dirt, a short time after we moved to New Mexico, these desires were amply fulfilled.

Both of us were employed as lookouts during the fire season, which usually extends from May to September. Along with our cat, Little Sister, we were helicoptered up to the highest lookout station in the vast Gila National Forest. The district ranger, Ralph Rainwater, spent the first two days with us to show us the lookout ropes, but from there on we were on our own.

However, before he left he made out a long list of jobs that I was expected to do. And most of them involved a lot of hard physical labor. One task was to dig a substantial garbage pit. I could easily see that previous lookouts had neglected this particular chore. Fifteen or twenty years accumulation of rusted cans and debris were in shameful evidence in several rusty heaps just a short distance from the tower grounds.

When I started to excavate our garbage pit I discovered why the others had given up and dumped their cans behind the trees. That whole mountain top was almost nothing but rocks, and each one I encountered had to be pried loose with a heavy, miners pinch bar. Another job I had to do was cut heavy, new post and fence timbers to replace the rotted ones that formed a protective corral around the cistern.

This construction was necessary to keep the horses from clomping over the top of the partially buried water tank. I also had to cut wood for the little cook stove and carry it up forty five feet to the twelve by twelve foot box on top of the tower which was our windy home for the next four months.

After the fire season was over, there was extra trail and fence work to do in the forest. As this work was too far from any base area, five or six of us would camp out for ten days and then take four days off. I really got my fill of sleeping on the ground, back to nature and hard labor. Nevertheless, I was immensely pleased and fascinated with the whole experience. There is a special gut satisfaction from strenuous physical exertion that is, unfortunately, unknown to those who think they are privileged to be excused from such degrading work.

Of course, all of this was only one aspect of my reaction to new thinking emanating from the perfection-now concept. One cannot help but realize a strictly personal factor inherent in this new approach. The directions I have taken and the experiences that have come to me can be of no direct value to another. And surely, no one else could have, vicariously, provided me with the wealth of benefits I have extracted for myself.

Rather than implying an idealistic, conditional, utopian attainment in the future, the perfection-now position places each of us in an immediate, down-to-earth, no-nonsense encounter with all the gut facts of our existence. We feel an inclination to intelligently use whatever we have at hand and make the most of it.

In considering that everything contains its own inherent perfection factor, one finds no tendency to either ignore, or rationalize out of existence, disturbing aspects as lacking in reality. In fact, just the opposite occurs. Excluding nothing, all of the factual evidence of reality (including the troublesome parts) are accepted and evaluated for what they are, just as we perceive and experience them. Those features which prove out to be correct and beneficial are gladly used, while that which is found to be disturbing and false is rejected and avoided.

The month of August, 1974, saw the high point culmination of the long Watergate hassle when President Nixon became the first Chief Executive to resign under the pressure of almost certain impeachment. A lot of inadequate standards are being dumped--and something more satisfactory will eventually emerge to fill the vacuum. Countless individuals are always moving ahead with more practical and just proposals to increase our physical benefits, and decrease the pain and trouble that has plagued us all for too long. Dedicated educators are continually looking into new methods to facilitate learning. Admirable progress has been made in the crime and punishment field--but we still have a long way to go in this vital area.

All of this is presently managed under the unnatural and unnecessary obstacles erupting malignantly because of our condoning of the imperfection postulate. But due to the innate excellence of our natures, we manage somehow, despite the confusion and turmoil we have thoughtlessly created for ourselves.

While the perfection-now concept may appear strange and unusual at first, I feel certain that, eventually, it will be recognized as a valid and self-evident factor which can help us to peacefully reestablish our important thinking to be more in constructive harmony with the factual nature of existence as it actually is.

One neglected area of our fundamental thinking concerns the basic question of who and what we are. The next chapter considers this somewhat intangible but nevertheless knowable subject.

CHAPTER III

SOUL PERFECTION NOW

As a shocking part of the watergate exposure, the whole nation was disturbed to discover that various "dirty tricks" were maliciously used as a destructive tool to accomplish political aims, by and for some of those already occupying the highest realms of government. In this chapter we are attempting to examine in a new and different light, a delicate topic which, in my estimation, has been subjected to the ultimate of dirty tricks.

I can't imagine anything more corrupt than the degrading assertions mankind has suffered from ecclesiastical and scientific authorities regarding the innate nature of his soul. On one hand, religious thinking leads us to believe that our souls are hopelessly imperfect, lost and destined to a variety of horrible ways to spend eternity--if we refuse to go along with their exclusive salvation programs. And on the other hand, scientific authorities dogmatically refuse to seriously consider the many, rational indications to establish that man even has a nonphysical soul which continues to exist and perform after his physical body ceases to function.

The sorry consequences of such irresponsibility are extensive in their destructive reactions. We are all compelled to contrive some form of self-protective shield in adapting to this unnatural problem. I suppose that many manage fairly well by just ignoring the deplorable soul dilemma as long as they can. Usually we keep busy with work and recreation. For quite a few years, any spare time I could afford away from my work was occupied with the fascinating hobby of catching fish. During this period, I didn't care whether I had a soul or not, or what might happen to it after I had gotten on out of here.

But it was a little different in an earlier period of my younger days. If you are gullible enough, exposed enough, and scared enough (as I used to be), you might decide to go wholeheartedly the religious way--hoping that somehow you would escape the terrible fate predicted for those wicked souls who choose not to join up.

Or, if later on you find, as I did, that you just can't stomach any more of the repulsive religious information you are required to consume, you might choose to say as I finally did, "I'll manage the best I can without religion."

Luckily, in my case, I found something better to take the place of the religious ideas I rejected. But the distressful aspect about this whole deplorable soul business is that some go to extremes in their disgusted reaction and, apparently, choose to make the very worst of it all. There is a daring tendency to rationalize that, if we are likely going to hell or oblivion in the hereafter, we might just as well raise a whole lot of hell here and now.

Under the imperfection setup, there is no logical basis for morality. You are condemned, damned and doomed any way you care to look at it. And if we ever expect to see a cooling of the hot fires of desperation, strife and brute belligerency in the world, the solution will have to come from something that correctly considers the <u>whole cosmic existence of man</u>.

It will have to be a simple, valid understanding that anyone can easily cope with on his own intuitive judgment. It will have to be free of conditional restrictions and requirements, such as we are now subjected to in traditional religion. And surely, an effectual resolution of the morality debacle can never be formulated as a part of a soulless, Godless, imperfection structure, such as we are plagued with in contemporary, evolutionary-based psychology.

The reactionary distress involved with incorrect behavior would be sufficient in itself to turn us off from immoral, harmful practices if we were able to function naturally without the complications presently associated with our condemning and punishment programs--both secular and religious. I'll never forget the time that I, unintentionally, frightened my little sister. We were living in Chicago at the time. I was about six, and Margy was three years old. I had been playing with a toy wooden pistol that made a sharp "clank" when the trigger was pulled.

Without thinking of the consequences, I pointed the play gun at my baby sister and clanked it a couple of times. Margy responded as if I were a Chicago gangster, and she was about to be the victim of a massacre. She bellowed out such a pitiful and convincing performance that I determined, solemnly, then and there, that in the future, I would be extra careful to refrain from adding to the fear and distress which older persons thoughtlessly inflict on those unequal to them in age, comprehension and experience.

I shudder to think of the great gobs of inhumane terror children needlessly suffer with the rash of horror pictures and stories imposed on them today. And the particular fiendish fear of losing their souls forever to a satanic monster in hell is still one which trusting, but immature, little minds must endure.

If the uneasy trepidation usually associated with our misunderstanding of soul existence could ever be effectively nullified, we could then investigate this fascinating subject without fear, and with rational judgment. The perfection-now position suggests the pleasing possibility that our souls are perfect now, and are never in jeopardy--regardless of how much deceptive material our surface thinking might have to put up with.

In this chapter I will try to provide a thorough accounting of the direct-knowing, soul experience mentioned briefly in the first chapter. Without the first-hand, soul knowledge gained directly from this mystical occurrence, I feel that the perfection-now position would be imcomplete and virtually impossible to comprehend or accept.

More than fifteen years have gone by since that unique, soul-awareness incident took place. At first, I was appalled to think that I had lived forty five years with, apparently, no valid comprehension of what my soul existence actually is. My utter ignorance on this subject seemed even more incredulous in view of the fact that I had been given an ample religious schooling--even to the extent of finally embarking, at the age of twenty four, on a theological course with the noble but somewhat demented idea of becoming a professional religionist in the Seventh Day Adventists denomination. Fortunately, my evangelistic ambitions and education were terminated by circumstances of the depression before I was qualified to enter the ministry. And my enthusiastic efforts were directed toward more sane and constructive endeavors.

The good years we have had here in New Mexico have provided me with an ideal opportunity to first explore freely what I consider to be the cosmic storehouse of knowledge inherent in my own inner being. Many novel conclusions presented here have come from an extensive tapping of this intuitive source. However, during this time I have also managed to delve carefully into related fields of traditional philosophy, mysticism and comparative religions (both Eastern and Western).

And from all the information researched and intuitively acquired, I have concluded that it is next to impossible for anyone to extract any reliable understanding of our factual soul natures while their perceptive abilities remain partially atrophied with traditional soul misconceptions. The restrictive mental shackles are even more binding by the fact that they are formally locked in place by respected leaders in philosophy, theology and psychology.

Later, in this chapter, I will point out specifically what I consider to be so terribly wrong and detrimental in traditional thinking regarding our soul natures. In addition, we will look into attractive, nonreligious alternatives which could prove to be immediately beneficial to our personal welfare. We will also explore the somewhat ethereal nature of mysticism and its vital importance in any thorough investigation into the factual innate make-up of man.

MYSTICAL OCCURRENCE AT SANTA MONICA

Before we get into the details of what actually happened in my direct-knowing incident, I think I should set the scene a little in order that you might possibly understand how I arrived at my conclusions on the matter--which, in some respects, are quite different than mystical information generally derived by others from similar episodes. Of course, there are various factors in my experience which I have found correspond exactly with pertinent features evident in other genuine transcendental happenings recorded by mystic writers down through the centuries. The principal differences are in my deductions regarding certain features of the mystical occurrence.

It is obvious (to me) that direct-knowing indications obtained by religious mystics have been rationalized by religious scribes, having no mystical awareness of their own, to fit in with established church dogma. And it is equally obvious that my conclusions are influenced by my previous intuitive discovery that <u>existence</u> <u>is</u> <u>perfection</u>, that nobody's imperfect, and that we are all existing in cosmic perfection now.

When this startling concept of unconditional, universal

excellence first became a dominating part of my thinking, it was so delightfully fascinating in its infinite scope of including everything, I was not at all bothered by my lack of valid knowledge concerning our soul natures. Whatever I thought my soul to be, it was sufficient to consider that we all had soul-perfection now.

Apparently our surface minds are never required to consider and assimilate any more information than whatever is essential for us at any period in our developing adventure. Coming into this physical environment at birth, it is enough that we just know how to eat and defecate, and raise a lot of commotion when we are either hungry or uncomfortable.

Generally, in our growing experiences, it is not too serious a matter if we are innocently unaware of information which will likely come to us naturally when it is most needed. However, trouble is brewed when we are conditioned ahead of time with false knowledge which prevents us from learning valid, intuitive information at the proper time when it might be vital to our mental and emotional, as well as our physical well-being.

As mentioned earlier, I had made a somewhat determined effort to unshackle my mind from all postulates and theories regarding humanity that were unsatisfactory and disturbing. It seemed impossible to extricate the unquestioned goodness involved in the personal endeavors of many, trying their best to manage in the complex difficulties of religious thinking, from the repulsive rationalizations commingling with it all. So it appeared easier and more sensible to just mentally separate myself from the inadequate, entire structure of organized religion.

Morality has an independent existence, and is not structured on any man-made, ecclesiastical system for its recognition or its function. I felt assured that whatever goodness I required could readily be found outside the religious dogma. And I have not been disappointed in that conclusion.

Placing myself wholly on the discretion of my own innate resources, I simply considered myself for whatever I obviously was--just one more Homo sapien going along for the ride on this earthly spaceship. I observed that somehow I could think and reason, as well as experience a variety of emotional feelings that seemed to be mostly reactionary to the changing circumstances of my environment.

In my forty five years, I had been aware of various degrees of joy and sorrow. At times hunger and sickness, fear and even terror had been a part of my adventure. However, most of the disagreeable aspects had been somewhat balanced by a fair measure of good health and some good fortune.

But somewhere near the end of this forty five year segment, I often had a perplexing feeling that something very essential was missing from my awareness; something which, could it be found, would make reasonable sense to replace the bullshit intellectualism we were supposed to accept and condone as substantial citizens of the community.

I should also mention here the nature of my work at that time, because it had a lot to do with my determination to find out what I needed to know, as well as how I reacted to that unexpected mystical happening.

For the past twelve years, I had been operating my own custom upholstering shop, doing specialty work for the wealthy people in Beverly Hills and the surrounding affluent territory. Along with the new custom pieces we turned out, there was always some cherished old furniture which had to be repaired and reupholstered. Since this old stuff was expected to endure along with our new pieces, it was always necessary to look for any original structural imperfections and strengthen these weak areas so they wouldn't fall apart after we went to all the work of refinishing and reupholstering them.

Our new chairs and sofas were expected to be of the highest quality, so it was necessary in the design and construction to see that no "commercial" inadequacies were ever a part of our product. Most of my business was conducted on a wholesale basis with top interior decorators who dealt directly with the wealthy clients. The decorators trusted my judgment, and I always had a free hand to create something always a little different and pleasing in design; and above all, I was careful to see that the quality of the work was far above reproach. Therefore, I had a lot of experience and responsibility in spotting troublesome situations and making necessary adjustments to bring the finished product up to a high standard of furniture excellence.

When I finally switched part of my endeavors from providing physical comfort and beauty for others to enjoy, to exploring the field of mental and emotional comfort (mostly for myself), it was somewhat of a natural transition from "fixing" furniture to searching out what was so distressfully wrong with our long established, but terribly inadequate living process.

Remember too, that I had already gone through one profound experience of sudden intuitive enlightenment. But this was simply a startling idea which came just like all other thoughts, except it was so powerful and certain and so expansive in scope, that it has taken me fifteen years to finally express in words the essence of what I felt was involved in that one moment of shocking awareness. My perfection-now idea had a fairly good start, but I was trying to be careful in handling this block-busting concept which implied a different measure on almost every aspect of our living experiences. Also, I was very pleased with the new freedom of thinking I had initially managed with just my mental house-cleaning.

And so it was in this very investigative and open state of mind that something occurred in my consciousness that was unique and delightful, but of a particular nature that our usual understanding of word symbols is somewhat inadequate to relate <u>exactly</u> and <u>fully</u> what took place.

Nevertheless, there is still a lot that can be told, even if it is impossible to describe correctly in physical terms, a sphere of existence and experience that, apparently, is thoroughly nonphysical in its peculiar, mystical make-up; at least nonphysical in respect to our usual comprehension of things as we normally observe and try to understand them from our seemingly, mostly physical nature.

Although it is necessary to make clear distinctions in various segments of existence for purposes of understanding, I am inclined to believe there is much to indicate that both the seeming physical and nonphysical aspects of reality are, ultimately, all one and the same thing. In the main, nonphysical soul-level of existence, there are outstanding characteristics of absolute changelessness which, apparently, function as a necessary balance to the continual changing, or developmental growth and decay, involved in all living, material creations.

Because there is so much in religious absurdities that is unacceptable to rational common sense, scientific thinking has carelessly gone to the other extreme of rejecting nearly everything having any taint of religionism connected with its establishment. To some extent the vital knowledge and beneficial comprehension available to us through various mystical occurrences have been distorted and misused by a basically nonmystical, religious corporation for purposes other than man's immediate enjoyment and well-being. This is another reason why it seems essential to me that we have an alternative, nonreligious approach to consider the knowable soul facts revealed in nearly all genuine mystical experiences.

I should make it clear that my own shedding of unsatisfactory religious features was managed in a gradual procedure over a long period of about fifteen years, and culminated when I finally made a determined mental rejection of whatever remnants still remained as a pollutant in my surface intellect. The point I want to make is that the nonreligious basis for thinking was firmly established in my common-sense judgment, and the final clearing out was more of a positive recognition of a fact, almost already accomplished.

I think this alternative, nonreligious factor is very important in view of the historical fact that most mystical happenings have been considered almost exclusively within the imperfection-based religious thought structure. And because of this extremely biased situation, mystical information in general has been, to some extent, rightly regarded with suspicion. But I have found that by stripping away the absurdities of religious dogma heaped onto the experiences of the saints and mystical writers, there is an acceptable, clear ring of truth apparent in the essence of the mystical incident itself, before incorrect, rationalized, religious implications have been made.

One important thing in considering this subject is to realize that a true mystical occurrence is a natural phenomenon of the general human experience. I am quite convinced that the full mystical experience is not the ultimate attainment of a religious quest. There must be a logical reason and essential purpose for its manifestation. I feel that the transcendental happening takes place of its own accord, despite the unnatural difficulties imposed by false religious dogma--and certainly, not because of it. We have made a sorry mistake in surrendering the whole mystical sphere to the domination of narrow-minded religious thinking.

But it will be easier to consider more of the true nature of mysticism and our personal soul relationship to this fascinating dimension of reality, after you are acquainted with the details of the direct-knowing, mystical occurrence which happened to me as I was driving alone to my upholstering shop in Santa Monica. It was about seven thirty in the morning, and I had just turned off the Pacific Coast Highway and was about halfway up the ramp that takes you to the top of the Palisades and right into the business district of Santa Monica, when I first noticed the beginnings of this unusual experience.

There was an unexplainable sensation of strange pleasantness seemingly centered in the interior of my body, below my chest area. The best way I can describe it, is that it seemed as if there was something or someone in there smiling at me. I remember thinking and almost saying to myself, "How can I be smiling at myself, and the smile be coming from deep inside me where there isn't anything in there to make a smile?" The next quick thought I had was that perhaps I had passed through some peculiar, atmospheric condition that might be responsible for such a delightful sensation. Maybe a truck loaded with perfume had turned over and hundreds of perfume bottles had broken on the pavement of the Palisades Drive above me.

With this thought in mind, instead of crossing Wilshire Boulevard as I usually did, I turned left, went one block, then turned right and circled the block, coming back onto the Palisades Drive, crossed Wilshire again going the opposite direction, and drove about two blocks into the residential area where there was no traffic and I could easily park my car. But by this time I knew that what was going on inside of me was not connected in any way with the condition of the air I was breathing or any other external situation.

I should mention here that all during the thirty five or forty minutes that this soul awareness incident lasted, my normal consciousness was functioning exactly as it always had--except that it was thoroughly amazed at what was going on. Our regular thoughts always seem to be located somewhere in our heads, but all of this mystical knowing was not in my head at all. Rather, it appeared to be centered in my body clearly below my head--but not confined to any definite position. Also I know I could have started up my car at any time and gone on to work--but that would have been unthinkable, in view of what I was experiencing.

By now the inner "smiling" sensation had increased and extended out beyond my body a little ways. It was as if I were in the presence of a wonderful friend, who was radiating a glowing fascination of supreme happiness and contentment. Yet, I was positive that this mystical friend was a very vital part of myself. While I was, to some extent, dumfounded, there was absolutely no apprehension or fear-- because this other part of myself was really no stranger to me. It was a little like going up into the attic and finding something you had been fond of and had used a lot, but had finally put away for a long time, and had forgotten about it--and now, after all that time, there it was again.

But there was more to it than just a startling awareness of my soul consciousness. My soul appeared to be existing in, and seemed to be a part of, a whole new dimension of cosmic reality that is incomparable to any conditons normally known to our physical perceptions. What started out as a subtle, mystical smile in my chest area, gradually expanded into an experience of peacefulness and enjoyment that was of a quality and degree that I had never imagined was possible in this life.

Never was there the slightest indication that my soul was imperfect, impure, lost, or in any trouble whatsoever. There was, certainly, nothing to show that my soul needed my help to get out of a bad situation. Actually, it was just the opposite of that idea. There was a glowing assurance that everything and everybody were absolutely perfect just the way they were now.

In addition, I felt a solid and positive impression that this delightful, nonphysical area of my being would always be available and ready to take over, regardless of whatever might happen to my expendable physical body, and my vulnerable surface mind consciousness.

In the first chapter I said that this was a direct-knowing experience. While most ideas coming into our minds from various sources are always regarded with a proper degree of uncertainty, a mystical, direct-knowing incident is entirely different. It's like being there and seeing for yourself, instead of having to take someone's word for it. Perhaps you have had the experience of first seeing pictures of the Grand Canyon in Arizona, and hearing others talk about it. Then later, you actually stood on the edge of that great excavation, and at last, knew for yourself what it is like, because <u>you were there</u>.

But a mystical experience is even more positive than this. You know first-hand with your soul intelligence, which is far different than just perceptual "knowing" with your mind. At every moment of this mystical occurrence, I was fully conscious of the two separate areas of my being. And at the same time, I realized that these two segments were individual aspects of one primary source. One was the familiar, thinking, feeling, wondering state that I was so used to, and the other was the marvelous soul consciousness, that, in a way, was somewhat strange and new to my normal awareness, and yet, in another sense, it was old and dependable, and more myself than the former.

The principal difference seemed to be one of degree or intensity. For instance, the joy of my soul existence was something like the pleasure I have known in my normal awareness--but this soul ecstasy was physical enjoyment magnified perhaps a hundred or more times. Also, soul pleasure seems to be a constant and enduring characteristic of our soul nature; while physical enjoyment tends to come and go in various degrees--usually depending on environmental circumstances. From what I experienced, there seemed to be no way that my soul nature could be anything other than joyful.

Later, in wondering how my nonphysical soul could manifest such unspeakable happiness and peacefulness, I became convinced that the explanation is related to the cosmic fact that our souls are not dependent on any aspect of material reality for their security or well-being. A somewhat lesser degree of this mystical pleasure is known to our physical consciousness, but nothing I have ever experienced, so far, could compare with the extreme delight that seemed to be the constant nature of my personal soul existence. This inexpressable, mystical joy is one of the outstanding features common to all genuine transcendental occurrences recorded throughout the past centuries.

While forty minutes might seem like a very short time for someone to become acquainted with his soul, you should realize that we were already good old friends of very long standing. Also, try and understand that the "ideas" derived from this mystical occurrence were actually soul "impressions or feelings," rather than verbal thought concepts communicated to my mind consciousness. My normal thinking had nothing to do with all that went on, except to just remain quietly pleased that somehow it was able to be a witness and an observer to the whole business.

Of course, after the mystical incident was terminated, I was right back with only my mind memory of all that had transpired. But that is the way it is for all experiences. I stood on the rim of the Grand Canyon and I saw for myself. I know how it is from personal experience because I was there.

Still, that too, is just a memory. And when I hear others talk of, or when I read about the imperfect ego, the irrational subconscious or unconscious mind--I realize they are just speculating in the dark, and their conclusions are way off course. I know something of what it's all about because I was there. I "saw," I "felt," I "heard," I "perceived." I put these words in quotes because the "seeing, feeling, hearing and perceiving" (which are not adequate terms) were all managed without physical eyes, ears or the usual mental processes normally associated with sensorial perception.

If this is too difficult to understand, don't be overly concerned. If you have a mystical experience of your own, you will know then for yourself. I am now inclined to think that such transcendental occurrences are far more common than is generally known. And it's high time we look at these miraculous, but very natural, happenings from a common-sense, nonreligious approach in order to find out as much about our total cosmic nature as we can.

Consider the first, subtle, smiling sensation I experienced in the interior of my body. My soul was actually doing the smiling--but not with any of the usual functions we ordinarily employ when we smile or feel like smiling. Of course, I was actually doing it too, because I am my soul, even though I had been wholly ignorant of that aspect of my total being for forty five years.

In some unexplainable way, my soul and my physical consciousness were communicating directly with each other on a wide-open, no interference basis. The fine tuning adjustments necessary for this face to face, soul and mind incident, were clearly within the discretion and ability of my soul nature. And no doubt there is a good reason for this sort of, "Don't call me--I'll call you" communication system. I am sure that if I could easily turn up my mind-awareness volume control, I would likely be pestering my soul nature for a lot of information which I need to discover on my own with the existing abilities I already have.

Another thing, the extra dimension of cosmic beauty, peace, contentment, intelligence, security, joy and especially love (which appears to be a composite mystical factor overlying all these features) is so desirable and attractive--in comparison to the relatively meager amounts we know in our physical adventure--we would all be very dissatisfied with our material position with its seemingly unavoidable chances of some difficulties and pain, if that sphere of reality were always available to us.

One of the very worst misconceptions imposed upon us by imperfection-based religion is an exploitation of this possibility. Mystics have always told their contemporaries of transcendental delights available for us in an extra dimension of reality difficult to describe in physical terms and symbols. But misguided religionists (unable to fully comprehend what the mystics have attempted to communicate) have gone to extremes in their promotional endeavors. They have discredited and devalued the cosmic excellence of the material "here and now" in zealous attempts to enhance the "perfection" thought to be found only in the nonphysical, spiritual reality.

It is utterly senseless to consider any aspect of our short, physical trip imperfect because of some <u>essential</u> measure of adverse contingencies possible here, compared with a seemingly more wonderful, trouble-free existence waiting for us when we leave this material experience.

And it is tempting insanity for anyone to imply or impose a conditional factor connected with this attractive nonphysical state of being, automatically available to all of us in our future existence.

From the perfection-now position, it appears that our souls are already existing in that marvelous condition of joy and peacefulness (right now--at this precise moment), completely free of any of the physical distress and turmoil, which can bug the hell out of our surface minds and bodies.

It seems to be a necessary requirement of this physical journey that we be sensitive and responsive to irritation. When we are either too hot or too cold, we need to know it. And our discomfort motivates us to do something constuctive about the undesirable condition. We have pains in our stomach when we are hungry and occasionally we puke when we have hogged in too much food. When our bank account gets too low, we worry, and this mental irritation usually compells us to get to work to provide the financial security that is necessary.

I have often thought back to what it might have been like if my mystical experience had not been discontinued as it was. I feel sure that I would have just stayed there and, likely, would have happily starved to death if I could have remained in that delightful state of mystical cosmic consciousness which, apparently, requires none of the physical necessities of material survival.

I think the one part of mystical information that is most difficult to comprehend is the actual nonphysical dimension of reality that is usually revealed in most full, transcendental, mystical occurrences. There is just nothing at all in our normal, physical awareness that this <u>extra</u> realm of existence can be compared to.

It is a little easier to grasp the possibility of our souls becoming better known to us because our regular consciousness is, evidently, a limited (though a sufficient and proper) extension of this more primary segment of our cosmic being. To some extent, we are all a little intuitively aware of a mostly concealed, <u>extra</u>, inner-consciousness and are quite familiar with the psychological terms of the subconscious or unconscious parts of our make-up.

But it is hard to consider that there is a whole cosmos around us filled with this seemingly nonphysical reality that all mystics know of, but find it almost impossible to communicate effectively with nonmystics regading this somewhat intangible realm.

If you should have a full mystical experience of your own some day, you will discover as I did that, although this transcendental level of reality might seem a little startling at first, in short order, you will find that this extra area tends, also, to be somewhat familiar--just as your own soul nature is clearly not a stranger to you. We have all been there before and it doesn't take very long to realize it.

I had a particularly strong soul impression <u>that the composition of this nonphysical reality is the underlying Creative Force and Universal Intelligence providing Infinite Power and directional control for every atomic particle, as well as each nonphysical component of the entire cosmos.</u>

As the mystical occurrence at Santa Monica finally began to diminish in "volume or intensity" and the very last remnants of it were still available for my careful scrutiny, I noticed a distinct, musical vibration--exactly like a bell tone. But this was not heard especially with my ears. It was still a faint, inner, soul-awareness "hearing" which is related to that mystical knowing. But my receptive, surface mind, taking it all in, can only describe it as something like physical hearing.

SOUL INTERCOURSE

For a long time, no one had any idea of what the backside of the moon looked like. But finally, the astronauts got up there and photographed it so that no longer is it any great mystery. It seems incredible that for an equally long time period we have had no really acceptable and valid understanding of the mostly concealed aspects of our personal soul natures. And yet, the natural means to intelligently investigate this important segment of our total being has been available all during that time.

Of course, we managed all right without photographs of the backside of the moon, mainly because we were allowed to remain in comparatively harmless ignorance regarding that particular part of the vast unknown. Also, we could have flubbed through quite well without much valid, soul information if we had been left alone to muddle through somehow with our natural lack of knowledge on soul matters.

But this has not been the case. From the time we are

first able to think a little ways beyond our initial eating and pooping occupations, we have been slathered with a disgusting spread of misinformation concerning this marvelous inner component of our being.

Despite the discouraging, extensive scope of the world's problems, I am personally confident that, eventually, every serious difficulty can be resolved by simply adjusting information programs to provide the essential knowledge we require. And at the same time we will cease feeding young minds invalid, mental garbage regarding their unconditionally, perfect soul natures. This degradation of our innate nature is directly causing much of our emotional disorders and unhappiness. To some harmful extent, we all have suffered from this general downgrading of the human animal.

I do not believe that the seemingly great task of separating the enormous amounts of sickening, soul propaganda from the wholesome goodness of much factual information available is as difficult as one might first think. Our biggest trouble has been caused from a very wrong approach. We have been desperately searching with eyes half blinded by false basic assumptions.

Somewhat late in my life I determined to find, and hopefully fix or adjust, the alleged imperfect area of my make-up. But instead, I discovered that the presupposed object of my search was nonexistent. I was mentally awakened to the simple fact that there was nothing in our innate nature that could properly be considered imperfect. Therefore, I would never find anything but more frustration, more hopelessness and unhappiness if I continued to struggle with that impossible goal in mind.

So I began to look with an entirely different purpose. It was almost like a return to my very early, natural fascination with all the interesting facets of sights, smells, feelings and sounds I thoroughly enjoyed before my parents sent me off, at the age of fourteen, to two years of boarding school. There, I was a captive audience for the dogma of religious fear, despair and even terror, in contemplating the awful things which were sure to befall on those who did not submit themselves to the dreary demands of religious damnation and salvation.

But looking back on it now, I can't blame my mother and father for doing what, evidently, they thought was best for me. Nor can I, in any way, condemn the officials and instructors of that small denominational Junior College and High School Academy for following along in the way they had been trained to function.

In all fairness I should give proper credit to the good aspects involved in those years of religious training. Mixed in with all the embarrassing, mournful, daily praying and pleading with God to save our supposedly wicked, sinful souls was a certain amount of "moral" exposure that, no doubt, was somewhat beneficial--despite the blackmail trappings. But damn-it-to-hell, I would have willingly taken on every bit of the good stuff without all of that repulsive material mixed in with it. Why did I have to have the poop scared out of me in order that I could learn the difference between right and wrong, good and evil? Why did I have to be taught that my soul was condemned, damned and doomed by God, just because I happened to be the human creature that I was?

I feel that the subject matter needs to be explored for the damaging and deplorable practice it is. The fact that we are all quite accustomed to it, and it has been an acceptable part of our heritage for thousands of years, in no way serves as a justification for a continuance of such a degrading program. If the perfection-now idea ever becomes recognized in religious discussions, religionists will either have to adjust their imperfection-based dogmas or defend them--and there is no rational defense for such nonsense.

It was a great shock for me to realize that the principal

fear germs of the imperfection sickness were being administered to its victims through the seemingly respectable and even noble efforts of almost all religious organizations. It required several years before I discovered that it was possible for me to separate the fact of false religious ideas from the host of individuals and groups who are infected with degenerate thinking implied from invalid fear doctrines.

It is not inconceivable that in a more rational, future time, the word "religion" will eventually develop a more respectable and truly moral meaning. And all the Dark Ages, imperfection-based inquisitional, fecal features of present day religious thinking will be a forgotten relic of the past.

If such a desirable adjustment ever could be managed within the future religious thought structure, the first concept religionists would have to set straight would be their misunderstanding of our soul natures. As I have no ambition to involve myself in any such corporate hassle, I am satisfied to merely adjust my own thinking on soul matters--and religionists can do whatever they please.

It should be understood that everything I am recording here is only my own personal estimation, and I make no claim of any divine inspiration. Of course, all of this material has been subjected to my intuitive judgment over a long period of fifteen years since that mystical occurrence at Santa Monica took place. But during my mystical experience, I did not submit any verbal questions, and certainly, no statements were issued by my soul nature. However, there were actual soul "feelings and impressions" involved in what I would call a mystical direct knowing. Still, the word composition of those soul impressions are the relatively, inadequate, literary endeavor of my surface mind with its usual ability to speculate, exaggerate or understate.

Also, from a nonreligious position, when we attempt to talk about a nonphysical soul existence, we are trying to consider something which doesn't even exist from the traditional "scientific" materialistic point of view.

But I have found that the principal features of a mystical happening <u>which can be expressed</u> have occurred over and over again to various individuals both in and out of the religious sphere. In almost every true transcendental occurrence there is invariably a remarkable experience of cosmic joy, peace and happiness.

It is also a distinct mystical feature that, in attempting to record his or her encounter with this extra dimension of delight, each mystic seems compelled to express his utter inability to relate properly in physical terms something which is seemingly nonphysical in its peculiar make-up. In addition (in the one outstanding mystical incident above all others), there is, almost always, a realization of a transcendental personality and a strong, unmistakable feeling of union or oneness with this marvelous mystical being.

But besides this extra soul personality, there is a positive, soul knowledge of an imageless, Cosmic Power and Intelligence which clearly extends beyond any single personality to be immanent in everything and everybody.

Now my own concept of these main features, which can be found in nearly all true mystical happenings, can be simplified in a nonreligious determination to be: (1) Our regular consciousness (which is a somewhat limited but adequate part of our souls); (2) our nonphysical, cosmic soul natures (which are mostly hidden from the surface consciousness); and (3) the almost unspeakable, but clearly knowable, Universal Creative Force and Intelligence of the whole cosmos.

I am convinced that the main reason for mystical manifestation is solely to give us some degree of valid information regarding that concealed part of our total being which most of us intuitively perceive will continue to exist after we have terminated our direct adventure as a living segment of material reality.

Also, information gained from mystical, direct knowing provides us with some tangible comprehension of the infinite God power and unlimited wisdom revealed in the orderly functioning of the entire perfect universe.

But we are not dependent on mystical information alone. From the perfection-now position there is a whole visible world of valid material to establish the actual existence of our soul natures, and we will consider that evidence later on. But the fascinating mystical knowing is vital as a confirmation of common-sense conclusions derived from ordinary experiences available to anyone.

If we look at these main components of nearly all-- once in a lifetime--mystical occurrences (recorded by mystics over an extended time period of thousands of years) with new understanding gained from the perfection-now position, we will find certain, almost obvious facts about who and what we are as well as strong indications regarding the innate nature of our total cosmic being.

I feel that an acceptable comprehension of our physical and nonphysical make-up would be the first, essential, educational requisite if we ever expect to have a mature, rational and pragmatic basis for learning, where moral integrity and constructive goodness can develop naturally in our ever expanding and seeking surface consciousness--rather than the frustration and belligerency which is predominate today. It seems reasonable that these principal features of our partially hidden nature are shown to us in mystical experiences for the express purpose of informing us about who and what we are--at least to the extent that we need to know and to the degree that we are able to grasp with our normal thinking ability.

Let's consider one segment of mystical knowing which the term "soul intercourse" perhaps implies more than any other word description. Having discovered the particular delights of sexual intercourse, no doubt a lot of young people wonder if their physical, pleasure experiences must be sacrificed in order to qualify themselves for the reported enjoyment possible in a mystical happening. In my own experience, I certainly didn't give up a thing that was desirable, good and enjoyable. In fact, I believe that the more we can enjoy ourselves, the easier it would be for our soul natures to accomplish the mystical occurrence.

I am convinced that our souls have always existed. Just because there are beginnings and endings in the physical realm is no indication that there must be beginnings and endings in nonphysical reality. But these conclusions do not exclude the fact of a cosmic experience of potential pleasure that is actually better than sex.

I think most mystics would agree that there is something better than sex--but God didn't keep it for Himself. It is freely and equally shared with our soul natures. Religious mystics have been handicapped in their attempts to describe the delights of a mystical "divine union" by their strict conditioning, where the enjoyment of any earthly pleasure was considered a stumbling block in their spiritual progress. Nevertheless, they have used such verbal symbols as "spiritual marriage" and the "bride being prepared for the bridegroom." But these expressions have always been considered in a very sexless implication. The general derogatory attitude toward sex, engendered in religious thinking, implies that the ideal attainment would be to enter into the transcendental soul-thrilling state as a virgin and remain that way through all eternity.

In my own mystical encounter, there was no doubt in my mind that the personality smiling at me from inside my body was, positively, another part of myself. Later in the transcendental occurrence there was, also, no question about the fact that my personal soul nature was absolutely "one with" that almost indescribable Universal Creative Force of the cosmos.

A lot of additional information regarding mystical experiences can be found in two books by Evelyn Underhill, *Mysticism* and *The Essentials of Mysticism,* E. P. Dutton & Co. She portrays the genuine mystic as one who is struggling to attain this "union with God."

There is no question but that most mystics were involved in a struggle--just as I was surely striving to make some reasonable sense out of the great conglomeration of religious and scientific nonsense. But I don't think that anyone fortunate enough to experience a full mystical encounter has any preconceived idea of what he or she is instinctively seeking. What is discovered is so thoroughly different than anything he could expect to learn about in the corporate religious structure, that the mystic is usually incapable of communicating clearly to others any intelligent understanding of what has occurred.

For sure, the religious mystic would hardly think of comparing his personal transcendental ecstasy, his "soul intercourse" or his "divine union with God", as something better than sex. But the normal soul delights which are there for all of us <u>are</u> <u>far</u> <u>better</u> <u>than</u> <u>sex</u>. I am not downgrading sexual pleasure, and certainly, it is no impediment to a mystical encounter. But I am saying that you will not be disappointed with what you find. And the best thing is the fact that the main, hidden part of our personal soul being is enjoying that unspeakable pleasure right now. Also there are no qualifications which will admit some and exclude others.

While the mystical occurrence makes it possible for us to get a little more acquainted with our nonphysical souls, at the same time, we are privileged to directly experience and know something of the God power of the cosmos. The traditional, religious concept of God will also have to be adjusted a whole lot if it is ever to correspond favorably with the factual truth regarding that profound Cosmic Creative Force.

A NONDRELIGIOUS GOD? OR "X" FACTOR

In the beginning of the perfection-now exploration, when I disassociated myself from the traditional acceptance of religious thinking, I had no intention of excluding any valid facts of existence. Just because it is distorted by religious dogma, is no reason to divorce one's self from a proper consideration of the cosmic x-factor or God Force that is the underlying power, eminent in every atomic particle in the universe. I was equally disturbed with some conclusions of authoritative "scientific" opinions. But this partial rejection did not turn me off on the whole package of apparently valid scientific information.

As I see it, and as long as religion means what is does today, the perfection-now position easily recognizes some type of nonreligious Cosmic Intellect and Power. And as long as we stay out of deified damnation and salvation, it doesn't matter too much what lable is attached to this omnipotent x-factor-motivator. Anyone having a full mystical experience is privileged to come into unmistakable contact with this God-force through the unique awareness of their personal soul natures.

During the mystical phenomenon the surface consciousness remains unchanged. Contrary to orthodox thinking about purification, it has not reached any special, transcendental level of attainment--other than perhaps having a simple desire to know and understand the truth about existence. It is our main, soul consciousness (which psychology calls our unconscious or subconscious) which, on its own option, increases the perceptive volume of its own existence to the transcendental state, where our amazed surface mentality is able to realize its innate oneness with this tree would have if it found itself extended through a hole in a tall, solid fence. For years this branch would develop on its own, unable to see the principal source of its energy and intelligence. Then, one day the fence was removed and this limb was finally able to realize how grand a tree it really was.

In my mystical encounter, I could not perceive any real difference between the impersonal God-intellect (which is clearly beyond any individual confinement and infinite in its location) and the cosmic knowledge and wisdom evident in our personal soul natures.

While in this respect they both appear to be one and the same, there is a noticeable distinction between our individual soul-personality and the x-factor God Force which is radiating out in all directions to a never-ending infinity. Even with my very immature, perfection-now comprehension, it was clear to me that my body, my mind and soul, and my inherent God-energy were all existing equally in the same unconditional cosmic perfection.

Shortly after the mystical experience had ended, I remember thinking what a perfect arrangement it all was-- something like a cosmic back-up system. When the expendable, physical body can no longer function, the surface mind consciousness (which is an extension of its main soul being) simply is withdrawn back into its principal, soul counterpart.

It's not any big deal for your nonphysical soul, because it is always independent of any physical discomforts or material restrictions. And it's something like a homecoming for our physical consciousness--because we quickly realize we have all been there before. Though we have been mentally consumed with other (mostly material) interest in our brief physical soul journey, no doubt, we can easily take up again our eternal, nonphysical soul existence with the greatest of pleasure, a degree of cosmic enjoyment, which, in comparison to normal physical delight, is utterly beyond symbolic literary expression.

There is absolutely no fearful question of eternal security within the make-up of our primary soul natures. And when it realizes its inseparable relationship with its principal soul-being, that same God-like fearlessness and confidence in universal perfection is possible for our superficial physical natures, too. If I had to pick out the one outstanding impression above all others, it was that my soul and my x-factor God accepted me just the way I was. There was positively no consideration of qualifications. Also, it was a lot more than just acceptance. They were both happy and overjoyed in their enthusiastic approval of me.

When the mystical occurrence had run its course, I knew for certain there was nothing I had to accomplish, nothing I had to become, nothing I had to think, believe, say or do that could--by omission or neglect--jeopardize my future, eternal existence and well-being. I also fully realized that I was nothing special, and the same delightful future was assured for everyone--irrespective of their belief or any unfortunate contingencies that might happen to them in their physical adventure.

With my crude and inadequate attempts at verbal communication, it seems almost futile to try to describe the nature of the x-factor or God Force; or (more correctly), to relate the impressions I received regarding this infinite cosmic Creative Power. If you could imagine an awareness of the totality of cosmic goodness, the immensity of cosmic love and the thrilling experience of cosmic pleasure, all mixed together into a knowable nonphysical substance; and this omniscient God-intellect was radiantly pleased that you were in "His" presence--that would still be a very inadequate telling.

The word "His" is not used here to indicate a cosmic form or personality, for there was nothing in the mystical occurrence to suggest a single God person. Neither was there anything to establish that this omnipresent Creative Force was either male or female. But in another sense there was nothing lacking either, for this omnifarious God substance was clearly the unquestioned source of everything required to be a person--both male and female.

There was also the essential stuff it must take to be a star or a whole galaxy of stars. This certainly sounds (even to me now--fifteen years after the experience) like a contrived exaggeration, but if anything, it is really an understatement.

I can easily see how the very real personality of our main soul beings (saturated as they are with this God-substance) could well be mistaken for a superior personal God being. This could happen if we limited our own soul existence to that lesser part we usually think of as our surface consciousness. In my own transcendental experience I was very aware of my normal self sitting there in my car taking it all in. And I definitely recognized this God-filled, nonphysical soul personality as the so-called unconscious or subconscious part of myself. That left only the impersonal, imageless, x-factor God Force to fill out the total experience.

I was not at all bothered by any religious dogma, and feel that I was able to judge the whole mystical happening for what it actually was. On an individual basis, where the mystic is thoroughly impressed with his "oneness" with the mystical God Force existing in his own personal soul nature, such a mistake would not diminish the effectiveness and purpose of the transcendental happening.

However, when an incorrect idea of a superior and separate, personal deity is taken on as a fundamental, religious postulate, and then embellished with additional gobs of invalid information regarding the precise character and nature of a God contrived in man's material image--this becomes a serious misconception, for those who, trustingly, accept such conclusions for the real thing.

It is degrading, too, when we discredit our surface

selves in comparison to the God-like segment of our soul being--which, in contrast, appears to be the ultimate in cosmic excellence.

The factual nature of our nonphysical souls seems to be identical with that of the nonphysical x-factor-God-Force. One outstanding impression of my experience was that the high degree of mystical love, joy and peace revealed in the make-up of our souls and God were of a constant, unchanging and enduring nature. These pleasant qualities were everywhere--just like the atmosphere of air which we always experience as being constantly around us.

Radiating from this God force was a powerful assurance that everything was absolutely all right (in fact perfect) regardless of adversities sometimes bothering us in our material adventures. It's as if our souls and God know well how miserable we can get--but from their position, it is of little concern. They know for certain that we will manage through it all somehow, and the happy, ultimate results will be right and good--irrespective of our various degrees of difficulties.

I am not trying to speak for God, but from what I perceived, the factual nature of God is far different than the wrathful, demanding, commanding, inhumane, illogical, unreasonable, inept, inconsistent, unloving, disordered, condemning, damning, punishing and destroying, ungodly character portrayed by the alleged "word of God" biblical records.

From what I think I know, the most predominate characteristic of God's nature is an almost inexpressible manifestation of love. This mystical understanding of cosmic love is related to something we all know a little of, because that same love is an integral segment of our personal make-up. But a full mystical occurrence usually gives one a clear understanding of God love that seems almost unbelievable to our normal understanding.

Love appears to be the principal ingredient inherent in the very real composition of nonphysical existence. It is as definite a portion of both God's nature and our soul's innate make-up as our flesh and bones, blood and guts are to our physical bodies.

It is also clear that this cosmic God and soul love permeates throughout the whole of material existence. It has an inseparable relationship with an understanding of universal perfection, and we will look into this important aspect more fully in a later chapter.

It would be futile to attempt to duplicate this high degree of God love from our present position of limited abilities. The amount of love we are able to manage in our physical make-up is plenty and sufficient for our purposes here. But it is good for me to know that such a tremendous amount of cosmic love is continually coming to each of us (without exceptions or conditions) from this inexhaustible source.

Even the most idealistic, sexual love fulfillment or any aspect of physical love falls far short of our soul comprehension of cosmic love. This love substance is the recognizable character and innate nature of God, and every mystic attempts, somewhat unsuccessfully, to tell his contemporaries something about it.

With the direct knowing of our soul's awareness in a mystical experience, there is a positive indication that no conditions are involved in the universal dissemination of this basic, first-cause love-energy. From what I have read, it seems that almost every genuine mystic is impressed with this pantheistic concept of God being in everything--the rocks and trees as well as the birds and animals. And though it is not spelled out, there is an implication that the mystics are not too concerned that this heretical idea includes the fact of God being in the evil or painful aspects of reality, as well as the good. I surely cannot speak for anyone else, but I would bet a couple of bucks that anyone who has actually experienced this transcendental direct-knowing of the x-factor God-force would agree to this conclusion.

When that startling concept of cosmic perfection being innately a vital part of all existence first entered my mind, I could intuitively grasp how simple it all was. But it has taken a long time for me to adjust my previously screwed-up thinking to the place where I feel I can at last put these unorthodox concepts into somewhat understandable statements. There is nothing faulty or imperfect about existence or reality. The only aspect that has been messed up is our erroneous thinking about ourselves, our souls and the God forces of the cosmos.

And eventually, I found there was a perfection factor, even in our mistaken conclusions. This was evident in the proper disagreeable reaction emanating from incorrect ideas--indicating that we were on the wrong track and needed to revise our thinking into a more pleasing and truthful direction.

A COMMON-SENSE APPROACH TO MYSTICAL NONSENSE

Just having a powerful soul-awareness experience (such as the one I encountered at Santa Monica) does not, in itself, make someone an expert on specific matters of the soul, the "x-factor" or God. I claim no such expertise for myself. And by the same reasoning, I cannot consider anyone else involved in somewhat similar happenings to be an infallible authority on mystical or metaphysical information.

Scholars who diligently study and synthesize the recorded conclusions of many mystical writers may, in one sense, become very knowledgeable about the mass of alleged transcendental material available; but their inept credulity is showing when they specifically attempt to clear up those indistinct, mystical areas about which most mystics readily admit are virtually impossible to accurately portray.

Of course, researchers are entitled to express their opinions, but in the transcendental realm the genuine mystics usually qualify their personal literary efforts as a very inadequate attempt to speak of the unspeakable or express the inexpressible. So, regardless of other admirable qualities, ecclesiastical writers, having no personal, mystical background, can hardly be considered as ultimate authorities on such intangible subjects as God and the human mind and soul.

Nevertheless, that conglomeration of alleged "inspired" religious literature, including much that is represented to be holy scripture is mostly an accumulation of this second-hand, much embellished, hearsay evidence which would never be admitted as reliable information in a court of law.

The obnoxious development of these misconceptions finally emerge as sacred "commandments of God" or "God said" this or that absurd statement. It becomes progressively more repulsive as these contrived mistakes become binding requirements for a futile salvation we don't even need.

And then frustrated scientists, somewhat disturbed by the imperfection dilemma, go to irrational extremes in a materialistic direction--preaching that we have no nonphysical souls at all, and that there is no nonphysical, Cosmic, Creative Force intelligently controlling the intricate functioning of our bodies, the stars, and all the atomic particles in the universe.

Therefore, in view of the sorry situation that is fundamentally responsible for much of our distress, it seems essential for us to discover the available facts about our own soul make-up, and to learn as much about the x-factor God force as is possible from our somewhat limited scope of investigation.

The first common-sense conclusion we should recognize is that from neither our normal human position, nor the full mystical experience, are there adequate verbal concepts which can precisely represent, classify or picture our mostly concealed, <u>nonphysical</u> souls, or the <u>nonphysical</u> x-factor, God intellect and power commingling with them.

The scientific label of "x", representing that which is unknown, is certainly a reasonable term if it had been allowed to stand that way. But scientific speculators have followed the example of their religious predecessors and added their own absurd evolutionary assertions, which only increases the deranged confusion of the imperfection dilemma.

In one sense we are better off to simply hold no binding belief at all in God and soul matters, than to adamantly cling to unsatisfactory, religious or psychological dogma claiming to be the exact final determination.

There is something very comforting about this no-precise-thought starting and returning point in regard to metaphysical concepts. Once we are free of the goddamned fear of losing our God-damned souls forever, it is really the most natural, contemplative tendency we have in our human existence, a miraculous blending of both material and nonmaterial God or x-factor substances.

Considering that all that you are and feel at this very moment is the ultimate of cosmic perfection (which includes our limited ability to fully comprehend all the intricate facts of our body, mind, soul and God existence), it becomes simple to realize that our normal and proper state of mind is one that is never immobilized by unreasonable, blackmail-fear-doctrines--threatening our existence in the eternity of the future--but is always open for any worthwhile thinking, should such beneficial indications come our way.

But the x-factors of cosmic excellence, making us what we already are, surely are not depending on any mental endeavor from us to enable them to perform their function. The great ocean of thought substances we delve into isn't even ours to keep very long. Rather, the little dab of it we experience appears to be a free-flowing panorama of ideas or segments of concepts which come and go almost as if they had a will and purpose of their own.

It is mystical nonsense to believe that we must use this receptive thinking, feeling, emotional area of our being in some specific way, in order to purify, perfect, change or even improve any aspect of that which we <u>already are</u>. Intelligent mental activity is vital in helping us to survive and enjoy our earth trip. But we are only spinning our wheels when we attempt to think or meditate or mortify ourselves into becoming something better or more perfect than that which we are now.

It might seem a little strange to think that we can empty our minds of all information on any given subject. But our thinking ability works equally well in both directions. However, what I am suggesting <u>is</u> <u>not</u> a negative mental effort to control our thinking along any certain direction. It's more of a mental relaxation, a no-concern or perhaps a respectful, "to-hell-with-it-all" attitude, which allows us to be properly concerned with pertinent things that might really need our full attention.

In another sense, it would be the more natural feelings you would have regarding your soul and God if you had never been bothered with the religious fear and dread, soul damnation and salvation, or the "no-soul, no-existence-after-death" implications of irrational scientific determinations.

If we simply <u>let</u> <u>them</u> <u>go</u>, disturbing, senseless thoughts can leave as effectively as they can come. Happily, this is one vital area which is always under our personal control.

Also, it is mystical nonsense to accept that we can mentally push ourselves into a state of transcendental direct knowing, but should you be so fortunate as to experience a direct-knowing mystical occurrence of your own, you would be in a more favorable state of mind to grasp the true significance of that unique event if your receptive mental faculties were open and uncluttered by disturbing thoughts.

Nevertheless, <u>after</u> the startling mystical incident occurs, the enlightened individual must still consider that which he has experienced on the same nonmystical basis that he used before. Having a mystical encounter does not change your normal method of consideration and understanding.

You may think you know a little more first-hand information about your soul and God, but one of the first things you realize is that it was your previously concealed soul nature which really knows; and your surface mind must now deal with that additional scrap of evidence, just like it must consider all other thinking which comes within its scope of rational discernment.

When the mystical happening is terminated, your main, soul knowing returns to its former place of partial concealment, and you are left with only a memory of what briefly transpired in your presence. So, you attempt to put wordless soul impressions into verbal statements. It's tough to communicate clearly any idea, regardless of its simplicity. But try and tell someone about something which is almost incomprehensible to the usual meanings we rely on in word communication.

However, while I may find it difficult to express clearly what I think our nonphysical souls and God <u>are</u> (or appear to be), it is not at all hard to say what, in my estimation, they certainly <u>are</u> <u>not</u>.

After careful consideration, I am thoroughly convinced that, above all else, our souls are not impure or imperfect in any way, shape or form. Our souls are not lost, or, in any manner, separated from God. How can they be when this x-factor God substance is ingrained in them as thoroughly as water is inherent in a block of ice? This God-force-permeation applies equally to that lesser (but not less perfect) segment of our souls we think of as our physical mind consciousness, as well as it does to that principal part we feel is hidden, sort of "below the threshold" of our usual awareness.

The sorry fact that we have been conned into believing otherwise, does not in the least change this inseparable, eternal, God-soul, God-body, and God-mind relationship. There is simply no place you, or your soul and mind, could ever go where you could get away from God.

It makes no difference if you are a saint, a dirty old man jackass, a criminal or a prostitute--there is nothing you could become, nothing you must do or believe, that would bring you any nearer to God than you are at this moment. So you could forget the whole business of soul and God, if you choose, and go to a football game, or go fishing, or go gambling at Las Vegas, or eat, drink, smoke or dope yourself to death; and you would be no better or worse off <u>in</u> <u>that</u> <u>respect</u> than you are now.

Irrespective of who you are, or what physical condition you are in, <u>you</u> <u>have</u> <u>soul-perfection</u> <u>now</u>. That is the ultimate and the ultimate is now.

It is further mystical nonsense to accept that our souls are degenerating in ignorance and must struggle to learn how to become acceptable to God. The truth is, our souls always have direct contact with the totality of Cosmic Intelligence. There is a host of more practical things that should be the object of our earth learning adventure--rather than striving for a mystical union with God-- when such an arrangement is already an accomplished fact.

Mystical enlightenment only informs our surface minds of a God-soul, God-mind relationship that, apparently, has always existed--without beginning or ending. Believing it or not believing it, considering it or ignoring it all, can have no effect on the cosmic fact of what you, your body, mind, soul and God--already <u>are</u> <u>now</u>. So, believing this as I do, you must see why I am not too concerned whether or not you go along with all the information that I am suggesting you consider.

I am inclined to believe that before we leave this material undertaking, most of us will likely encounter some degree of personal transcendental soul awareness. In June 1974, Victor Solow appeared on a television interview to tell about his experience of being apparently dead after suffering a heart attack. Fortunately, his wife, who was with him in their car, quickly got help from a policeman who applied heart massage until an ambulance came.

Doctors at the hospital jolted him back to life with electric shocks. In describing how it felt to be dead for twenty three minutes (no measurable pulse, no heart activity or vital signs), Mr. Solow said it was all a very pleasant experience. He remembered nothing about the efforts to save his life, but he was conscious of entering some kind of "energy field--I can't say much about it."

However, he did mention that he no longer had any fear of dying. A brief account of this unusual incident was also reported in the June 16, 1974 "Grit."

"The Pleasures of Dying," is the title of an article appearing in "Time" Magazine December 4, 1972. One of several experiences reported was that of Literary Patron, Caresse Crosby, recalling her rescue from drowning. "I saw the efforts to bring me back to life and I tried not to come back. I was only seven, a carefree child, yet that moment in all my life has never been equaled for pure happiness."

There are many more documented incidents and others that I know of personally, similar to these, which clearly indicate to me that when our regular physical consciousness ceases to function in our bodies, our main, nonphysical soul consciousness takes over and we simply return back to the delightful state of cosmic nonphysical existence we were in before we embarked on this material adventure. This is the same state which our main soul beings <u>are</u> <u>in</u> <u>now</u> and are continually in, while only a minor segment of our souls is involved in that which we call our living consciousness.

My mystical encounter at Santa Monica established for me that this unbelievably happy, untroubled, main soul existence is not something which begins only at or near the time of death. I wasn't at all sick. It took several minutes after the mystical incident started for me to drive around the block and then travel a couple of blocks farther down the Palisades Drive to find an open area where I could easily park my car.

But an adequate awareness of our souls and some knowledge of a controlling God Force is not dependent only on outstanding transcendental occurrences given to some and withheld from others. There is much in our everyday, normal experiences to indicate that we do have nonphysical souls. This same available evidence is also sufficient to show that our total existence is managed through and by an extra, nonphysical dimension of cosmic God Power that is not usually discerned by the regular perceptions of our physical senses.

And it makes a whale of a difference if we look into such phenomena from the common-sense, nonreligious point of view possible in the perfection-now position. We have been so confused that something basic is terribly wrong with human nature that we easily tend to overlook the many natural wonders and even miracles that we all experience every moment of our lives.

In considering these marvelous features of our ordinary experiences, I am not suggesting that precise proof of a nonphysical soul existence, and a nonphysical, x-factor, Cosmic, Creative Force can be established absolutely on the same basis that we require for physical facts. It is futile to expect nonphysical, soul or God substances to reveal themselves through procedures normally employed in considering regular, material facts which are always responsive to our perceptive senses of sight, sound, touch, taste and smelling.

Actually, the most enchanting feature of this soul and

God business is that they are completely free of any limitations or painful consequences encountered in physical laws or material relationships--although they do have the ability to blend into physical substances while still remaining independent by the unique nature of their nonphysical make-up.

For our purposes here, it seems enough to me if we can just show within reason that there actually is an extra nonphysical ingredient or aspect of our total existence capable of functioning on its own without assistance from its sometimes physical counterpart. This is not too difficult to accept when the x-factor, God substance is felt (by most mystics) to be the ultimate, eternal nature of both material and nonmaterial reality.

Consider the common, everyday fact of memory. We can all easily recall, in vivid detail, various incidents of our childhood when none of the material substances that made up our small bodies then, are a part of our adult bodies now--twenty, thirty or forty years later. In fact we have all used up and discarded several physical bodies in that time period, but the memories of those early experiences have somehow remained with us.

I think this simple memory evidence becomes a strong indication that there is within each of us an eternal, nonphysical "element" which manages its memory function and others without dependency on any precise material relationship.

Thought transference is closely related to the phenomenon of memory. But when it occurs between two individuals separated by great distances, this miraculous feature of mental telepathy could hardly be accomplished without some aspect of a nonphysical nature existing as a vital segment of our make-up.

Cleve Backster of the Backster Research Foundation in New York, has shown that some degree of apparently nonphysical thought communication can take place between plants and man, or plants and animals. Novel experiments with the electroencephalograph (lie detector) have proven that such a phenomenon does occur and can be demonstrated repeatedly.

I think this contemporary scientific development effectively nullifies the illogical, psychological concept that mental experiences are only responsive, neuroid sensations of matter--or energy, which scientists have substituted as a more proper term for their latest idea of the primary, basic, building blocks of the universe, which isn't too far from the mystical, x-factor-God-Creative-Force.

If we simply observe the unquestioned fact that our bodies actually are (in their visible form and substance) the food we eat, we can hardly ignore the common-sense conclusion that intelligence, memory, thought transference, and such things as love, sexual pleasure, and appreciation of beauty, art and music, could hardly be cooked into a hot serving of roast beef and mashed potatoes, with a touch of mystical direct knowing baked into the apple pie we enjoy for dessert.

It would seem almost the essence of reason to conclude that something extra is inherent in our make-up besides the material stuff we extract from the food we consume. And it does not seem unreasonable to speculate that this somewhat unknown dimension is somehow nonphysical in its mystical cosmic nature.

Thinking along these lines, our common sense is not at all insulted if we further calculate that this almost indescribable, nonphysical feature could hardly be considered imperfect when almost all of our contrived ideas of alleged imperfection are related to adverse aspects of the better known physical reality. When even in a full mystical transcendental experience (which in itself is practically incomprehensible until you have encountered it yourself), you can't really see it, hear it, feel it or touch it (because all of that is accomplished with your intuitive soul "hearing, seeing" etc.) It is mystical nonsense to assume that any aspect of this intangible, nonphysical reality could possibly be less than unconditional, cosmic excellence.

And then, if you carry over the idea which almost all mystics feel strongly about (that is, the pantheistic concept that this x-factor God element is an inseparable, innate part of the entire visible and invisible cosmos), it becomes a common-sense conclusion to understand a little more of the perfection-now position.

I think I should explain why we are considering these almost obvious facts when it is common knowledge that most of the people in the world already believe in some concept of a nonphysical God or x-factor power. And also, many intuitively feel that they have nonphysical souls which will continue in existence when their physical living is terminated.

The main reason is that from the beginning of this writing endeavor, I have felt it was most important, and in one sense almost vital, to keep the perfection-now exploration on a nonreligious basis. Conclusions I have determined for myself have developed entirely from simple observations (available to anyone) which are clearly outside the grasping "domain" of commercial, evangelistic theology. And I desire to keep my reasoning on an unbiased level of common-sense understanding that is never dependent on "authorities" who usually are only vicarious experts on that which a lot of other supposed authorities have established.

Let's look into some novel features involved in dreams. This is a phenomenon well known to all of us, but it is such an ordinary part of our usual sleep experience that we seldom consider what all can easily be determined from a careful examination of this unique mental activity.

From even the most common dream experience, we can all realize that, presently within our make-up, there are alternative ways of seeing without using our eyes; hearing without the help of our ears; touching without physical contact (even making love without a real live partner); in addition to thinking and reasoning without the employment of our regular, awake, conscious minds.

Moving just a short step past ordinary dreaming, with only a slight amount of very relaxed attention, we become aware of the novel realm of daydream, reverie visions. This is almost the same as dreaming, or perhaps the prelude to regular sleep dreaming, but somehow our conscious minds are still alert enough to pay attention and we can observe a sort of television picture within our mental perception. I discovered this simple vision technique some while after we came to New Mexico, when much of the former pressures of business and general, rat-race turmoil were happily forgotten. We were faced with a whole new way of living and thinking in our more down-to-earth employment with the Forest Service.

After spending most of my working life inside dusty and lacquer smelling shops, tending to the many details of furniture construction, it was blissful to sit in a naturally air-conditioned (forty mile an hour wind blowing through the cracks) glass enclosed room on top of a steel, lookout tower anchored firmly (we hoped) to the peak of the tallest lookout mountain in the vast Gila National Forest.

Our primary job was simply to observe a big hunk of the beautiful world in a way and from a position which few persons are privileged to enjoy. Of course, our main purpose was to report fires (mostly lightning caused) while they are still small enough to be easily contained by a couple of smoke-jumpers. But mostly it was just looking, and for me, it was the first time in my life I was earning money without having to produce something of saleable value with the effort I was expending. I was paid to observe.

The first day the District Ranger impressed upon us the importance of careful and thorough observation; for it is very easy to overlook a small patch of smoke that, because of constantly changing atmospheric conditions, can easily blend into the camouflaged, abstract pattern of lights and shadows, rocks and trees. He suggested that after a quick, general, all-around look, it would be wise to cut the area into sections, as if you were cutting pieces of pie with your tower position in the center. Then we were to examine carefully each cut of pie area separately--starting from right in front of the tower and going back and forth horizontally with your looking until you have reached the limit of your effective vision which might be sixty or seventy miles away.

This detailed looking at what was there became almost second nature to Hazel and me. And when we returned to our home at the end of the fire season, it was difficult to stop our acquired habit of careful observation.

I think it was during the second winter of our new life in New Mexico that I started to explore the fascinating phenomenon of mind visions. Because of the cold and snow, we had to spend much of our time near the comforting warmth of our big wood heater which occupied the center of our living room. At last there was ample time to read and study or just do nothing--which seems to be a favorable atmosphere to consider the illusive mysteries of the mind and soul. Later, I learned that mental visions are quite common and familiar to many; however, they are unknown to a lot of others--just as they managed to escape my unaware attention for more than forty years.

One feature I noticed about these reverie visions is that the things, places and people you might observe in your mind's eye are mostly strangers and new to you, while in some of your regular dreams you are often involved in bizarre situations with individials and circumstances related, somewhat, to recent happenings of your conscious awake experiences. Much of the time with visions, the scene observed dissolves after a few seconds, and a new face, place or intricate design appears for your amazed examination.

I have no explanation for how this miracle of extra visual perception occurs. Nevertheless, I did discover that, <u>to some extent,</u> you were able to contrive, or at least encourage what you were seeing. For instance, one time I started to observe what seemed to be the crude beginnings of a dragon-type face. With only the faintest of intentions, I encouraged an exploration in that direction--and to my surprise, I was able to see clearly a whole series of grotesque, beastly faces; until I finally cut them off with again, only the merest of conscious effort.

I am not relating these experiences with the idea of impressing anyone with my ability in exploring psychic phenomena. Actually, I have never felt there was any special value in pursuing this delving into <u>visual</u> <u>imagination</u>--which might be close to a valid description of this mental seeing. But this speculation is not intended as a satisfactory explanation.

The beginnings were almost always the same. First, you would just be aware of the abstract pattern you would "see" when you closed your eyes. Then, your attention might fasten itself onto some little spot which almost appeared to be perhaps an eye, or a whole face. The next thing you knew, it actually became a living eye or face, or something else, and remained clearly in view for a second or two. And then like the dragon faces, these images would repeat themselves, as if someone were putting on a television fashion show for you.

On several occasions, when a particularly strong and vivid vision would be there for me to see, I would open my eyes and the same "vision" would be projected seven or eight feet away into the dark space of my bedroom. But every time I did this, the scene remained only a few seconds and the whole mental show would be terminated.

I have ceased pooh-poohing or discrediting any aspect of the fascinating psychic manifestations we are privileged to experience. But still, I realized that what I was observing was hardly anything more than what drunks likely encounter when they see snakes on the walls and floor. Sometimes, I would see groups of people and occasionally individuals of these groups would even move about a little.

But I finally quit deliberately experimenting with these visions because it got so that almost everytime I closed my eyes, I found it was getting to be a habit for me to see what might emerge next on my mental television screen. Frankly, the somewhat boring show just wasn't worth the slight effort required; and I was not really interested in that much extra seeing. As I could not realize any real benefit coming from it, I figured I would rather spend my relaxed time just thinking in the ordinary, non-visionary way.

However, once in a while the vision business would occur spontaneously without any effort from me, and when this happened I would go ahead and look. Mostly it was just a short and sometimes interesting prelude to sleep.

But on a few occasions, usually after I had been asleep for some time and had partly awakened, the beginning reverie vision would develop sharply into something positively beyond the simple vision phenomenon. This might best be described as an extra clear dream. In fact, it was so vivid, so real and factual, that I am inclined to believe that some part of my being was actually at the scene to behold and experience all that was occurring.

I speculate that it could be some form of soul-mind journey--but nothing at all like the direct-knowing soul awareness happening I experienced at Santa Monica. Rather, the whole presentation seemed to be confined to my regular mind consciousness, released somehow from its normal location in my body.

Although I was awake enough to be aware of this extra clear dream starting, after I was into it a short time, the stark reality of what I was observing caused me to forget the fact that a part of my being was still at home in bed. Also, at the beginnings of these unusual mind journeys, I often say to myself, "Oh boy, here we go again," and I am certainly very pleased when they occur.

On one occasion I found myself on a party fishing boat, something like the deep-sea sport-fishing, day boats operating from Santa Monica and Malibu which are very familiar to me. However, this one was of a foreign type and design that I had never seen before. And the area near the beach where we were drift fishing was also new to me. On the shore I particularly noticed something which appeared to be a highway or an old ship-launching ramp extending into the water on a slant.

The beach, the water, the ocean atmosphere, the distant view, the boat and the people fishing, talking and milling around, and especially this road, or abandoned launching ramp were all so very real that I still feel that I might someday go to that spot on the earth and see it all again. I could positively identify it from the ancient stone launching ramp or submerged highway.

My position was a little above the wheel-house superstructure, and I was looking down on the boat and its passengers. I thought we were drifting in too close to the shore as I noticed a large wave forming--but it passed harmlessly under us before breaking. Then the craft started its engine and proceeded into the nearby harbor. During this traveling time, I observed closely various details of the boat construction and the sound of the engine--all of which were somewhat different than the many deep-sea, fishing boats I personally know about.

We entered a harbor channel and I looked with amazement at the clear reality of the buildings adjacent to the harbor shore. On one was a rectangular carved plaque which I think I would recognize if I should ever see it again.

About this time, I again recalled that I was really at home in bed, while this vivid experience appeared to be taking place in a foreign country and sea, perhaps somewhere on the Mediterranean-maybe near Venice. I knew it was nighttime where my body was in New Mexico, but it was daylight here on this fishing boat somewhere else in the world.

During the time I was marveling at the carving on the plaque, I found I had left the craft and was moving through the salty air above the water directly toward the roof of the house having the plaque on its smooth stucco siding facing the channel. On this short flight, I thought to myself, "Good, I'll feel of that wall with my hands and see if this is just a dream or something more."

But when I got to within a couple of feet of the top edge of the building, I found that my interest in the composition of the stucco seemed to cause it to sort of open up, and I realized that instead of stopping for a look at the outside--I was actually going on <u>inside</u> the wall itself!
Seemingly, it hadn't bothered me too much to figure that I was home in bed and flying over the harbor waters of some little seacoast village thousands of miles away at the same time; but the shock of, apparently, being able to go right into and perhaps through that solid wall was too much for my wandering mind which was used to stopping at the outside surface. It was the actual reality of this seemingly impossible situation occurring which jolted me back to the more acceptable reality of my normal self resting in my bed.

Another possible soul-mind journey incident began in much the same way as my fishing boat experience. I had been sleeping and was partly awake when it started. Again I was pleased. This time I found myself at a place I recognized and knew very well. I had been part of a Forest Service crew hacking out a new trail above the Catwalk Camp Grounds in White Water Canyon.

This was a particular spot where we had camped for quite a while during the time we erected a swinging, cable bridge over a small chasm. This bridge brought the trail to a spot under an overhanging ledge we called the Cave Walk. At the upper end of the Cave Walk, we made another solid, steel bridge to cross the canyon again, directly above a small waterfall. And about two hundred feet beyond this second trail bridge is the place where we made a campfire and rested during coffee, lunch and smoke breaks.

When I found myself in this place, again I was impressed that this kind of extra clear dreaming is surely more than just an ordinary dream or the somewhat contrived mental imagination of visions. It was just too real to be imaginary. I did notice that it wasn't daylight. Nevertheless, I could see fairly well. Perhaps there was good moonlight, but I wasn't too concerned about these aspects.

While I was pondering the miracle of how it could be, I decided to look closer at the running water. To manage this, I just floated in the air above the little stream and under some overhanging brush. I thought to myself, "I'll test this out by putting my hand down in the water (which was only about six inches deep) and feel the sand and pebbles on the creek bottom."

I did this, and could feel the wetness of the water, but I was not bothered by the coldness of it. I got myself a handful of sand and felt and saw the grit of the sand as I rubbed it with my thumb and fingers. I suppose it was the convincing reality of the experiment which seemed so impossible, that wrenched me back to my more believable position in bed.

These returning jolts are quite an emotional shock that seems to occur when your mental consciousness is, apparently, hurried back into its normal place where it once again is comfortable within your physical make-up.

Prior to the perfection-now period and before my New Mexico experiments, I experienced a few other extra clear dreams or mental adventures. They were of the same nature as the ones I have just related and were equally clear and real. But at the time they occurred, I hardly knew what to think about such a marvelous phenomenon.

I will mention only one briefly, in which I found myself in a place of strange and unusual structures. Some of the building material appeared to be somewhat of the consistency of fire--not flames but more like glowing coals. It was most beautiful and not at all disturbing. I noticed this unusual condition in what seemed to be the remains of some walls that were about twenty inches thick with window and door openings but no windows or doors.

The firey walls were something like transparent burning embers, but they were not being consumed, smoking or burning up. Whatever it was seemed to be the almost living nature of their composition. There was no feeling of heat or danger from them.

Many years later I arrived after dark at a small forest fire. Five or six large logs were burning clear through from one side to the other and from end to end. They were enormous glowing embers, seemingly almost transparent. And this is the only thing I have ever observed which comes close to describing those firey walls I saw long ago in that strange soul-mind journey.

In another area of this same trip I found myself examining the base of an enormous stone structure. But the remarkable part was that the entire building appeared to be studded with large, jewel-like stones of exceptional beauty, color and design. These gems were five to six inches across their widest dimension and were artistically arranged with three to four feet of space between them. There was more in this experience, but these features were the principal highspots which still remain clear in my memory. At that earlier time I didn't have the investigative interest in such unusual things as I developed later.

It would be senseless to accept that these spectacular

mental events occur without some logical purpose. Putting it all together, I am inclined to believe there is something much more significant to these living, technicolor, mind adventures than just chance mental fantasy or hallucination. But, of course, I know of no way such a conclusion could ever be proven, and perhaps it is just as well.

Nevertheless, these phenomena have occurred in my own experiences and in countless, similar episodes documented by others. From what I know of personally, I feel that the combined weight of the evidence is, at least, sufficient to establish that you and I are, actually, partly nonphysical in our total nature.

Also, if we can figure that our familiar perceptive mentalities are able to temporarily leave our bodies <u>now,</u> while they are still alive and functioning, it is not unreasonable to think that they can easily detach themselves and take off when the body is of no further use or responsibility to them.

Even now, it seems incredible and almost unbelievable (at least to me) that I and millions of others were able to "see" through the miracle of television, the actual event itself when man first set foot on the moon several years ago.

In evaluating this outstanding accomplishment, managed through a clever use of materials and forces that, apparently, have always existed in the cosmos, I find it much easier to speculate that some part of my total make-up was actually there on that fishing boat while my body was resting in bed, perhaps thousands of miles away from that particular spot on the earth.

Moreover, it becomes most logical to think that my curious, nonphysical God-soul-mind could easily have gone inside that stucco-surfaced wall and had a good look around. In fact, I really <u>was</u> inside the wall! I'll never forget the strange experience. I actually was cruising through a spaceous, wide-open universe of atomic particles for a short time, before the shock of the unexpected experience abruptly ended my mental adventure. I see no point in trying to describe what I "saw" inside the wall, except to say that it was a real experience and there was no mistaking where I was, as far as my thinking is concerned.

There is a clear-cut difference between ordinary dreaming, reverie visions and these remarkable mind excursions. And, of course, a direct-knowing, mystical, transcendental, soul and God awareness experience is in a category by itself. Now that lunar exploration is no longer an impossibility and almost commonplace, serious investigators will be able to look into other forms of space traveling without fearing the stigma of being considered a crackpot lunatic. The recent establishing of The Institute Of Noetic Science by Edgar Mitchell, Apollo 14 Astronaut, appears to be a healthy breakthrough in the right direction--at last!

Since I know of nothing on this earth which corresponds to the walls of firey composition and the jewel-studded construction encountered in that unusual episode, I do not consider it beyond rationality to speculate that my soul-mind awareness could have traveled to some other earth-like planet in the universe where such features may be quite common.

The basic idea of unqualified perfection for all existence has an obvious relationship to the factual reality and excellent nature of our souls. Believing that our release from physical living is an unconditional emergence into a fully conscious awareness of another dimension of existence, seemingly by contrast, more desirable in some respects, than that which was vacated, would dispel much of the emotional agony caused by traditional ideas of either a hopeless, no-soul, no-more-existence concept, or the impure, imperfect, damned and condemned, lost-soul condition of religious contrivance.

The eventual termination of this present, material relationship could well be considered perfect if we had some reasonable indications that it would immediately culminate in a desirable compensation at least equal to, or perhaps more than that which was given up.

Starting our thinking on such matters from the disgusting assumption of inherent imperfection as the existing make-up of our soul natures, reason and logic will not function or apply in our calculations. Subtle suggestions of mind comfort emanating from our intuitive awareness must be ignored, and we face the eternal cosmic unknown with little assurance or confidence regarding our future position. In fact, we wonder if we will have any position at all.

The obnoxious complexities of conditional, soul salvation held over our gullible heads like bait for a sucker fish by commercial religionists has no comforting satisfaction. Eventually, it becomes a frustrating, boring burden if we seriously attempt to conform to the dismal requirements usually concealed in the small print of the typical, ecclesiastical, salvation contract.

The fact that ancient authorities were badly misinformed and, in turn, passed on incorrect information to us does not alter the enduring truth and reality of cosmic perfection being inherent in all existence.

Considering our souls and mind consciousness in the framework of total, unconditional excellence, any uncertainties of our metaphysical speculation would not be a depressing, bothersome affliction. Combining ordinary common sense with an awareness of all-inclusive perfection, we are satisfied and even pleased with our estimations. At least that is how I feel about it.

The perfection-now position allows us to look carefully and without fear at any and all phenomena which might help us extricate ourselves from the nonsensical, occult and scientific mess which has, unfortunately, been heaped upon us as our secular and religious heritage. We are badly in need of an alternative, stable, middle ground where we can just live and enjoy, look and learn without struggling through sickening accumulations of scientific or religious, false doctrine.

Hazel and I figured that our move to the tranquil, high country of New Mexico was at least one step in such a direction. But as time rolled on, we discovered that imperfection pollution had degraded even the purity (we thought) of the good-guy Rangers of the U. S. Forest Service.

Nevertheless, unexpected adversities we encountered provided a thorough test of the value and validity of my maverick brain child--the perfection-now alternative to chaos.

CHAPTER IV

ALTERNATIVE TO CHAOS

"Listen Bob, if you don't spell it out exactly <u>how</u> this crazy instant perfection idea of yours can be of some immediate, practical use to help people get themselves out of their depressing troubles, no one is ever going to pay one bit of attention to a lot of babbling about whether it is valid or not."

Hazel put it pretty straight to me, and, like a lot of things that she observes, I knew (after spending five years writing two unsatisfactory book-manuscripts stressing validity aspects) that she was right in this case.

When I first started out in this writing endeavor, the question of validity seemed extremely important--at least to me, and for sure, it still does. But now I realize that ideas must have a lot more than just validity if they are to appear attractive and valuable. Astrology is a good example of what I mean. Nearly anyone can tell you what his astrological sign is. That is, whether he is a Gemini, a Leo or a Pisces--which is my sign. But I have yet to find anyone who can give me the slightest bit of valid information that would even tend to establish the authenticity of that well established business.

But I must admit that, despite the lack of evidence, a lot of people are fascinated with the material the astrologers provide them. And to some extent, it perhaps makes them more thoughtful and careful about their attitude and behavior. I think, too, that most astrologers incorporate a lot of good common sense in their advice, even though they seem to be short of it in the foundational structure of their pseudo science. They also tend to spotlight the admirable qualities in people--and this welcome uplifting is worth something.

As far as the perfection-now position is concerned, I certainly didn't want to be responsible for someone splitting away from one mental cesspool condition and rushing ass over teakettle into another situation that might turn out to be as bad, or perhaps worse than the former. However, after all these years of intimate living with my perfection-now idea, I realize that it is not really my responsibility to prove its legitimacy for anyone else. So, if you decide to adopt a perfection-now concept of your own, you will have to take on the responsibility for its character by yourself.

Your perfection-now brain child would likely be quite different from my perfection-now baby, and that would be exactly how it should be. I surely wouldn't waste any effort to persuade you to accept my particular creation. But this doesn't mean that we will not look into the question of validity; we will consider it in Volume II. It only denotes that I am placing that segment of the story in a somewhat secondary position.

I agree with my wife that the most important aspect of any new proposal is--what good is it? Will it work? Especially, will it help you and me resolve our personal problems? And what about the malignant turmoil of insane drug abuse, increasing crime and explosive foreign affairs involvement? Is such a concept as instant perfection for everyone able to help us keep Uncle Sam's big, generous ass out of another futile hassle like the disastrous Vietnam debacle?

How about the mad bombers and demented kooks who think they can straighten up the world with their assassinations, bank robbings and terrorist's activities? Can taking on the perfection-now position serve as an effective deterrent to prevent the soulless, Godless, slavery shackles of communism from eventually taking control over this whole beautiful world? Could it possibly counteract some of the shocking lack of integrity still festering in our post-Watergate land of the free and home of the brave?

And let's not overlook the antagonism forever boiling over between men and women struggling through unholy matrimony. Will perfection-now thinking tend to diminish the screwed-up sex debacle existing as a deplorable obstacle to a happy home experience?

If there is not some reasonable hope that this incredible alternative to chaos can be applied beneficially to all disturbing problems--then Marmalade is right. Who is going to consider some novel idea for the heck of it?

I have been irked at writers who ask profound questions (such as I have just done) but never get around to offering a simple answer. Therefore, I will answer my own questions promptly. And the answer is yes.

There are a lot of indications that the perfection-now alternative can help us resolve all the degrading messes cluttering up our beautiful world, rip-offs and fecal situations that we have foolishly (but perhaps unintentionally) created for ourselves.

But at the same time, you and I know that no single idea could ever be adequate enough, in _itself,_ to resolve all the countless complications that are presently bothering us as individuals, as communities, as nations and as a world family of nations. Fortunately, you and I don't have to come up with answers to every problem.

We need to be concerned only with that which is vital to our own well-being and pleasure. We live in a big world and there is always much going on that is beyond our ability to do anything about. But along with the limited scope of our personal influence, there is also a boundary on one individual's obligation. It is important to understand something regarding responsibility, and we will get into that later.

But in a few words, the essence of personal obligation in any situation can be expressed in one simple statement:

The creator is responsible for the creation. So my own liability is confined to just that which I have created for myself. And you are responsible only for your creation.

In addition to the alternative aspects of the perfection-now position, the how part of using your own intuitive thinking will also be considered in this chapter. So far, we have taken an introductory look at the main perfection-now concept itself and the soul-perfection now assertion which, to me, is a vital part of it. These two mind-boggling ideas came to me spontaneously--the first in a bursting moment of enlightenment and the second in what I call a mystical direct-knowing experience lasting about forty five minutes. What I think I know and understand about tuning in on intuition has taken a lot longer for me to realize--coming in subtle bits and pieces over an extended long period of time.

This intuitive information might be more useful and more significant in some respects than the other two, principal ideas of the perfection-now "big three." But they are all so interrelated that it is hard for me to place one above the others in importance. I don't think I could have found out about the perfection-now position at all if I hadn't accidentally flubbed into a state of mind where my atrophied intuitive faculties were able to function somewhat naturally again.

And I think the same is true with my mystical soul awareness experience. But I wouldn't want you to think that learning about your intuitive channels is a guarantee that a full mystical encounter will come to you. There is no sure way that I know of that will cause such an occurrence.

Actually, all three of these features worked together for me. And I doubt if I could have arrived at some understanding of my instinctual nature without the help of several other related ideas that eventually presented themselves for my eager exploration.

I also had a lot of help from Hazel in grasping this

rather intangible, intuitive subject.

Maybe you are not too concerned with the possible cosmic excellence of your total existence, or even how your mind consciousness is hooked up to your somewhat concealed soul consciousness. But if you are the normal curious creature that I think you must be, I am sure there is plenty that you are seriously concerned about.

Whatever it is (and it doesn't matter what it might be), if you want to find out a lot more about it--perhaps discover the very essence of it--your own intuitive nature can provide you with that information. The same goes for problems. Any situation troubling you can easily be resolved when you learn the simple procedure of tuning in on your intuition from the perfection-now position.

But first I would like to explain what I mean by alternative aspects.

INSTANT PERFECTION
THE INCREDIBLE ALTERNATIVE

I suppose that most writers develop an interest in words. They are the only material an author has to work with. Somehow, I rather like the word, alternative. To me, it is an important verbal expression, as far as the perfection-now position is concerned. The incredible part of the perfection-now alternative is that it has always been available, but (as far as I know), it has never been seriously considered before.

No matter how significant it might turn out to be, and regardless of all implications and applications contained in its potential influence--or disregarding all that if you would rather--the perfection-now position is still a fascinating, alternative way of looking at yourself, your problems and the rest of the existing creation. To me, it represents something valuable which a lot of clamoring complainers wish they had but don't.

Like a lot of people here in the Southwest, we leave our radio on station KFI, Los Angeles, all night. Hilly Rose comes on with his Open-Phone-Forum talk show at eight o'clock, and Ron McCoy takes over with his telephone conversation program at twelve midnight and continues until five in the morning. These days and nights (and especially since the Mary Hartman-Mary Hartman TV show started) you can tune in on just about any subject imaginable.

On nighttime radio, there seems to be a lot of interest in the "new morality" (known in the old days as shacking-up). And then occasionally you will hear some serious talk about the many acute problems that appear to be forever increasing to near chaotic porportions. But through the years, I have noticed that, although almost everyone is able to point out some great injustice or the damaging aspects in various fecal conditions, no one seems capable of providing reasonable answers and solutions to resolve the predicament. A lot of time, Ron and Hilly both say to their exasperated callers: "I agree with you. But where is the answer? What do you have for an alternative?"

Mostly, the indignant protesters register their disapproval of the shenanigans going on and want the world to know that they are disgusted with it all. But in general, there are no sensible, pragmatic aternatives suggested that might possibly ease the ever-growing tension-buildup of the imperfection nightmare dilemma.

However, there are plenty of crackpot alternative ideas thrown out on the air waves. One Los Angeles citizen thought that the County Sheriff should be equipped with several attack bombers, so that, if the Watt's rioters should go on another rampage, the cops could retaliate with napalm incendiaries and block-buster bombs. Someone else thought we should use mine fields along the Mexico border to stop wetbacks from coming into the United States.

A few days before Christmas, 1974, NBC Nightly News considered an important question: Should law-enforcement agencies use hollow-nose bullets in their futile efforts to stop crime? The principal arguments for the special bullets were that they make a much larger and more ragged wound. They can shatter bones more effectively and almost guarantee to put the victim out of action--maybe for good. Or, perhaps, bad would be the proper word in such a case.

A few weeks later in January, 1975, there was some speculation in the land about whether the United States should use armed forces to straighten up the oil-exporting countries. I was surprised that a lot of callers thought they should. Somewhat exasperated himself, Ron McCoy commented that the only alternatives people seem to have is to just kill off the adversaries.

In May 1975, President Ford got the biggest popularity boost of his career for ordering the use of armed forces in rescuing the crew of the freighter, Mayaquez from the Cambodian "pirates." I don't suppose that it was his fault that there was possibly some overacting (or over-killing) which resulted in the tragic loss of a lot more men (NBC News said perhaps more than one hundred) than the thirty nine they were attempting to save. Nevertheless, the entire crew of the Mayaquez was released and their vessel was recovered.

After our big credibility losses in Cambodia and Vietnam, this somewhat successful rescue did help to raise the nation's sagging spirits. And, irrespective of my recently acquired feelings regarding condemnation and punishment, I tend to think President Ford performed properly in this emergency.

I mention this personal observation, here, so that later in our consideration of the possible abolishment of condemnation and punishment thinking from our natural thought structure, you can see that I hold no extreme, fanatical attitude that we should neglect our right and responsibility of self-protection.

If some crazy kook is breaking into my home, clearly intending to harm me or my family, I wouldn't hesitate to shoot him--if there were no alternative way out of such a debacle. But I surely never intend to provoke anyone to the extent that he might want to take his belligerent frustration out on my hide. In fact, from here on out, I am going to be very careful not to pester anyone to any extent at all.
Still, if somehow such a hassle ever occurred, such self-protective response would be a natural, spontaneous <u>reaction</u> on my part. The unwise aggressor would become the recipient of destructive measures caused by himself.

But I should add that I would use beforehand every possible alternative available to prevent any such violence--because my only purpose from now on, is to get all the enjoyment I can out of this earthly trip. And I know from a lot of unhappy, personal experience, that you can't very well enjoy yourself when you are engaged in some bullshit hassle--no matter what its nature, or the assumed righteousness of your personal position.

That goes for the perfection-now position as well. For a while, I used to argue about what I thought was right. And looking back, I realize I was often pretty superior and obnoxious in defending my position. But I know now that such an inconsiderate attitude is stupid. And, if carried too far, it could very well lead to dangerous complications--which it did for me. I was lucky to escape with my ass intact, but I'll tell you about that a little later. I wasn't thinking too much of the value of alternatives in those early days, but I realize now, that if I had considered alternative attitudes and behavior, my welfare would not have been in so much jeopardy.

Perhaps a lot of additional lives could have been saved

in the Mayaquez action if those in direct command had considered all the alternatives. The instant perfection concept can be boiled down to one single statement: <u>Existence is perfection</u>. Nevertheless, countless implications and applications obviously suggested in this new thinking, opens up a whole new world of unexpected alternatives.

Various new choices are available for our selection that we couldn't see before. In grasping just a little of the significance, that an instant perfection factor is inherent in absolutely everything, we tend, almost automatically, to look a little beyond the irritative walls of our self-made, basic-imperfection rut.

The damned dilemma that we thought was impossible to resolve, suddenly appears to be not so complicated as we previously thought it to be. Certainly, we never can see that which is always hidden past the next turn in the road. But we can now see far enough ahead to take a few steps in a more promising direction. Perhaps a fresh adventure is indicated, containing desirable features, likely canceling out bothersome conditions--irksome involvements we are clinging to--that probably are out-grown, used up, finished and done for.

That's how it was for Marmalade and me when we made our big decision to give up everything that had become our imperfection-rat-race, security blanket out in California, while taking our chances on whatever we could manage in the mountain, ghetto boondocks of New Mexico. Hazel and I were both forty seven years old. And by this time our daughter was well-launched on her own matrimonial hassle up north in Nevada.

We let go of a lot that ordinarily would seem desirable. I was well established in my own business. It wasn't any big deal, but it had been enough to provide us with a good living. We had made the last payment on our home and didn't owe anyone a dime for anything. Although it was paid for, our abode wasn't much compared to the grand residences most of my custom-made furniture went into. But it was adequate, comfortable and plenty satisfactory for us.

We called our place Pine Point. It was situated on a choice view location overlooking Topanga Canyon and much of the Santa Monica coastal mountain range. There were several large pine trees, rock retaining walls and terraces that were something like Hazel's old South Fork Canyon home in New Mexico. That was one of the main reasons we liked it so much. The site consisted of three lots providing plenty of ground space. And with the patio and outdoor barbecue, an abundance of trees and shrubbery, we enjoyed lots of freedom and privacy.

An old-timer in the area told us that our place, and many others nearby, were built during the time of prohibition in the twenties. It was a status thing for those who could afford it to have a weekend cottage far enough back in the hills, so they could have (he suspected) drinking and fornicating parties without the fear of authorities checking up on them.

As a result, our little house was not much on size, but we had it furnished just about as elegantly as the big estates of our wealthy clients. We even had a special French Provincial wing chair upholstered in top-grain leather, exactly like the original one I had designed and made for Frank Sinatra.

When I delivered that chair and some other furniture, the famous singer was there, but he seemed somewhat strained and unhappy. While I was there, he acted as though he didn't even notice the special chair I had contrived for him. This was in the late forties when the Sinatra kids were small and Frank was still married to his first wife. Of course, neither of them had seen me before. Probably thought I was just a delivery man--which in fact, I guess I was. The reason was that the Sinatras had their dealings with George Hall, who was one of the top interior decorators, and well established with the big shots of the movie bunch.

Some of our other star customers we had through Mr. Hall were Bing Crosby, Gary Cooper and Celeste Holmes. Through the years there were quite a few other movie celebrities, and of course, we had other interior decorator clients. Gwen Carde was one of my main clients.

I am sorry that I never saw Bing Crosby or Gary Cooper. They were not at home when we made our deliveries. But I recall an incident when we were hauling in a whole room-full of furniture for the Bing Crosby mansion.

A young man and woman took advantage of the open-door situation as we were bringing in a large sofa. Without an invitation they just walked into the foyer with us. The capable black maid standing guard asked them what they wanted. They put on something of a cock and bull attitude of big-time importance, telling her they knew positively from reliable sources that Bing was flying in from New York that afternoon. And that it was imperative that he should be given the package of songs and manuscripts which they handed her. The maid was diplomatic and pleasant, and assured them that Bing would get the package as soon as he arrived home.

When they had gone, she gave a disgusted grunt, and shaking the large envelope, told us, "This stuff is going into the trash can with the rest of the garbage. If them two big-shots knew half as much as they claimed, they would know that Mr. Crosby never flies. He always takes the Super Chief." (This, too, was in the late forties).

When we delivered Celeste Holmes' living room furniture, which was all upholstered in white fabrics--a bit unusual in itself--I was surprised to find the entire, large living room to be also in white; white walls and ceilings, white draperies and carpet. Even the woodwork was finished in white.

And the famous actress was wearing a matching off-white housecoat. I have been in a lot of wealthy homes, but

I can remember this one most clearly because of that all-over white treatment. It sort of made you feel a little like you were up in the heavenly clouds.

Hazel and I used nothing but real leather on our own upholstered pieces. Fabrics get soiled easily and wear out too soon, while leather always looks rich. You can clean it with little effort and it lasts a long time. But we sold our home completely furnished, and gave up just about everything of material comfort that we had accumulated when we moved to New Mexico.

We had only a very small cabin to go to, one that had served as a vacation place for a few weeks each summer. The little shack was already furnished with local, Early Fanny Hill, ghost town furniture. Fanny Hill was a shanty settlement--or what was left of it--near one of the mines.

It was quite a contrast from the custom stuff we were used to in California, a conglomeration of anything that could be scrounged together. Instead of comfortable sofas and chairs, we parked our behinds on hard-seated chairs and a couple of rockers. In the Silver Creek area no one ever bothered to keep up with the Joneses, because there had never been any hinky-stink Joneses to keep up with.

To someone else, the change might have seemed like quite a come-down. But to Hazel, it was at last a glorious homecoming. She loved every crummy, junk piece of furniture that we had acquired. When she made the final break, she didn't want a thing that would be a reminder of her long, unsatisfactory, California hassle.

Our servitude relationship with the Hollywood Stars didn't mean a thing to Hazel. The only stars she was concerned about were the real heavenly ones we could always see so clearly at nighttime in the pollution-free atmosphere of New Mexico. As for my feelings, I had put in twenty seven years with my nose on the furniture grindstone, and I didn't care if I never saw another fine piece of furniture again.

I guess I must have felt like the Basque cook who worked for my daughter and her husband in their J&T Bar and Restaurant in Gardnerville, Nevada. One evening when I was there on a visit, I had my dinner in the kitchen at the big table next to the range. Instead of eating steak that he cooked for everyone else every evening except Sundays, I noticed that Basillio was roasting three hot dogs in the oven for himself.

We did our cooking on a small wood cook-stove. And it took exactly one hour to get a fire going hot enough to boil water for a cup of coffee. Waiting that long for coffee in the morning was just a little too long, even for Hazel. So, one of the first improvements we took care of, was the acquisition of a two-burner, gas hot plate and a one-hundred pound tank of butane. A butane truck serviced the ranches in the valley ten miles away, but our mountain road was too difficult for the large truck to navigate. So we had to haul our own fuel.

The "State Highway" into our little mining camp community was a corkscrew, rocky, single-track road with wider places once in a while, so two cars could carefully creep past each other. Fortunately, you didn't meet many, and you could always tell when one was coming by the cloud of dust that was kicked up.

For some it was a flatlander's nightmare. A few travelers who were not familiar with such rugged mountain driving were often petrified with fear at the prospects of having to go back over that tortuous, narrow, wagon trail, blasted by the miners out of solid rock on the steep sides of the canyon walls.

After turning off the valley highway and climbing up some small hills, there was a couple of miles of easy traveling across a big flat mesa. But once you left the elevated table land, and started up the mountain itself, it was a different story. There just wasn't any place at all to turn around, and the worst stretch of all (Rocky Cut) was only about a mile from the edge of the mesa.

So, for the timid travelers it appeared easier to keep going than to attempt to turn around and go back. Some continued on, hoping they could find an easier way out after they arrived in Silver Creek. In winter there was no other way out. But in the summer, after the snow in the high country had melted, you could go on through the forest.
However, it was twenty times as far that way. If anything, the road was even worse in spots, and there was always the danger of getting stuck in a wash-out.

From our elevated front balcony, I overheard a couple talking about the charm of our mountain area. The man said, "Well, how do you like it? Isn't this place something?" And the woman answered, "You know, now that I am here, I think it is beautiful. But that goddamn road nearly scared the shit out of me!"

Another thing, there wasn't any electricity since the big power-house was dismantled in the early forties, after the mines were all closed down. We were not at all bothered about this feature, as we were well supplied with coaloil lamps. But it turned out to be more of a problem than we figured. One thing we thought we were going to have was a lot of peace and quiet. In the whole Silver Creek area, there were only eleven people, and we would make a total of thirteen. However, our tranquil expectations were shattered early the first evening after we arrived.

Someone had taken over the property next to ours and had installed a light plant. They ran it without a muffler, and it was unbelievable how much racket that machine could make. Whether it was intentional or not, we will never know, but they kept that blasting monster on until two-o'clock in the morning that first night. The mechanical beast was stabled in a shed at the rear of their property. The way our little cabin was situated, our bedroom window was less than forty feet from the flexible exhaust pipe hanging out of a hole in the wall and pointing in our direction.

It almost looked like a conspiracy to discourage us from staying and send us back to California. And after a few sleepless hours that first night, we were both wondering if that might not be such a bad idea. Although we had given up the lease option on our business location in Santa Monica, our house was only listed with a real estate company. We figured we would have at least a few months before it was sold, and if things got too tough, we could always run our gutless asses back to Topanga. I could either get a job or start another business.

Our new neighbors even ran their irksome contraption at times during the day. They were remodeling an old frame store building into an art gallery and small museum, and started the plant up every time they needed power to run their electrical equipment.

But irrespective of the noise pollution, it didn't take long for us to realize that our little, chicken-shed cabin would not be adequate for a permanent dwelling. So we soon purchased a substantial rock and adobe structure on a large lot that had been one of the town's main general stores.

It had two stories with living quarters on the second floor. Still, we didn't get away from the light-plant racket. Ironically, our new home was just as close--only on the opposite side of the noise-pollution source. But the twenty-four inch thick, rock and adobe walls of this solid building served as an effective sound insulator, and somehow we adjusted to the pesty disturbance.

Finally, we did get relief from the unearthly clatter of that light-plant when Hazel and I were helicoptered up to Mogollon Baldy, which became our lookout tower home for the summer months.

But we lost our butane hot plate, and were back to waiting one hour for our morning coffee again--brewed on a small wood-burning stove almost identical to the one we had in Silver Creek. After Labor Day when we returned to our thick walled adobe home, the offending mechanical beast was silenced, because our industrious neighbors had returned to their Silver City residence to spend the winter and look after their rental property there.

Through the winter months, Hazel and I had the "town"--or what was left of it--practically to ourselves. The only close neighbors were three old timers who lived a respectable distance away, sort of on the edge of town. If you can picture in your mind that our building was located about in the center of town, and these people occupied the outskirts, perhaps a quarter of a mile away, you can get some idea of just how little town there was. The few others lived in the suburbs, a mile or more "out of town."

The water in our adobe came from a well in the basement. That is, it came when we hauled it up out of the well in a bucket and carried it up the stairs to our living quarters. On the lookout tower we had a similar water situation. Our water there was rain water collected from the roof of the cabin where we stored our wood and all the equipment required to run that operation. The water was filtered through a sand and gravel box and was stored in a tank buried in the side of the mountain.

We had a rope and pully hoist at the top of the tower. After I hooked on a five-gallon water container, Hazel would pull on the rope from the top while I pulled from the bottom. And together, we hoisted our water forty five feet up to just above the steel guard rail around the tower catwalk. Then, as I held the rope, Hazel would pull the can inside, and I would lower it gently to the catwalk floor.

Mr. Spooner, who sold us the adobe building, told us how we could get water up to the second floor from the basement well without going through the bucket brigade procedure. His idea was to combine an ordinary hand pump at the sink with a well-cylinder pump directly below in the basement.

Following his suggestion, I ran fifty feet of large plastic pipe from the cylinder pump across the basement floor to the well and down into the water. With the guts of the hand pump removed, the handle was fastened to a long sucker rod which connected to the fittings in the cylinder pump eighteen feet below. The whole thing was like a windmill setup, but we used elbow power instead of the wind. It all worked perfectly just as Mr. Spooner said it would, and we are still using it fifteen years later. Actually, we wore out the first pump machinery and replaced it a couple of years ago with a much better one that should last for the rest of our lives.

Even though we now have electricity and have our own pressure tank with water piped to the sink in the normal way, we still prefer to use the hand pump. When the power goes off as it sometimes does, we are never out of water. With one or the other, we always have an alternative water system.

I guess we are fortunate to have a lot of other alternative systems also. Since the State Highway into our ghost town is now improved a little, and black-topped somewhat, the butane truck comes and fills our three-hundred gallon propane storage tank. In Hazel's large modern kitchen, she has three stoves. There are two regular gas stoves (one apartment size) sitting side by side, which gives her two ovens and eight top burners.

As an alternative cooking system, she also has a large, wood-burning, old-fashioned kitchen range (it came with the building) which she uses in the wintertime anyway. It provides adequate heat for about half the house and does a good job of cooking, too. But of course we always use the gas for our morning coffee.

In the living room, we have a substantial, gas, circulating heater set up as an alternative heating system. But we never use it. We really prefer the heat from our big, wood heater and the wood is free. It is free, that is, if you have a truck and a chain saw, and the energy to go into the forest to get it--which we still seem to have.

When I rewired our place for modern electricity, Hazel insisted that she didn't want electric lights in the kitchen, although she permitted a wall plug for her cake mixer. The idea was that she wanted to keep our coaloil lamps in good working order, as an alternative lighting system.

So, when we get up in the darkness before daylight, as we often do on winter mornings, we light the coaloil lamps as a lot of people have done for so long before us. And, as I am the one who always gets up first, I find I really like it that way. Of course, we have regular lights in the rest of the house, but the soft yellow glow from that coaloil lamp in the kitchen during the early morning before daylight is something special.

In addition to our truck, we still have our old car. Isolated as we are, and having more time than money, I have learned how to do all of my own mechanical work. If I am repairing one vehicle, the other is always available as our alternative transportation. And in my old Pontiac, I even have an alternative fuel supply. It is equipped to operate on either gasoline or butane. I can change from one to the other with the flick of an electrical, solonoid switch.

Having all these alternatives for our various physical needs is a good thing. In our situation, I suppose they are almost essential. In any case we consider ourselves fortunate in that respect. But of even greater value is having satisfactory, alternative ways of thinking--which, after fifteen years, has, positively, removed the usual perplexity, hopelessness and pain of the human dilemma for us.

Though I suppose there will always be plenty for us to figure out, to a large extent, Hazel and I have both resolved our own personal problems in our minds and hearts.

Therefore, in a small way, I feel that we are no longer contributors to the insidious, imperfection madness, polluting gullible minds all over the world.

From the instant-perfection, alternative position, I can at least see a possible way out of the absurd complications the world is embroiled in. Though the religious, social and political distress appears overwhelming in its explosive pressures, at the same time, it is also, just an accumulation of a lot of personal problems for a lot of individuals. The solution is a simple, alternative way of thinking--a new, intellectual experience capable of beneficially influencing hearts and minds.

When that is accomplished, the greater, community and national problems of social injustice, crime and war will gradually diminish from a lack of disordered militant instigators. From the perfection-now position, individuals will easily see the intuitive wisdom of simply avoiding the unsatisfactory alternatives because of the unhappiness and trouble they cause. And they will choose a better way to function because of the pleasure it provides.

TUNING IN ON INTUITION

Looking back on our early New Mexico experiences, I now wonder how we ever had the guts (or some might think the insanity) to attempt such a revolutionary change in our living setup as we did. But of one thing I am sure, and there is no mystery about it. We managed as well as we did, mainly, because of Hazel's strong intuitive nature. It has always been a special reserve part of her make-up, which somehow, she held onto during the turmoil we both endured, as we floundered our way through the unhappy years of our long imperfection dilemma.

In order to explain how I learned what I think are the

essentials of intuitive knowing, it is necessary to tell you a little of what occurred to make Marmalade the fascinating, highly intuitive person that she is.

Hazel was born in a little house not far from the Deadwood Mine and Mill. She was still a baby when the Brixner family moved just over the hill to South Fork Canyon which runs into the main canyon of Silver Creek. In some ways my wife was like an only child, because her two sisters and one brother were almost grown up when she came into the world.

Compared to the bewilderment encountered in the big city when she left her mother and father and her South Fork home thirteen years later, her childhood experiences seemed like a heavenly shangrila existence. Just the physical differences alone were revolting to Hazel. In Silver Creek on her way to school, she walked (or usually ran) about a half mile down South Fork Canyon, which is an especially fascinating spot with a magical quality of its own, then up Silver Creek about a half mile through town.

The Silver Creek Elementary School (it burned down two years before we moved to New Mexico) was located on the side of the canyon overlooking the town and some of the most inspiring scenery anyone could ask for. Hazel knew almost everyone she came into contact with. And in a way, they all cared for her and sort of looked after her.

In Los Angeles she stayed with her sister and brother-in-law at their home in Hawthorne, which has little to offer as far as inspiring beauty is concerned. Being religious, her sister wouldn't let Hazel attend the public high school which was only one block away. Instead, she had to ride the streetcar into downtown Los Angeles, transfer at an intersection on skid row, and then ride a long ways to the Los Angeles Academy, a Seventh Day Adventist church school.

During this long trip every day, her eyes hurt her from the smog, and she had to contend with sex perverts who took advantage of the crowded streetcar to annoy a pretty young teenager. Hazel soon developed a serious case of homesickness, from which she didn't fully recover until we moved back to Silver Creek, thirty four years later. And she still hates cities with a passion.

The food situation also was changed drastically for Hazel when she had to leave her South Fork home. Her mother was a good cook and there had always been plenty to eat. Her father saw to it that there was always a good supply of venison on hand. I'll never forget the breakfast I had when I first visited Hazel's parents after we were married. The main feature I recall was a generous platter of fried venison steaks with fried potatoes and bacon gravy. A little later, came homemade apple pie and delicious coffee. I think it was the only time in my life up till then that I was able to eat all the meat I wanted at one meal.

The only job Mrs. Brixner ever had before she became a housewife was helping to cook in a boarding house. After she was married, preparing three meals a day and looking after her family was the only occupation she had ever known. Another special meal I remember on that first visit, was highlighted by a huge pan of roasted venison ribs. What a feast that was. Hazel told me that when she first went to the Los Angeles Academy, they had a race for all the kids, boys and girls together. "I found myself so far ahead of all of them I got embarrassed. So I slowed down and allowed someone else to come in ahead of me."

Having had that kind of food all her young life, I could see why Hazel was in such good condition. She said she used to run all the way home for lunch and then run back to school during the lunch hour. "But in California, I was hungry nearly all the time. My sister sort of expected me to act as a maid and housekeeper to help pay for my expenses.

"I guess she thought I could look after my own eating. But I wasn't any cook, and as Seventh Day Adventists weren't supposed to eat meat, there didn't ever seem to be much food in the house and damn little cooking was done. Alta's husband was a car salesman and he ate out most of the time.

"I had to get up awfully early to catch the streetcar, and usually, I went to school without any breakfast at all. I guess I was too shy to ask for any money other than my carfare, so I couldn't eat in the school cafeteria. It was a real relief for me when I finally got to go to La Sierra (the boarding school where Hazel and I met) because then, I could at least eat all I wanted in the cafeteria. And I didn't have to ride them damn streetcars any more."

Her sister kept her out in California for two years before bringing Hazel back to New Mexico for a visit. "I told my mother and father that I did not like it at all in Los Angeles, and definitely, didn't want to go back with Alta. We had a big argument and my father ended up going out in the yard and crying because he thought I needed the education they couldn't give me if I stayed in Silver Creek.

"Another thing, Alta wanted me to become a nurse, and I hated that idea worst of all. So, when my sister promised me that I could take the beauty course, as well as typing, and have piano lessons, I gave in and went back to California with her.

"But when it came time to go back to school, Alta had changed her mind. The beauty course and typing were out, and so were the piano lessons. Alta insisted that I take the pre-nursing course, and I felt I had to give in to her because my father had told me to make the most of my opportunity, be a good girl and mind Alta."

Of course, the thirteen years that Hazel lived in Silver Creek as a child were a lot different for her than the many years we have lived here since we moved from California in 1962. Where once there was a hustling, little, mining-camp town with a post office, a sheriff, a jail, a doctor, school and churches; also saloons, an ice house, power houses, whore houses, mines, mills, stores, restaurants and lodge halls; gas stations and garages, and even a motion-picture show house, plus a conglomeration of people to go with it all--now there are only five ancient, decaying, commercial type buildings (without the commerce or the people) something like our rock and adobe, general-store structure.

Four of these store buildings are clustered together at the lower end of town, while our place sits somewhat by itself in the middle of town--that is, by itself, as far as other commercial buildings are concerned. The few other remaining structures are mostly small, decrepit board and batten, deserted dwellings with rusty, tin roofs that somehow escaped various fires that gutted several areas of the narrow canyon community.

Some of them are used by their absentee owners as camping places to spend a few weeks during the summer, just as Hazel and I did before we made Silver Creek our permanent residence. Of course, because of the isolated mountainous terrain--which is still the same now as it was during Hazel's childhood--the Silver Creek area was, and still is, like a heavenly world in contrast to the metropolitan madness of Los Angeles.

On that first visit I asked Hazel's father what he thought of California? He had been there just one time for a few weeks. "Well," he said, "I guess it's all right, but I never could get used to shitting in the house."

And now, after all these years that we have become accustomed to answering nature's calls in the outhouse, I can well understand what Adam Brixner meant. He wasn't trying to be funny. In the outdoor facility you can blast away with no concern that someone will hear your sound effects. And with the wide-open ventilation, you are not worried that you could be stinking up the atmosphere. Mr. Brixner wouldn't even use the outhouse at their South Fork place. He preferred to hike a ways up the canyon and into the oak brush where he could squat down and "take a dump."

The only times I have missed an indoor toilet were on a few, rare occasions when, in the middle of a winter night during a snow storm, you have to bundle up in boots and heavy warm clothing, then wade through the snow in the back yard, climb up the stairs and park your warm behind on a frosty outhouse seat. In time, you see to it that your defecating urges come after breakfast, in the morning daylight. But even those extreme experiences are not too bad, in reality. It's mostly the thought of having to go out in that cold, freezing weather that seems disagreeable.

In her early years, Hazel was spared any serious, religious exposure. Although there were several small churches in the mountain community, her mother and father never attended them. They were simply good people with an admirable, nonreligious integrity, engendered from a close association with the basic gut realities of living close to nature. "The only religion we knew were the few times when Alta would make me and mama kneel down with her while she prayed for God to forgive us and save our souls. Mama and I were always embarrassed and didn't pay too much attention to it. We only went along with Alta's program to keep from hurting her feelings."

But in California her sister took her to church every Saturday where she was subjected to the fearful, horror story that the world was soon coming to its end, that Jesus would come down from heaven to kill off the sinners and save all the good Seventh Day Adventists.

After we had moved to New Mexico, it took about eight months to find a buyer for our property in Topanga. Hazel and I made one last trip to California to close the deal and ship out some personal items we wanted to keep. Going back to the big city after only that short time away, I felt something of what Hazel must have experienced when she came to Los Angeles for the first time.

Unlike my wife, I had grown up in cities with streetcars and freeways--in San Francisco, Chicago and Los Angeles. But after four months on the wilderness lookout tower, where even a dirt road in the mountains looked strange to me when I first came out, on this trip back to "civilization" I was really disturbed at the fury of all those vehicles moving with such great speed and so close together.

The beehive hum of commercial activity was overwhelming for me to behold--even though I had been a frantic participant of it all for a long time. None of it had ever really bothered me before, and in a way, a lot of Southern California was *my* South Fork home.

Nevertheless, after we had finished our business and were on our way back to New Mexico--I think we were somewhere in Western Arizona--I noticed a most welcome feeling of relief and freedom to be getting far away from all of that frenzied civilization. At last, I had experienced for myself, the essence of what Hazel had been lecturing about for so many years.

On this trip we had passed the point of no return. But neither of us had any worry about ever going back to the rat-race life we had given up. By this time, we were enthralled with our new adventure. Our part-time employment with the Forest Service gave us a big part of the winter months to just live and do as we pleased.

For the first time in my life, I had a lot of free time to search out the many answers about life that I felt were just waiting to be found. For Hazel, it meant that after thirty four mostly frustrating years, she had been liberated from at least one irksome situation, that, in her case, had prevented her from the full enjoyment of living that each person is entitled to.

My investigative interest in intuitive awareness began a little before my Perfection-Now Baby idea was conceived in the latter part of 1960, two years before we came to New

Mexico. Like so many in California at that time, Hazel became interested in painting pictures. She had worked for a couple of years as a ceramic decorator, and therefore, had developed some skill with paints and brushes. She was especially adept in fine detail work.

I had always done sketching as a part of my furniture designing work, and Shirley was taking an art course at High School. So, for a while, we were all dabbling around with oil paints and canvas boards to see what would develop.

But Hazel stayed with it, and it soon became apparent to me that she had a natural talent. She really was an artist. Each evening, when I returned home from my shop in Santa Monica, I was amazed at how much Hazel had accomplished and at the quality of the work she was turning out.

Lee Hanks, who lived just across the street from us in Topanga, was also a beginning painter at the time. And for quite a while around our place, there was a lot of falderal conversation about art and artists. It didn't take long for Hazel to become bored with realism, and soon she was experimenting with abstract art.

Somehow, in this area she was able to excel. To her, it was an avenue of complete freedom of expression. As far as she was concerned, there were no rules to follow, no standards to live up to. Mrs. Hanks stayed with realistic painting, and couldn't understand how Hazel could paint the way she did. One time she asked her, "How in the world do you ever make your mind think that way?"

"The truth is," Hazel answered, "I really don't think. I may have some idea of colors I want to use and some vague objective in mind when I start out. But after I get going, I sort of forget my own ideas and just do whatever seems called for at the moment with hardly any planning or concern for how it turns out."

Most of Hazel's work was done with the canvas flat on a table. And often she never set it up for a critical look until she was completely finished. Also Hazel never worked over or adjusted any part of a painting. She always said, "Let the record stand." She felt it was always better to let it stay as it developed the first time.

In the course of our discussions, we concluded that Hazel was able to follow some, inner creative force, an intuitive intelligence, that was somewhat different than, and superior to the directions she was able to command with her surface mind alone. She even demonstrated this for me one time with some linear drawings. Deliberately using only her conscious mind she began a new drawing, and the initial results were obviously less than we both knew that she was capable of. Nevertheless she kept on, and in a few minutes she told me to observe what was taking place.

"Now look, I am beginning to go with my intuitive directions, and you can easily see the difference." Where before there had been a somewhat childish doodling (about like what anyone could do), now I could see the lines were clearly beginning to form a part of some orderly arrangement.

I was impressed that with such a careless--almost don't give a damn--attitude, Hazel could produce such pleasing paintings. One afternoon I came home and was startled to find an exceptionally fine painting completely finished. (We call it Blue Lagoon and still have it.) That same morning, when I had left, it was nothing but a large bare canvas.

I remember saying, "My God, if I could ever learn how to use the creative forces in my endeavors like you use them in your paintings--I could end up with equally good results."

Spontaneously, Hazel answered me back, "Your trouble is that you are always trying to use the force. Quit trying to use the force! Just let the force use you!"

This cogent bit of advice was something like a mental spark that ignited a glowing new awareness in my mind. To me, it was a turning point, where I quit my frantic rat-race struggle to accomplish so much. For the first time in my adult life, I thought it would be wise to just relax my frenzied effort a little and see what would happen. Of course, I knew I had to keep on working. But somehow, the intensity and importance I had placed on so many things for so long, gradually began to diminish.

A few months earlier, I had made an experiment to see how many jackpots I could win on the Malibu deep-sea fishing boat. Usually, I went out once a week, either on Saturday or Sunday. Nearly every fisherman would put a dollar in the pot, and the one who had the biggest fish at the end of the day took home the loot along with his big fish.

Of course, I had been fishing for years in this area, and I pretty well knew all the local tricks of the game. But catching the biggest fish always requires a little something more than whatever an angler can figure out by himself. Also, there were a lot of other regular, fishing maniacs besides myself, and they knew all the angles, too.
The previous evening, I had carefully worked over all the physical requirements, such as fishing pole and reel, hooks and line, to be sure that nothing would fail me in that department. And by always paying an extra dollar for my ticket, I managed to get a choice place to fish on the stern of the boat.

Before the anchor was down at our destination, just outside the kelp beds, my live bait was already swimming in the water close to the kelp. Every second of the day I was alert and ready for anything that came along. But I had done all these things many times before.

Once in a while I had won the jackpot--but not very often. On this occasion, however, I was using a little "mind stuff" to see if that would make a difference. Winning athletes have a name for it. They call it "psyched-up", and I suppose that comes close to describing my state of mind. I was determined to win.

And to my surprise, at the end of the day, I found I

had the biggest fish. Usually, whoever won the pot gave the deckhand a couple of dollars out of it, which he split with the skipper. If you had a really large fish, you depended on the skipper or the crew to gaff it and haul it up over the side and into the boat. I had always insured good cooperation in this operation by always giving five dollars to the deckhand, whenever I was the winner--even though there might be only twelve or fifteen bucks in the pot.

The next weekend I "psyched" myself up again, and once more I brought home the winning fish. This day it was a fifty four pound halibut, caught outside the surf and up the coast a little beyond Paradise Cove. There was only about a half an hour more to fish for the day, and I thought it a little strange that no sooner was my giant fish on the deck than we moved to a different location.

I went up to the flying bridge and asked the skipper how come we were moving when there was a good chance of getting more big fish in that area. He laughed and said, "That's what I am afraid of. Some one might get a bigger one than yours. I am going to a spot where there hasn't been a fish of any size caught in years." This unexpected announcement sort of made me wonder if it was "mind stuff" working for me or the five dollar tip the skipper felt he could depend on from me.

The third weekend nothing unseemly occurred, but we did run into a school of large, white sea bass, which, among knowledgeable ocean fishermen, is rated to be the most delicious fish you can eat. I usually caught so many fish that Hazel and Shirley were not too enthused when it came to cooking and eating them. But whenever I brought home white-sea bass, we always had a grand feast. There seems to be no fishy taste to the meat of the white sea bass. It almost is more of the consistency of chicken than fish.

On this particular day, all the fish caught weighed from about twenty to thirty-five pounds. By keeping at it and hard work, I managed to catch the most in numbers, and somehow, one of mine was the heaviest by a close margin.

But on the fourth trip, something happened which caused me to discontinue my determined, mind-stuff effort. It was late in the day, and I already had a fairly large fish that looked as if it would take the pot.

Shortly before our fishing time was up, an inexperienced young man with a rented pole and reel, hauled into the side of the boat a monster halibut which easily was twice as heavy as the one I had. The barn-door fish was not struggling at all, but was just quietly laying there, flat on the surface of the water. There was a lot of excitement and the bait boy came running with the long gaff. But instead of gaffing the heavy fish properly and lifting it out of the water, he just gave it a terrific jab.

In the thrashing and commotion that followed, it appeared to me that he deliberately jerked the gaff downward and out. The big fish took off like a spurred racehorse. Evidently, the novice fisherman had tightened up on his star drag (brake) thinking to keep his fish from getting away. If he had known better, he would have loosened the tension for such a situation. Anyway, the pole was slammed down hard to the railing and almost jerked out of his grasp, but he hung on. Because of that solid resistance, the line easily snapped and the prize fish was gone forever. Again it was "lines up", and we moved immediately to another fishless location to finish out the day.

Of course, I was pleased with winning the jackpot four times in a row. But when I started out with the mind-stuff business, I never had any intention of becoming involved, even indirectly, in such obviously crooked shenanigans just to get a little extra money.

I didn't say anything, but I quit going out on that boat and switched to one based at Santa Monica. I quit the mind-stuff, too, as far as my fishing was concerned. It seemed that the questionable benefits were not worth all that mental and physical effort. I always contributed my dollar to the jackpot and got back into winning occasionally, as I had before my mind-stuff experiment. And I found this easier attitude to be more enjoyable than the almost demented endeavor to be number one, that I had gotten into during those four, straight, winning weekends.

Sometimes, Hazel and I would use mind-stuff to get a good place to park near a favorite restaurant in Santa Monica. A lot of times it seemed to work. Often, just as we were driving up, someone was pulling out of the exact spot we wanted. There is hardly anything tangible one can do or think in such mind-stuff effort, except perhaps to mentally register a request for whatever you want to happen. It could be there is some mental telepathy involved, combined with the mysterious power of suggestion, and the unique energy of desire.

In some respects, it's about the same procedure a person goes through in praying; or what a gambler goes through when he bets his money on a horse to win the race. Back in those days there was a lot of speculation on the power of positive thinking. If you had the attitude that likely you wouldn't find a good parking place--chances were that you got what you expected. Then you had to settle for a place a block or two away.

Although I quit using the positive-thinking approach on my fishing trips--for the special reasons I have given--something, evidently, was working for me in my experiment, as my four straight winnings seemed to establish. And I don't want to leave the impression that I am pooh-poohing whatever it is, that, apparently, does perform in such happenings. I have more to say on this subject in the chapter, Perfection-Now Powers in Volume II.

But I could see that all this positive thinking, this frantic effort to influence people and things with your surface mind, was not the same thing that Hazel employed in her artistic endeavors. Actually, in some ways it was just the opposite. Where the one was something of a mental hassle, and sometimes a disappointment, Hazel's involvement was almost an effortless one, as far as her conscious mind was concerned. Winning recognition or fame, or turning out an outstanding masterpiece was never a part of her effort. Good, bad or indifferent--it didn't mean a thing to Hazel.

Nevertheless, in her art work she always enjoyed what she was doing. Obviously, a certain skill was needed, and Hazel had that. But it was equally certain to me that the subtle enchantment of her paintings was directly related to an easy-going, aware relationship with her intuitive direction.

After Hazel told me to, "quit trying to use the force; just let the force use you," I began to look at things around me with a far different attitude than I was used to before (such as my jackpot winning hassle).

I began to approach what I was attempting in a somewhat similar, tranquil state of mind that Hazel used when she was painting. I recalled that she had told Lee Hanks that "I don't think." And this little clue is what gave me the idea to mentally get rid of the religious and scientific ideas about humanity that I couldn't stomach any longer.

Actually, it is almost impossible to make your mind stop thinking, or make your mind a blank, as some attempt to do. I found out that what Hazel really meant, was that she didn't consciously think out her abstract concoctions ahead of time, and then try to reproduce something she had in her mind on the canvas. Rather, she was simply allowing her special abilities to be used in a creative process. Hazel was just as surprised at the pleasing results as anyone else when she saw what had been accomplished.

Another thing, Hazel always had fun with her art work. Whenever it ceased to be enjoyable she would stop her effort. There was an important clue for me in this pleasure aspect, too. Intuitive information or impressions seem to "come through" easier when we are relaxed and having a good time in some way.

In thinking these various angles out, I realized that most of us use our intuitive knowing in a lot of ordinary procedures--perhaps without ever being directly aware of what was going on. Intuitive thinking, I found out, is no different than the regular thought process we use all the time for everything else. It finally occurred to me that I had been using it successfully for years in a lot of my furniture work.

As an example, I noticed it working for me, especially, every time I had to cut material for quilting. Rather than have the fabric quilted in one big hunk of yardage, we cut each piece separately ahead of time. This made it easier for the quilters to do their work on smaller areas, and it saved us the expense of quilting unnecessary material.

You had to allow a good ten percent extra for fullness, and the pattern had to be matched up and used to the best advantage. For instance, on hunting prints with horses, you had to use discretion as to just where you placed the horses' asses, which sometimes were featured quite prominently.

Anyway, there was a lot to think about, in addition to the things I have mentioned, every time I had to cut material for quilting. Usually I got the fabric out in the afternoon, draped it over the sofa or chair it was going on, and just looked at it awhile. But at the end of the day, my surface mind didn't seem to want to work on the many problems--so I would say, "The hell with it, I'll do it tomorrow morning."

I never gave it another thought, but when I came back the next day, I could easily see what I had to do. In some mysterious way all the problems had been resolved for me. The answers I needed were just there, in the regular thinking area of my mind. Putting these things all together, it occurred to me that if such an intuitive approach worked effectively for me on cutting quilting material, and performed easily for

Hazel in her art work, then, by all that's right and holy, it should be efficient for just about any situation at all that seemed to be a problem.

At that time there was a lot I wanted to know; about living and dying, loving and hating; and especially about all the damn foolishness we become involved in. I wondered why Hazel and I became so miserable at times, when as far as physical requirements were concerned, there was no tangible reason for such discouragement.

Years later, I recalled this same question, when in July 1975, Hazel told me she heard on the radio that Dan Daily, the famous movie star, had applied at one of the Hollywood hospitals and asked, "Please, this is an emergency, can you help me?" He was told there were no emergency facilities there, and that he should go to the hospital in Santa Monica. He went out the front door, put a gun in his mouth and killed himself.

A few months earlier on April 4, 1975, Garric Uttley was reporting for NBC in Saigon. A ship was unloading its weary cargo of refugees fleeing from the communist dangers in the north. Expecting to be on board for only one day, they had been confined to the ship in the harbor for four unpleasant days before they were allowed to disembark.

One woman with four small children told about becoming separated from her mother, who had been traveling with them in DaNang. Miraculously, just as they were leaving the dock, they ran into the lost grandmother who had managed to come down on another ship. The tearful reunion was something to see. But it was just one, small, happy incident, in a great sea of human grief and turmoil for so many unfortunate Vietnamese refugees. When I saw that, I couldn't help but wonder again how Hazel and I could have been so unhappy back in 1960, when our troubles were seemingly nothing in comparison to the heartaches these war-torn people were suffering.

But trouble is trouble, and pain is pain, regardless of its severity, its nature or its cause. Bullshit or otherwise, Hazel and I had our share. And adversities do not occur without a cause. You would think that in a proper state of mind, almost anyone would be more than willing to do whatever was necessary to live peacefully and without conflict. Still, the usual experience seems to be, that we are invariably involved in some complicated hassle--no matter how hard we might try to resolve the, apparently, irreparable difficulties. Often such a situation becomes the cursed crux of the baffling human dilemma.

Nevertheless, it seemed to me, there had to be a predominant, primary cause for this mental and emotional torment most of us screw ourselves into during some part of our adventures on this earthly spaceship. I figured that if I could discover the one principal factor that must be at the bottom of the human dilemma--surely it would not be too difficult to restore whatever was lacking, or repair whatever was out of order. In other words, I was hoping to isolate the basic, taproot, imperfection flaw in the human make-up.

When finally I did settle down from my rat-race pace and took a little time to observe what was so obvious all around me, I realized that cosmic orderliness (similar to a quality in Hazel's paintings) was abundantly in evidence in that great body of water that I looked at as I drove to and from work every morning and evening. In the oceans of the world, which occupy the greater portion of the earth's surface, there is a continuous regulation that was accomplished without any assistance from man's civilized contrivances. In fact, the oceans perform their vital function in spite of all our degradation, carelessness, and don't-give-a-damn stupidity.

Every creature in the ocean, apparently, knows how to manage their particular living experience--at least for their own benefit. Surely, the same cosmic intelligence which told the salmon where, when and how to perform their function of propagation was available on an equal basis to Homo sapiens. But what was so screwed-up about humanity, that men and women often behaved with seemingly less good sense than, say a mackerel or a shark?

It is true that every fish takes a smaller ocean creature for its food. But you seldom ever see a sick fish. This rather hard aspect means that nearly all ocean creatures have their living time terminated while they are still in fairly good physical condition--which perhaps, isn't too bad a way to go; at least for a fish. On the other hand, each species has its own peculiar defense adaptation, and manages to survive, despite the dangers of being eaten by hungry members of another species.

Compared to the fish, animals, birds and insects, men and women, apparently, have lost a large measure of their own defensive abilities. In fact, man himself has become his own worst enemy. Something is surely way out of order.

I have already described the way I experimented to see what I might have believed if I could have avoided the effluent, mental contamination of taking on so much irrational, cock and bull propaganda about the nature of humanity and man's environment.

The essence of the perfection-now position seemed to almost explode its beneficial alternatives into the open, receptive areas of my mind. And one of the most incredible aspects of this shocking idea is the gentle way it seems to restore our atrophied intuitive functions <u>in those areas we need them the most</u>. It was almost unbelievable to me that I was able, without any effort at all, to get directly acquainted with my subconscious soul existence and the cosmic x-factor-God-force, which clearly (as far as my thinking is concerned) is the creative source of all instinctual and intuitive directions, coming to all living creatures-- including Homo sapiens.

Out of my personal investigation, and as a result of my

own experiences during more than a decade and a half, I think I have found the basic essentials of intuitive knowing. And here is a brief summary of them:

(1) Answers and solutions are available to each individual from within the cosmic intelligence of his own, total being.

(2) A strong need or desire to know is all that is necessary as a request for valid information.

(3) A simple rejection of unsatisfactory ideas is all that is required to open your mind to receive pertinent intuitive information.

(4) Don't try to use the intuitive forces. Let the force use you. (As Hazel put it so well.)

(5) After requesting information on a certain subject, dismiss the problem from your mind and enjoy yourself in any way you can.

(6) Valid, intuitive knowing comes to you in the ordinary thinking you use for everything else.

(7) Fed up with academic brainwashing forced upon you so far, you surely won't settle for any more crap rationalizations. You will easily recognize the difference between superficial fantasies of your surface mind (or someone else's fecal conclusions) and genuine intuitive directions--hot off your personal, cosmic, soul computers.

Truth, when you find it, always has a delightful, satisfying character. In time, you will learn to know the ring of truth. But don't expect too much too soon. All worthwhile growth and development in nature is a subtle, gradual process--especially for a perfection-now baby.

PERFECTION-NOW BABY

On that day after I had my mystical soul encounter at Santa Monica, I went on to my shop as usual. When my work period was over, I returned home and attempted to tell Hazel something of what had happened. And I discovered then how difficult it is to tell another person about such an intangible occurrence.

When a baby is born, it takes a long time before it develops an ability to communicate its ideas and feelings. It was sort of that way for me when I tried to tell my wife about my strange soul-perfection-now happening, although I didn't use that term at that time.

A few weeks earlier, I had attempted to explain my initial, perfection-now concept, but that didn't make much of an impression on Hazel either. I suppose it was because there were just too many questions that I was unable to answer intelligently at that first disclosure.

I was only able to say that I was firmly convinced in my mind, even though I didn't yet have the words to make it clear and understandable.

On this new, mystical, soul-awareness development, about the most I could utter were some thoughts I had hooked up to the expression, "double whammy." One impression that I thought was significant, and I felt I could talk about, was that it no longer mattered so much to me if I should die at an early age or be killed in an accident.

I was confident that I had discovered a part of myself which would not be bothered at all if my material adventure should suddenly be terminated. This was a very positive and real experience for me, and was not any temporary, false courage regarding physical harm or even death itself.
And it is still the same, fifteen years later. Hazel has no dread of dying either. But she is determined to die well, like the fish. Of course, after making my discovery, I wanted

to continue living the same as always, if not more than before, because now there was something new, vital and exciting to consider that had been lacking before.

The scope of my thinking on existence had doubled. For the first time, I was able to see or at least think a little way beyond the death-barrier mystery. And I liked what I saw. The "double whammy" term seemed to convey one aspect of what I had retained from that exceptional, mystical encounter.

Through following years, I have found various other dual-thinking situations connected with the perfection-now position, where an acceptable ambivalent assessment was also possible. For instance, as I mentioned earlier, I am now able to separate, or make a clear distinction between a dirty deed and a dirty-deed doer.

I could never condone injustice or mistreatment. But I now find it is possible for me to excuse the deranged perpetrator for his damn-fool error in judgment. Actually, I do this more for my own benefit than for the good of the antagonist who might be conspiring against me. As far as my own mental tranquility is concerned, I know now from some sorry experiences, that it makes a lot of sense to be more forgiving than to always react belligerently, in the traditional retributive manner.

Of course, these ideas came to me much later. At that earlier time, I was thinking about a lot of other pertinent things besides the possibility of being killed in an auto accident. One rather serious concern I had was; how could I ever manage the novel experience of living in a somewhat new world, a fresh experience, where all my old established thoughts contrived on top of a crumbling foundation of basic imperfection were now obsolete and invalid, at least, as far as my personal thinking was concerned? To that extent, I suppose I was sort of a perfection-now baby.

Of course, at the same time, I was also a typical, big-mouth, know-it-all, overbearing, middle-aged man jackass. There were no authorities to consult with, no one at all who could help me adjust to this completely new environment which had so unexpectedly developed around me.

Obviously, I did a lot of talking about my theory with Hazel until she got sick and tired of constantly having to listen to me expound about my "damn perfection idea." And as I said before, it took eight years before she could finally grasp what my initial babbling was all about.

I suppose it took that long because, after a while, I quit trying to convince her. Eventually, however, Hazel finally agreed with me when she got around to using her own intuitive thinking on the subject. One day she surprised me in one of our discussions when she said, "Well, if we don't have that (meaning perfection-now) as a basis to go on, we may as well just say, 'To hell with everything.'"

My parents told me that their doctor informed them, that I was the first white baby to be born in Kramer, California, which at that time (March 1, 1915) was merely a freight train service stop, almost in the center of the extensive Mojave Desert. Forty-five years later, in the latter part of 1960, you might say I became the first perfection-now baby; although I hardly realized the significance of what was occurring--on either occasion.

When I first started thinking about this baby hook-up business, what I had in mind was that the concept of universal perfection, <u>without qualifications</u>, was, in essence, <u>my baby</u>. It sort of came into existence to fill a need in my life, and I have been stuck with the infant concept twenty-four hours a day, every day since.

All babies require a lot of attention, and my perfection-now brat has demanded plenty from me. But idea babies are quite different from regular babies. They have to have a mind to develop in. And when you take one on, or maybe you allow the idea to take you on, you become the idea, and the idea becomes you. Or at the least, that is one way to think about it.

I found that as my maverick brain child began to grow, there was a gradual letting go of parts of my old feelings and reactions that wouldn't fit properly into the unique nature of this newly developing creature. In comparing my old, obnoxious self to the inclinations of my perfection-now baby's character, it has been a shocking experience to consider how much damaging influence the insidious, imperfection postulate has had on so many vital aspects of our Western culture. The thing sneaks up on you, gives you the shaft, and at first, you hardly know that you have been skillfully inoculated with the vitriolic, imperfection toxin.

It's something like being injected by a kissing bug. It seems they anesthetize the spot where they jab you, and the poison spreads over a large area before you realize what has happened. It was that way for me one night. I awakened, and thought I was having a heart attack. I had pains running from my left shoulder down my arm clear to my finger tips.

I had never heard of a kissing bug, but Hazel had. She looked and found a big red swollen area on the back of my upper arm where the little devil had given it to me. We looked around and found the black-winged culprit under my pillow.

Finding that I could no longer base my new thinking on a false, toxic assumption, I realized that I would have to look for a whole new set of alternative ideas on just about everything that was worth thinking about. Satisfactory new conclusions that I hoped to find would have to fit easily into my allegation of unqualified excellence for all existence.

This perfection-now baby of mine would require a completely new manual on how to get along and find happiness in a perfect world, inhabited with only perfect people. Of course, it was necessary for me to make allowances that all these creatures of cosmic excellence were terribly misinformed about their factual, innate nature.

At the bottom of this whole investigation, I was hoping to uncover basic understanding that would be helpful to Hazel and me so we could experience more enjoyment and less turmoil for the remaining years of our lives. But Hazel was already involved in her own independent search.

My proposed new adaptation looked like a tall order, and I wondered if I could ever manage such a project. Nevertheless, I figured it would be at least a start in a promising direction if I could unravel some of the perplexing questions for myself alone.

The complicated problem of just how much responsibility one person has for the welfare of another, or for the community, or the world itself, seemed extremely important to me. And, in relation to my metaphysical speculations, it appeared imperative for me to learn just how far my personal obligation extended.

And while I was going to find these answers, I thought I might just as well learn why we all are here <u>as we are</u> in this complicated, social quagmire. It didn't seem at all unreasonable that thinking Homo sapiens should be able to discover and understand a valid, <u>satisfying purpose</u> for their physical existence in this world.

There were also other important subjects that I felt needed resolution. Exactly why had all the great thinkers of the ages been unable to devise a simple and reliable test for truth? The problem of establishing reasonable validity, in vital metaphysical aspects of human experiences, appeared just as impossible in 1960 as it, apparently, was thousands of years ago.

I really wondered if I could ever establish a convincing case of validity for the perfection-now concept. And I needed to be able to make sense in my conversations about universal perfection. I would have to have understandable, concise statements that would express clearly, and also explain this shocking speculation, about the cosmic quality of all existence.

My perfection-now baby required reliable information on various, vital subjects to avoid the mental and emotional turmoil that Hazel and I had stumbled into before. Of course, I was certainly encouraged in that, already, two new and exciting fundamental concepts (existence is perfection and soul-perfection now) had emerged spontaneously for me, shortly after I had managed an open, unbiased state of mind allowing me to recognize and evaluate such welcome information when it was presented. Also, I thought it was significant that these two main ideas had something of the satisfying, natural quality that I could perceive in many of Hazel's paintings.

During this early time in my new search for understanding, Hazel had managed to sell a few of her paintings. I thought it would be worthwhile if we had photographs so we could still look at them, even though someone else had the original.

For years I had taken pictures of my furniture creations with an inexpensive flash camera. The results were good enough because I only needed a record of the shape and tailoring details. But when I took a flash shot of some of Hazel's paintings, the developed picture had a large bright spot, where the flash was reflected back and recorded on the film.

I realized that for improved results I would need a much better camera and a lot of information about photography. This was the beginning of a fascinating, additional, new interest for me. I purchased an Edixa, a single-lens, reflex camera, made in Germany. The salesman at the store gave me some basic instructions and helped to get me started. After a while, I found several good books on photography at the library, and I was eager to learn what others had figured out about the art of taking pictures.

Of course, photography was only a secondary interest. My main concern was finding answers to the perplexing problems of living. Usually, I fastened my strong desire for information on just one subject and stayed with it until the response I was looking for came.

So, after I began studying about the fundamentals of photography, I was occasionally surprised to notice, that while I was reading about cameras and lenses, at the same time I found that, with another area of my mind, I was thinking about the particular metaphysical subject I was investigating. These extra thoughts seemed to sneak in and take over most of my conscious awareness.

I often found I had read a half a page without paying any real attention to the meaning of the words my eyes were seeing. When that happened, I would put down my book and concentrate on these intuitive thoughts that were almost demanding my consideration. When enough of these mental interruptions occurred, so that I had an accumulation of bits and pieces of new ideas, I would scribble down the main features of the intuitive knowledge that was coming to me.

My goal at that time was to find a simple, key statement that would briefly explain my perfection-now thinking and feelings on a certain subject. Sometimes, at the end of my writing period, I would have what I was looking for. The words seemed to be valid and have the ring of truth. And they were plenty satisfactory to my sense of reason and logic.

As an example, here are some of the condensed results of my intuitive search on a variety of subjects:

Existence is perfection.
Truth applies universally and eternally.
The creator is responsible for the creation.
Rational judgment is not determined by irrational abuse.
Experiencing enjoyment and feeling appreciation are

the primary, dual purposes for our existence.

If these statements don't mean much to you, standing alone as they are, do not be concerned about it. I will be explaining them as we go along. I mention them here, only to show what is possible in using your intuitive knowing to provide answers to perplexing problems.

In volume II, I have a whole chapter on the subject of truth, and the last chapter deals with the main purpose of man's existence. The big question of responsibility in a perfect existence is considered, mainly, when we look into the likely possibility of abolishing condemnation and punishment aspects from our personal and social thought structure. <u>Judgment</u> <u>is</u> <u>not</u> <u>determined</u> <u>by</u> <u>abuse</u>, is the key statement needed to understand man's inhumanity to man in relation to unconditional cosmic perfection. And, of course, this whole book is about my perfection-now baby idea that <u>existence</u> <u>is</u> <u>perfection</u>.

The perfection-now baby term is also an intuitive development. Sometimes when my wife was irked at me, she would call me a jackass. Now, she says I have improved a little, and have become a perfect jackass. And lately, she is beginning to add baby to some of her other words of endearment such as, "Booby-Baby" and "Turdy Baby."

After I started my writing endeavor, I realized that if I ever expected to introduce my perfection-now idea to the world (and that's all I care to do), I would have to cut the shock effect and the mind-boggling profundity to smaller, bite-size servings. It seemed the best way to do it was to garnish it up with something innocent and appealing that people are familiar and comfortable with.

Nothing is as attractive and compelling as a baby, and it doesn't matter if it's white or black, human or animal. I suppose the worldwide interest stems from the fact that we were all babies to start with. It occurred to me that presenting the concept of instant perfection for everyone and everything as a new-born infant would give it something that most anyone could easily relate to.

No doubt, more people have become Christians from the Babe-in-the manger Christmas story, than from any real sense of needing redemption. Some religionists that I know of personally, would likely say that this contrived, baby hook-up for the perfection-now position was clearly the work of the devil. But I have already told you what I think of false demon possession.

My education started with the first two grades in a Catholic school in Chicago, and ended with a ministerial course at a Seventh Day Adventist's College at La Sierra, California. Of course, I learned more about Catholicism at La Sierra College than I did in the Catholic school in Chicago. The SDAs claim that the devil and the pope are conspiring to send the people of the world to hell by having them break the fourth commandment, requiring everyone to go to church on Saturday.

On the other hand, Catholics think the devil is leading protestants to their eternal doom by taking them out of the mother church. In fact, most Christians are obliged to consider the devil as the great conniver and deceiver. When you won't take on their doctrine, it's the old devil in you that is keeping you away from the "truth."

But, as I said before, <u>only</u> <u>ideas</u> <u>about</u> <u>something</u> can occupy the thinking area of your mind. They can represent something very real such as a book or a chair. Or your mental creations could be only fantasy thoughts representing nothing at all, as far as actual existence is concerned. Still, whether fact or fancy, the ideas themselves are real--<u>as</u> <u>ideas</u>.

Therefore, there is a phenomenon I call <u>the reality of illusion</u>. This is another sort of ambivalent or double-whammy way of looking at existence. And a whole chapter in Volume II deals with Perfection-Now Reality.

But for now, if you are beginning to see the perfection-now position as I do, the perfection-now baby idea will appear to be something more concrete and factual than just a subject title in a book. If my conclusions are correct, I actually was a Perfection-Now baby when I was born on a homestead in the middle of the Majave Desert. But, of course, <u>not</u> <u>the</u> <u>first</u> <u>one</u>.

Regardless of color, race or religion, or any other qualification, all babies everywhere, and for all time, have been perfection-now babies. Only no one, before, has recognized that vital fact. And the cosmic perfection inherent in each baby at birth remains exactly that throughout his life--in spite of anything that might occur during his experiences.

When I realized for the first time that there was no factual imperfection to be found existing anywhere in the cosmos, I was already a perfection-now man. And, of course, Hazel was a perfection-now woman, even though she suspected I could be conning her into thinking I was not the obnoxious, male chauvanist pig that she had to contend with during the best years of her life.

Besides, through the many years of our imperfection dilemma, Hazel and I both were brainwashed to assume that I had started out as an imperfect baby (born in sin and raised in iniquity) and had developed into an imperfect, inadequate man, doing all the stupid things that imperfect, carnal, lustful men are inclined to do.

While the truth about my innate nature (as I believe now) may have been exactly opposite to my previous, conditioned assumption, my distorted concept of an imperfect Homo sapien struggling through an imperfect, God-damned and God-doomed existence <u>was</u> <u>potent</u> <u>and</u> <u>real</u> <u>enough</u> to make me perform and react somewhat like the imperfect, idiot slob Hazel thought I was. And although I felt I wasn't quite as much of a reprobate as my wife claimed, I sometimes wondered if, after all, she might be correct in her estimation.

Nevertheless, when I finally cleared out the intellectual garbage from my mental chambers, the fact of my true nature was able to make itself known to me. And it was the beginning of a gradual, slow process of adaptation. As the transition (almost imperceptible) began its subtle effectiveness, I thought I could discern slight mental and emotional, and even physical adjustments. Still, the profound concept of universal cosmic excellence for all existence was so foreign to me and so upsetting in its extensive implications, that I could only take it on in its initial embryonic, very immature form.

At first, all I could manage was to tolerate it on a conditional basis. My unexpected, perfection-now baby would have to establish its legitimacy for me on every count. No more anal inconsistencies would be acceptable. Neither would I be satisfied with any more rationalizations as a substitute when reason and logic wouldn't apply. I was fed up to my eyebrows with irrational, cock and bull, excremental information, and I would not condone any more of the stinking stuff in my new thinking.

Providing a favorable environment in which my newborn concept could develop, was one of the main reasons (as far as I was concerned) for the big move to New Mexico that Hazel and I made. So changing our whole lifestyle so completely was not as difficult a decision for me to make as you might think.

As mentioned before, Hazel had been clamoring for such a move ever since our daughter had married and moved to Nevada. There seemed to be powerful instinctual forces pulling on Hazel to get her back to the one place in all the world where she had been contented and happy. She was seriously troubled that she might die and be cheated out of experiencing again, the magic of a New Mexico autumn. And she had had enough of "one goddamn beautiful day after another" in California.

She longed to hear again, the wind in the pines, high up on the ridge of the canyon walls. Also, she wanted to be there when the first snow storm came in the fall, and search for the first tiny wild flower to appear in the promising months of spring.

I had no idea how I would ever make a living away from the affluent Southern California area in which I was already firmly established. Yet the intuitive call to return to the enchantment of the Mogollon mountains of New Mexico was so persistent in my wife that I knew that, eventually, she would go without me if I refused to go with her. Hazel and I had an uncanny ability to make each other unhappy. Our personal tendencies seemed always to cause us to want to go in opposite directions. The mutual misery whipped up between us was the cause of an earlier separation and divorce that lasted about two years.

However, we both found that we were no better off, no happier away from each other.

So, on a vacation trip to New Mexico to visit Hazel's mother and father, we stopped off at Globe, Arizona, found a Justice Of The Peace, and for three dollars we legalized our togetherness relationship again. Shirley, about six years old at that time, signed as one of the witnesses. And like most properly old married couples, we managed to have a good fight before the second wedding day was over.

Although there are some good features connected with it, and I am all for it--there is something asinine about our civilized practice of getting married. The first time Hazel and I did it, and about an hour after the mighty deed was done, we both wondered if the other felt any different. I can't remember what we expected it might be like, but I do recall saying, "No, I don't feel anything different. How about you?" And Hazel answered, "I don't feel any different either."

I haven't any idea now what we were scrapping about when we got married the second time. But it did seem strange to me, that we should end up bitching and bickering on such a day. On the second time around, it evidently did make a difference. Years later, I tried to figure out why married people get to hating one another as much as they apparently do. And in the following chapter on "Love, Hate and Sex," I'll try to give you some of my findings on the subject.

A young black man was partially responsible for whatever ever courage I was able to muster up to make such a drastic change in our living arrangement. Thinking we might sell some of Hazel's paintings, we had converted the front part of my shop into a small art gallery.

One day, this young man came in to look at the paintings. During our conversation, I found out that he, also, was an artist. At that time, I think half the people in Southern California were trying to be artists. Anyway, he told me that he and his wife had just returned from a year-long trip to Spain. It had been their honeymoon adventure, and they would have stayed longer, except that his bride became pregnant. They figured, under the circumstances, they had better come back home, get a job and be prepared for the baby when it would come.

I looked this world-traveler artist over rather carefully. And it was obvious to me that he certainly was not a part of the wealthy, Beverly Hills set that could afford to run around the world on money someone else had provided. I was curious, so I asked, "How can a young guy like you manage to get married, take off a year, go to Europe, play around painting pictures, and even visit places like Paris and Rome?"

"Hell man," he said, "it's easy if you know how, and don't try to act like a rich American."

"But good God, how did a youngster your age ever accumulate enough money to swing a trip like that?"

"Well, it doesn't take as much as you might think. I saved up $1500.00 from my salary, working as a janitor.

That's all we had. After we were married, we went on a bus to New York. And going by bus is the least expensive way you can travel. When we got to New York, we immediately booked passage on a freighter, going first to North Africa and then to Spain.

"The ship was not leaving right away, so we had about a week to see New York City. During that time we were able to live in our state room on the freighter at no extra cost.

"In Spain we rented a nice furnished house for twelve dollars a month. And we could buy all the food we needed for just a few pennies a day from the street peddlers. (He showed me a photograph of the house and it was a nice place). Do you know that an average working man in Spain earns only about thirty dollars a month and raises a big family on that small amount? (Remember, this was in 1960).

"And by watching how we spent our money, we could even afford train trips to Paris for a week or so, and then on to Rome, Venice and other places. Of course, we always searched out the cheaper hotels and restaurants.

"When my wife became pregnant, we came back on a passenger liner, got another bus back to Los Angeles, and arrived here with three hundred dollars left over from the original fifteen hundred. Also, I shipped back quite a few paintings that I might sell."

I told Hazel about these young kids, and we visited them at their apartment in Santa Monica. After showing us some of their paintings, they filled us in on a lot of other details of how to travel on a small amount of money.

The prospects of taking off and doing something like they had done--maybe going to Spain--seemed not too impossible for us. There was an option clause in my lease on our business property, where we could renew it for two more years or give it up. Hazel sort of went along with the Spain trip thinking, but later (in fact, fifteen years later) she told me she never had any intention of ever going any farther east than New Mexico. And the way things turned out, that's as far as we ever got.

Dana and Virginia Lamb, author and explorers, who were contemporaries with Hazel and me, were also somewhat responsible for giving me a little spunk, at least enough to help us break out of our boring, tight, little circle of keeping at the daily grind. In the early thirties, during the worst time of the depression, they had guts enough to build a sailing canoe and embark on an exciting adventure that lasted most of their lives.

All they had when they sailed out of San Diego harbor was their well-equipped, sixteen-foot, sailing canoe, less than five dollars cash, and one hell of a lot of courage. Of course, they had spent one whole summer getting themselves in shape. They practiced running the breakers through the surf because their plans were to sail along close to the coast and come in to shore each evening and camp on the beach. They intended to feed themselves on fish that could be caught and anything else that could be scrounged from the beach area.

Lasting several years, their first excursion took them down the wild coast of Baja California, Mexico, around the southern tip and halfway up into the Gulf of California. And this was when it was still rather primitive and practically unexplored in many areas. Then they sailed across the gulf to the mainland of Mexico. This was considered to be almost an impossible ocean trip for such a flimsy craft as theirs. They made their way down the west coast of Mexico and ended their initial trip after going through the Panama Canal as the smallest registered vessel ever to make the passage.

Enchanted Vagabonds, their first book about their travels is, in my opinion, a classic in the literary world of modern adventure. I was especially fascinated in reading it, because at the same time they were building their canoe and getting ready to go, I was also building my own canoe and paddling through the surf at Sunset Beach just for fun. Usually the canoe would swing around sideways with the breakers, fill with water and dump us into the foam. But we didn't care. By then, we would be in shallow water, and my friend and I would lift the craft out of the water upside-down, thereby getting rid of the water; then we would jump in and paddle out through the waves for another wild ride with the big breakers. Later, I built a small, racing sail boat (Snipe Class). But Catalina Island, twenty miles off the coast, was as far as I ever sailed in my ocean travels.

Of course, this was before Hazel and I were married. After we were married, she eventually revealed her intense dislike for the ocean and just about anything connected with it. Hazel managed to get seasick just about every time we went out together on my boat. It got so bad with her that she almost puked, just standing on the floating dock at Watchhorn Basin where I kept my little craft.

When she first came to Los Angeles, some kids took her to the beach for her first experience with the ocean. To Hazel it was strange and somewhat terrifying. Although she couldn't swim, these mean punks drug her out into the surf in water almost over her head. Then they left her to struggle back on her own. A big breaker knocked her into a deep hole and Hazel nearly drowned before she somehow thrashed her way back to shore by herself.

This was the beach at El Segundo, and in order to get there you had to drive through a gigantic oil refinery which stinks like rotten turnips. And fish harbor, where the commercial fishing fleet discharge their cargo, is close to the dock where I tied up my sail boat during the summer time. As you can imagine, this didn't contribute to the purest of smells either. The whole ocean deal was just too obnoxious for Hazel, who was used to the clean, unpolluted, blue-sky mountain air of New Mexico.

After we got hooked into the evangelistic hiatus, we

sold the boat to finance my ministerial college debacle.

But of all the influences that caused me to dare to change my life-style so completely, I think my new concept of universal perfection was the most compelling. As a result of the startling information I had already discovered, there was a burning desire in me to learn a whole lot more.

In the opening chapter, I told about my mental experiment, wondering if I could figure what my thoughts might be if I had lived alone on an island. Well, in one respect, our move to New Mexico was almost a fulfillment of that slight wondering. Again I say, be careful of what you want--you might get it. On that first summer lookout job, we stayed on that mountain top for four months and two days.

It was not an island surrounded by water, but we were certainly isolated with an opportunity to observe a special part of the world, just as it has existed in a natural state for thousands of years. My perfection-now brain child had several summers to develop in something like the unique setting I had thought would be a novel experience in my fantasy speculation. As it turned out, it was really better than Spain for my purpose--and we got paid for our time as well.

During these initial years of adjustment for my new thinking, I hardly realized, at the time, what was taking place, as I am now able to look back and consider what has occurred.

For a long time, we lived without television, although electricity and improved roads came to our mountain community the third year after we arrived. But in 1972, after a period of cabin fever and sick-of-everything syndrome, we snaked a couple of wires, about a quarter of a mile long, up through the trees to a place on the mountain where there was a good TV signal coming from Tucson, Arizona. With an antenna up there, and the help of some signal booster gadgets, once more we were able to look through an electronic window at the outside world.

Now I had my island and my special TV, so I could look and see what was going on. But this time, I was prepared to judge what I saw from the perfection-now position. For I had already started on my writing endeavor.

In California, and up till 1962, we had enjoyed television from its earliest commercial beginnings. In 1972, having lived ten years somewhat cut off from the general turmoil reported in news programs, it was again a fascinating novelty for me to observe what I call our imperfection madness running wild throughout our country and much of the rest of the world. Although, of course, it was not a pleasing or satisfying sight to see.

On April 2, 1975, NBC Nightly News featured the plight of one Vietnamese baby who had become separated from his mother. The scene revealed a large landing craft loaded with passengers and about to pull away from the beach. A woman is holding a baby up almost over her head, and the crowd on the beach is shouting that the mother of the child is on the ship. Nevertheless, the soldier guarding the entrance is adamant, and will not allow anyone else to come on board.

Then someone drops a large cooking pot from the overhanging deck above, and the infant is hauled aboard. The big ship starts to back off the beach. Then another wild cry is heard from the people on the shore!

"Wait! There has been a mistake. The lost mother has been found and is not on the craft. Here she is on the beach, and the baby is now on the boat."

Again, the departure is delayed, and the great ship comes back to shore. The baby comes back down in the cooking-pot elevator, and eager, helpful hands bring the child to its mother, who is already carrying another older younster on one hip. With her free arm, she takes the rescued baby and turns her back on the vessel on which, no doubt, she had hoped to escape the impending chaos of a communistic takeover. I suppose that millions of viewers along with me, have wondered whatever happened to that mother and her two babies. Was she among those who finally made it to the U.S.? Or is she still in Vietnam attempting to adjust to the obdurate forces of a communist "liberation?"

I have wondered if that particular baby will ever know that he is a perfection-now baby. If enough people in the world knew about universal excellence, would that knowledge make a difference? Do you think hatred, animosity and injustice would be tempered if a majority of the inhabitants were aware of their innate state of cosmic perfection?

What kind of a world would we have to live in, if all, or at least most of the people realized that basic imperfection was only a false, mental contrivance of their gullible, brainwashed conditioning? Isn't it a possibility that people of different cultures would have more respect for, and trust in one another, if they became aware that everyone everywhere, for all time, were absolutely equal with each other in cosmic perfection?

Is it too fantastic to speculate that there could be a time when perfection-now babies could grow and become aware of their factual nature in a perfection-now world, cared for by aware, perfection-now parents, and instructed by knowing, perfection-now teachers? Is there any chance the United States could become the first perfection-now nation? And how would it be if we had practicing, perfection-now politicians, lawyers, doctors, scientists, movie stars, mechanics and janitors?

My fifteen years of perfection-now experience has not made me a prophet. So I do not claim to know what will occur in the future. But knowing what I do know, my concern for the state of the world is not as hopeless as it used to be. And the reason for my optimistic attitude is that, now, I firmly believe, without any reservations, we are already living in a perfection-now world.

I am convinced that our nation is, at this moment, a perfection-now nation, as are all other nations, regardless of what they call themselves or how they behave. I feel sure that we have perfection-now babies being cared for by perfection-now parents. Our doctors, lawyers, scientists and all those in governmental positions are presently perfection-now people.

And, of course, we even have perfection-now religionists. In addition, we have perfection-now prostitutes, pimps, criminals and insane people. Then there are perfection-now homosexual people. The only trouble is that none of these creatures of excellence realize that they are all--<u>without exceptions or qualifications</u> whatsoever--absolutely perfect Homo sapiens living for a short time on this perfect, cosmic, space ship.

Although I am ignorant of what the future holds, I am inclined to speculate that somehow, when the perfection-now word gets around, we will all enjoy ourselves more. Likely, there will be less fighting, less condemning and punishing, less mental and emotional despair--and a lot more appreciation and love circulating on our beautiful earth.

In such an improved environment, perfection-now babies will have a better chance to know who and what they are, and why they are here as they are. And, perhaps the problems they encounter will not appear so devastating and hopeless as the damned dilemmas we have had to cope with.

BYE-BYE DILEMMA

"Turdy baby, it's all right for you to speculate about what might be in the future--that is, if your fantastic idea of instant perfection ever gets to be well-known. But what about right now? You are going to have to explain how just one individual can manage his own dilemma--and never mind waiting around for the perfection-now age of enlightenment to come. That might be like waiting until you get to heaven for a little peace and enjoyment.

"If there is any real truth to your concept of perfection existing for everyone, it should be possible for anyone to resolve his problems now--without waiting for the whole world to understand existence as you see it. Good God, that might take a hundred years or more. Or maybe most of the people of the world will never find out about their factual nature. The perfection-now idea may be your baby, but it is only a ridiculous way of thinking to most everyone when they first hear of it."

Hazel has always had an effective way of bringing me down out of the clouds to face the gut realities of contending with the here and now. So I will attempt to reveal how <u>you, as an individual</u>, might be able to say, "Bye-Bye" to your dilemma, just as Hazel and I, as individuals, have managed to dispose of ours.

Actually, your intuitive thinking will do the final revealing. About all I can do is tell you something of how I have been able to get rid of the perplexing problems of being a human being for myself.

Through all the years of hashing over most of the subject matter in this book, I don't feel that I have been of much direct help to Hazel with her various dilemmas. In some respects, I have been one of her big dilemmas. But <u>indirectly</u>, somehow we have been helpful to one another in our separate efforts to unravel the deep mysteries of existence.

A dilemma is a perplexing situation where you think you must choose between two or more alternatives which are equally obnoxious. Obviously, the solution to any dilemma, including yours, whatever it may be, is to find an additional alternative that negates the undesirable selection you thought you had to make.

But don't expect the perfection-now alternative to resolve your dilemma all by itself. However, it can start you thinking along a new, more satisfactory direction that perhaps you couldn't see before.

I think electric razors are a marvelous invention. Yet I have to get mine out, plug it in and use it for myself, if it is going to do me any good. And electric blankets are a super development. Still, it's up to you to regulate them for your particular needs. Psychiatrists say that their main job is to help the client help himself. And that's about all the perfection-now concept can do; indirectly help you to help yourself.

A while back, Hazel experienced a minor dilemma, but soon found its solution through her own effort and observation. She tried to explain the problem to our daughter in a letter: "...What I mean about tired is this: I am tired of life. I am tired of cooking, cleaning, getting groceries, talking to neighbors, reading, writing, enbroidering, quilting, painting, drawing, gardening; tired of all the old pursuits, and not much interested in taking up anything new either.

"But I always manage to keep alive one interest to keep me going. I've always had plants, and after you said you had eighty nine of them, I perked up, looked around at all this space, and suddenly got serious about plants! Now I am in it up to my eyeballs! (I don't get tired waiting on them-- Ha!) And it isn't hard on my old eyes or my old carcass."

I think I can add that likely, Hazel was fed up with knitting wool socks for me. I must have about forty pair-- thank God and Marmalade. And long ago, Hazel had heard all she could take about my perfection-now baby. Anyway, I am now living with a house-plant nut.

Hazel has always had a fondness for growing things. When we lived in Topanga, the best surprise I could bring home to her was a couple of sacks of manure.

Here in Silver Creek, the outside growing season ends

with the first freeze, usually in October. Fortunately, our thick-walled building is an ideal green house, and Hazel has always managed to have some house plants growing through the winter months. A few years ago she had several African Violets, but they all croaked when we were stranded for several weeks at our vacation cabin, the one that burned down. There was a freak, four-foot snow fall and it was impossible (even with the help of the army) to get our car out to the main highway.

With her new interest in plants, Hazel now had a longing to get some more African Violets. It would take too long to relate how, in a roundabout way, these new plants she wanted managed to come to Hazel. And she didn't buy them. It seems lately that about all Hazel has to do is have a strong desire for something, and whatever it is just comes.

Anyway, when the plants arrived, they were not in the best of health. However, in about a week, I was amazed at the beneficial change that had taken place. Hazel had placed them all under intensive care. And some of those delapidated plants were even producing new, little baby plants from just some almost dead leaves that had been placed in moist vermiculite. Hazel showed the new arrivals to me through a magnifying glass. She also told me that one woman could raise African Violets twenty- seven inches across from such infant plants in just one year. Some of the older plants were spreading out and taking a new lease on life too, because Hazel was providing the proper environment they required.

It is a well-known fact that horses, dogs and cats, children, husbands and wives, in addition to house plants, always respond beautifully to thoughtful, tender, loving care. And when I saw how much good Hazel had accomplished on those sorry plants in such a short time, (and especially seeing those tiny baby plants beginning to grow) I recalled the initial cerebral shock I experienced fifteen years ago when I first realized there was no factual imperfection to be found anywhere in the vast universe of existence.

That startling, newborn awareness was of a twofold nature. Of course, the first was a great relief, a new sense of freedom and a pure delight at the great intellectual treasure I had uncovered. The second feeling that came a little later was a somewhat distressful chagrin that this vital information had gone unnoticed for so long in a world that needed it so much. And it still seems incredible to me that clever Homo sapiens who can send astronauts to the moon and back, are yet groveling in inquisitional Dark Ages when it comes to caring for their own mental and emotional needs.

As the general human dilemma is so widespread, with hostile erruptions occurring in various, explosive places throughout the world, it is reasonable to think that the primary cause of the ever increasing chaos is also something that is global in its toxic influence.

As I clearly saw it in that intuitive flash fifteen years ago, and as I can easily grasp it now, after much careful consideration, the imperfection postulate we all subscribe to (Ha ha, nobody's perfect you know) is the infectious breeding ground for mental and emotional desperation and despair.

Damn it to hell, we have all been playing our cards against a stacked, crooked, imperfection deck. No wonder so many believe there is no way to win. But the truth of existence (as I see it in the overall picture) indicates there is no way that anyone can lose!

<u>And</u> <u>that's</u> <u>a</u> <u>big</u> <u>difference.</u>

Surely it's time for all the trouble-making cards (social, industrial, political, philosophical and religious) to be laid out face up on the table, so that we can realize we all have been playing a sucker game with ourselves. Looking at the world and each other through imperfection-tinted glasses has distorted our vision in every direction that we have attempted to explore. Imperfection-oriented rationalizations have complicated every important effort that has been put forth.

Going back to before _my_ perfection-now age of enlightenment started, the principal dilemma of my experience was the frustrating problem of coping with the seemingly self-evident fact of my supposedly innate imperfection. Every mistake made, each difficulty I encountered was an insidious, irksome reminder of the woeful lack of perfection in my make-up. And there was nothing I could do about that.

How many times have you read or heard, "The trouble with human nature is human nature?" Young people are still being conditioned, as I was, to deny and ignore the existing cosmic excellence that is already ours--and nothing can ever take it away from us.

To compensate for what is supposed to be lacking in our inadequate nature, we are urged by sick zealots to take on radical political conspiracies, impossible dream-world programs, or impractical utopian and religious plans to save ourselves from destruction when doomsday comes. In going along with the available programs, we seriously strive to modify our alleged inadequate nature to conform to the diarrhetic, regulatory system thought to be the least imperfect.

Some think their salvation can be earned if they devote themselves to scientific investigation, to medicine, education or social service. And there are plenty who con themselves into thinking they are called (as I once did) to evangelize, persuade and convert. With the best of intentions, we are all somewhat inclined to assist, aid and even go to war (if necessary), determined that our nation shall be the number one power in the world, having the greatest capacity to annihilate the ever-present enemy.

At some time in our life, it is likely we are encouraged into thinking that a serious, rat-race dedication to traditional programs will somehow remake the world into a more perfect place. To some extent, we are led into believing that, by struggling and fighting to eradicate the imperfection, thought to be in our adversaries, in wives and husbands, children, neighbors and friends, we will somehow root out the fecal circumstances causing individuals and nations to hate and contend with one another.

But the history of scores of past centuries have all been bloody records of disastrous failures to accomplish the peace and security which we, too, seem helpless to bring about--with all our atomic capability for global destruction.

For too long, we have condoned an imperfection-oriented, self-destructive program of forceful conformity, sanctioned by educators, governments, religionists and even the common man in the street. Now we are seeing our established, psychotic, condemning and punishing example adopted by angry bands of militants, who erroneously think their experiments in violence will eventually establish the long sought, "Brotherhood of Man."

Is it possible that these fanatical idealists are ignorant of the fact that great, organized armies throughout history have been unable, <u>through coercion and slaughter</u>, to engender attitudes of understanding, tolerance and love in the minds and hearts of the assumed, imperfect, human animal?

The consequences of our imperfection training should be clear to anyone who even considers the significant events of the last seventy- five years. When, through extensive corruption in the corporate (watergated) aristocracy (the haves), the oppressed and sometimes unemployed working class (the have-nots) are provoked and frustrated to extremes--riots and anarchy can be expected.

Promising food, security and a utopian society of equality and plenty for everyone, communist rabble-rousers have a golden opportunity to take forceful charge in such a chaotic debacle. But as I see it, freedomless, Godless communism is the most corrupt of all the imperfection-based alternatives.

In some respects it is even worse than the Dark Ages, inquisitional, religious conformity. The obdurate gods you must plead with to gain some browny points are the power-holding bureaucrats of the movement. We should not be deceived with proclaimed records of reduced crime, corruption, prostitution and poverty. When you are so restricted in your activities that you have to get permission from some block warden to go to the bathroom or visit your sick grandmother, do you think such an administration is going to admit to personnel troubles they surely encounter?

As far as poverty is concerned--they have made everyone poor. And the hard-core regulators are steeped in corruption. They have stolen from the people their freedom to think, to believe, to live and work and move about on the earth as they choose.

But the innate perfection of the enslaved people remains--despite their forceful confinement in a frustrating, reform-school nation. There is nothing anyone can do that will alter or take away the cosmic excellence that is as much a part of those in communist countries as universal perfection is inherent in disturbed Homo sapiens in our own thoroughly watergated, capitalistic system.

As it was in my own experience, problems originating with the invalid imperfection assumption are likely to adversely affect nearly everyone during some period of their tumultuous earth adventure. Although, on the surface, many appear to manage fairly well in spite of the irksome difficulties, there are times when the most stouthearted persons might become satiated with imperfection-oriented injustices, inconsistencies and runaround rip-offs.

At any time at all, the most optimistic individual is in danger of becoming glutted with the woeful lack of integrity, truth and security threatening the foundational structure of our unique country. Almost anyone could be afflicted with a loss of confidence in his own integral make-up, in the seemingly obstinate nature of associates, or husbands, wives and children. And often we hesitate to trust lawyers, doctors, educators and even law-enforcement officials. Also politicians, automobile salesmen and religionists have engendered for themselves a shabby reputation of being clever but unscrupulous con-artists.

Overwhelmed with a backwash of deception and corruption seemingly about to engulf us, it is no wonder that we are usually unaware of the inherent joy of existence always available to us from within our own, natural resources. But this tranquil, intuitive knowing will never force its gentle awareness upon us. Our instinctual intelligence never demands us to pay attention to its instructions.

The x-factor, God wisdom inherent in our soul natures does not insist that we line up to any precise, inflexible procedures. The subtle, mind-comforting suggestions offered are presented without conditions--other than perhaps a freewill, open mind and heart consideration, thankful recognition and possible acceptance. But most of us become so screwed up mentally and emotionally from all the fecal, imperfection thinking that is dished out to us, that we are unable to realize that a satisfactory solution to our personal dilemma can be found in our ever-ready instinctual feelings.

During times of increased tension and provocation, we are often gullible victims, easily conned into taking on a sucker program of regimented conformity. Of course, we are hoping to find salvation from the impending disaster we fear will overtake us. Scared out of our minds of a doomsday future, we become eager marks for the first, attractive, institutional master, claiming he can lead us out of our bewilderment into the saving light of his (usually exclusive) "God-sanctioned" program.

Most of these pseudo saviors have the same, almost stereotyped, religious, blackmail approach. There is an implication that, if we follow without question--that is, have faith in the master's instructions and dogmas, and contribute (pay your tithe--ten percent of your income) to his noble effort to save the whole world, we might attain enough spiritual development to escape the terrible cosmic punishment waiting for all who refuse to go along with the master's program.

In my opinion, they display about as much common-sense integrity as the bait boy who helped me win the fourth jackpot by knocking off the winning fish. When these young sailors have worked for three months as apprentice deck-hands, they are promoted to the rank of master-baiters.

In the simple equality of universal perfection, I have found no valid categories for masters and subjects. One is not above another because he may learn something first, which eventually becomes common knowledge--providing he actually has discovered something worthwhile and factual.

The finder of truth is not greater than truth itself. The validity of what is said is better to be determined than trusting in the authority of the speaker. Knowing who the author may be, is not as vital as deciding the authenticity and value (or the deception and possible harm) of what is suggested in the literary record.

Ignoring the integral, soul intelligence of our own perfect beings, we are exhorted to look outside of ourselves for some far-off intangible savior who, miraculously, might decide to provide that which we think is lacking within ourselves. But in metaphysical matters, I have found that saviors cannot actually save us--because we are never really lost and therefore don't need saving. Knowing guides are unable to effectively lead us. Dedicated instructors do not actually teach us. Capable governors are powerless to really rule us. And often, the best doctors are helpless to restore our health.

For no other person is able to accomplish for us that which we alone can do for ourselves. So by groveling low in fear and humility before some distant, vengeful deity--we are effectively denying and ignoring the absolute equality and Godly excellence of our own, fully adequate being.

None of the above should be misconstrued to indicate that I am suggesting that we do not need capable instructors, dedicated doctors, governors, lawyers, and even religious leaders in our modern society. Surely, we should seek out and take advantage of all the worthwhile and valid information that is available.

And of course, my denouncements do not apply to master mechanics, music maestros, or the host of technicians having expertise in all the fields that sustain and constantly improve our vast, technological developments. I recognize and respect hard work, honesty and integrity wherever it is in evidence. And for sure, we wouldn't have the great measure of goodness and security we enjoy now (at least in this country), if it were not for an abundance of common-sense morality and ethical endeavor still functioning quietly and mostly unnoticed behind the scenes--despite the more notorious shenanigans that we seem to want to know about.

This might sound like another ambivalent situation, and I guess it is. To some extent, I am giving everyone a little hell for their gullible support of the imperfection assumption. And of course, I am applauding them all for the creatures of cosmic excellence I perceive them to be. But it's an awkward position in which to find yourself--something like patting someone on the head and kicking him in the ass at the same time.

And I want it understood that I am not condemning these sorry devils who are sucking the life blood from the almost dry tits of uninformed, but trusting young people, as well as taking advantage of credulous, older people living somewhat in a state of fear and anxiety, but who have never bothered to figure things out rationally for themselves.

Likely, these sick, but clever deception artists are

victims of their own deception and are to be pitied, not condemned. Although I realize that most denouncements imply condemnation--<u>mine</u> <u>do</u> <u>not</u>.

In all this, I hope you can understand that the single notion I am trying to introduce is that, no matter how fouled up anyone might become, when at last you clean away the filth at the bottom, you will find that every son of a bitch is a perfection-now baby.

Isn't it ironic that the most outrageous deception ever perpetrated on an easily cheated, world population is often disguised as a humorous, comforting blanket to cover up inadequate, slipshod endeavors?

One incident that likely, millions recall, was when Flip Wilson flubbed and said, "Put the mantel on the cup", instead of, "Put the cup on the mantel." He got a big laugh when he corrected himself and added, "Well, nobody's perfect you know--ha-ha." What we need now in the world is a good, long laugh at the biggest joke of all time--the jackass, imperfection mistake we have all made.

But the consequences of our tragic mistake have not always been funny. Yet, regardless of how we react to it, a personal comprehension of universal perfection somehow performs its soothing adjustments. And the reason is that, unlike any other alternative, the solution to any dilemma emerges first as an intellectual option.

Bothersome, involved situations do not always require immediate, adamant alterations. In my own experience, as I was gradually able to perceive perfection in all reality, I found that a more tolerable and forgiving attitude was possible for most irksome situations. This dilemma dissolving, mind comfort emerges spontaneously from an application of the concept that <u>existence is perfection,</u> in the only place you and I can apply it--in our new thinking and, eventually, in our more satisfying conclusions.

When I began regaining my common sense regarding

this vital subject, (and it is a gradual, ever growing development), the perfection-now position became, for me, a simple solution for the complex, imperfection-oriented dilemma that had disturbed me for so long.

I discovered, too, that its beneficial responses are never dependent on a favorable disposition by our adversaries. Increased understanding on any subject, as well as greater emotional stability, begins to assert their welcome influence in our consciousness when we consider the perfection-now idea as the obvious solution to our imperfection dilemma.

One approach that has worked well for me in any conflict, (and I have been involved in a few hassles since I started in this business), is to look for the somewhat hidden perfection in the actual trouble itself, in the adversaries who are causing the squabble--and even the perfection you can expect in the eventual outcome of the disturbance.

In observing perfection in all phases of a dilemma, we no longer look upon complications with the painful concern that previously was such a bother to us. And I think you will find, as I have, that your new reaction to an awareness of cosmic perfection in, around and throughout the distressful involvement, is usually one of diminishing concern.

Most of my frustration had been a drastic, dreadful feeling related to my helplessness to manage circumstances that I believed were causing my unhappiness. Usually, these irritations are tied into the attitudes and behavior of others, and I am powerless to control their thinking and performances.

But with my perfection-now thinking, I can easily see that it isn't necessary for me to even attempt to influence and regulate what others around me believe, think, say and do. Instead, I resign my activities to whatever I can easily manage within the limits of my capacity and my responsibility, and leave the rest of the perfect mess up to the Universal Creative Power, having overriding responsibility for the entire creation.

It takes a while (sixteen years for me) to find that, in addition to a solution for our present dilemma, perfection-now considerations often function in a preventative manner. In time, you will likely find that your new thinking tends to keep you clear of difficulties that, previously, would have robbed you of your happiness. Enjoyment inevitably increases when you cease struggling and involving yourself in troublesome activities over which you have no obligation, no influence and no control.

But detaching our involvment to the extent that circumstances are no longer a dilemma for us, need not mean that we must develop an unfeeling, cold state of mind toward those who are still striving in their complicated turmoil. In fact, from a less involved, less bothered position, our sympathetic understanding and concern for those embroiled in trouble of their own creation is noticeably increased.

And we find that our own, somewhat happier attitude contributes somehow--but without direct effort on our part--to improve the unpleasant entanglement. At least, when we become accustomed to reacting from the perfection-now position, we can feel assured that our less-disturbed approach is not causing any further conflict or unhappiness.

Although the perfection-now solution to our imperfection dilemma is not conditional on immediate adjustments, there is nothing implied that we must resign ourselves to forever be contented with intolerable, exasperating circumstances. For instance, if a cow is standing on your foot, it is clearly your responsibility to get your foot out from under the offending beast.

However, at the same time, it is not your duty to educate all cows so that they will never again step on someone's foot. And, if we can see the wisdom of letting cows remain as they were created to be, wouldn't it make sense to adopt the same, rational attitude toward our associates?

Training all the cattle in the world to be careful where

they place their big hoofs would be far easier than attempting to control even one, obstinate hominoid so that he or she would always perform in the particular way that was reasonably pleasing to us.

Wouldn't it be better to accept cows and people just as they are and quit the futile struggle to refashion them into something more perfect than they are at this time? When you stop to consider that people and cows are perfect already, even though they may upset us occasionally, makes a big difference in our reaction to an occasional hassle.

I suppose that, in most cases when we are young, we have no choice but to go along with the program others push us into. Neither Hazel nor I wanted to go to the church boarding school we were sent to. But to our young minds at that time, it seemed we had no other alternative, so we went.

Nevertheless, when enough time goes by, reason of our own creation begins to make itself known in our comprehension. Finally we are fully capable of thinking and choosing for ourselves. And we realize we can use our own judgment for decisions concerning our personal welfare.

The main point I want to stress here, is that the means to equalize any misdirection that may have been imposed upon us eventually develops within our understanding. However, restoring common sense and repairing emotional damage have been difficult to manage under the overwhelming miasma of traditional, imperfection thinking. Yet realizing this, one cannot overlook the fact that countless millions of people have lived and died on this earth without ever consciously knowing the absolute excellence of their human nature. Or at least as far as I know, that is a fair assumption.

Of course, the inherent perfection of their make-up was always there--despite their not-knowing. Reason and logic were functioning in their experiences, too. Also, intuitive soul knowing, never completely deflected by false information, had always been emanating to some extent, for everyone in its subtle, comforting way.

Nevertheless, believing in basic imperfection caused them to question their instinctual confidence in their own reason and logic. And, of course, we all are doing the same thing today. But despite incorrect assumptions, of which our surface thinking is capable of being suckered into, there is always our deeper soul knowing providing a counteracting balance to some extent.

So, although the full, factual truth of existence (existence is perfection) may never spill over into our surface comprehension, intuitive indications of doubt and wonder likely will surround unreasonable assertions.

And for most practical purposes, irrational conclusions are somewhat nullified in their adverse effectiveness. It is some comfort to realize that this automatic, de-bullshitter function of our humanity was working for our predecessors the same as it is working for a lot of people today.

A few episodes occurred when I was about seven years old that I think will illustrate this point. At that time, we were living in the country, about three miles from the little town of Bristow, Oklahoma. My father had helped his uncle to build a two-storied, frame house which was located on top of the flat crest of a hill. Aunt Minnie and Uncle Dick lived upstairs and we occupied the ground floor. The new structure sat back away from the dirt road about one hundred feet. A large cement slab was all there was for a front porch.

One evening a little after dark, we were all sitting around the dining room table. We could hear a Model T Ford chugging slowly up the long hill from the direction of town. When it reached the top of the hill just outside our place, we heard someone shout, just like gun-men do in the movies, "Stick em up."

Almost immediately, there were two loud shots fired. Turning off the Coleman gas lantern and leaving us all in darkness, my father told us to be quiet and follow him. He led us out the back door and we all crept silently to a place in the underbrush beyond the outhouse.

While we waited, there was more shouting and commotion. Then after a while, we heard the car start up. From the sounds, we could tell that it had turned around and was going back to town. Still we waited quite a while, until everything seemed like it was back to normal.

Finally, while my mother, my two sisters and I huddled fearfully together, Dad made a cautious exploration of the area and found that the hijackers had cleared out and it was safe to go back into the house.

The next day we found a big sploch of blood on the smooth concrete of the front porch. Evidently, the victims of the holdup had tried to get help at our house. Then they had hurried back to town to get medical attention--which we couldn't have given them anyway, even if we had known they had come to us for assistance. We learned later that the armed bandits (two of them) had secured a little more than twenty dollars for their bloody violence. Also, two people were in the car and one had been wounded, but not fatally.

Not long after that hijacking incident, my mother woke me up a short time after I had gone to bed. She was crying, and had a telegram in her hand. Between sobs, she told me that her sister, my Aunt May, had died in Chicago. I wasn't much help to her--I cried too.

Then there was the time when Mrs. Ritchy, the lady who lived across the road from us, got lock-jaw and was very sick. After a few days had passed, her son, a young man, came by and my mother asked how his mother was getting along. "I guess she's going to make it all right," he said. "Hell, that old woman is just too darn ornery to die."

I thought this was a very strange way for someone to talk about his mother who had been close to death. And altogether, these three episodes made a strong impression on me. They were the first encounters I had made in my young life with insecurities and the dreadful aspect of living and dying. But shortly afterwards, something happened to soften these jarring, upsetting emotions of fear.

One day I was exploring with my dog in the forest near our property. The place was in a small, open spot by a brook with a few puddles of water left over from a summer shower. A large, rounded rock about five feet high, partly covered with moss, had attracted my attention. I had sort of leaned up against this boulder with my head up flat against the rock and my arms outstretched, almost as if I were embracing it. I was enjoying the touch of the smooth lichen when I experienced some kind of intuitive communication.

Judging from my later experience, I realize now there must have been a slight mystical aspect to it. I have never forgotten the strange feeling. The wordless information that seemed to make an impression on me was that, regardless of troubles, and even death itself, everything was all right.

But the religious teachings I was subjected to seven years later, when I was fourteen, knocked the hell out of the assurance and fortitude I received in this instinctual experience. And it took a future intuitive incident thirty-three years after that, to put me back on the less-fearful track I had found when I was seven.

The distressful dilemma of my experience began to diminish, the moment I first realized that I had been terribly mistaken about my alleged, built-in state of imperfection. The somewhat sickening frustration I had endured for so many years was dispersed in that instant of clarity when I could believe that I was not really an accidental, faulty, freak of nature, lost in a hopeless happening of impending chaos.

My factual nature of cosmic excellence began to assert its real presence in that startling second when I recognized that I was a valuable, important segment of a whole universe of unqualified perfection.

And a few weeks later, when my mystical, "Soul-Perfection Now" episode at Santa Monica occurred, there was too much of an exciting nature to consider, for me to be bothered with old, invalid fears of my imperfection years. Of course, nothing at all had actually changed in my make-up. I was exactly the same person I had been before. The only alteration was an intellectual one. My new thinking had managed a complete turnaround. And happily, I was discovering a new sense of respect and value for everything I encountered.

But firmly established, imperfection habits of thinking and behavior do not vanish completely overnight. And here is another ambivalent consideration. One part of my thoughts were eagerly contemplating new attitudes and feelings that were forming, in addition to challenging new directions I wanted to explore. And yet, another part of my consciousness was still clinging a little to old ways of thinking that, despite their unsatisfactory character, were somewhat comfortable because I had managed somehow with them for a long time--even though not too well.

So when Hazel and I moved to New Mexico, I went into my new life with something of a double personality. One was my old obnoxious self, with a lot of overbearing attitudes I had acquired through many years of imperfection, gut struggling. The other was a somewhat child-like character who was looking at everything he saw as if for the first time. Of course, I didn't realize this while it was happening. It is only in looking back that I can now see the gradual adaptation that was occurring.

It is no wonder that my new associates in the Forest Service hardly knew what to make of me. My years of turning out top quality furniture for those who were willing to pay for the best, helped me in some ways and worked against me in others. There were no problems as long as Hazel and I worked by ourselves on the tower. But when the fire danger was over, I found myself working with local men and spirited young cowboys who had lived in the area all their lives. It took several years for me to learn there is a big difference in the quality of furniture going into a famous movie star's home, and that required for a horse pasture fence built on a ten-thousand foot mountaintop in New Mexico.

And I didn't know any more about building a fence than a cowboy would know about diamond tufting on a Saint Francis chair. I may have been a jackpot-winner on the fishing boats at Malibu, but I didn't know my ass from a hole in the ground when it came to mounting a horse properly, or operating a chain saw, or using a diamond hitch to secure the load on a pack mule--or a lot of other things that are essentials for survival in that wild and primitive country.

But I was a willing worker and eager to learn. However, my enthusiasm didn't prevent me from occasionally making a damn-fool of myself when I was working with and under the direction of these native fellows. And I can see now, that an accumulation of these minor irritations eventually made serious trouble for Hazel and me. This adverse encounter (when it exploded unexpectedly upon us) socked us both into a new dilemma for which we were hardly prepared.

But in the end it also provided a positive test for our new thinking. Also, to some extent, it enabled me to gain a little clear insight into the complex emotions of love, hate and sex--which invariably are at the bottom of most dilemmas. Therefore, love, hate and sex from the perfection-now position are featured subjects in the next chapter.

CHAPTER V

LOVE, HATE AND SEX

A few years back, when the late Maurice Chevalier was making his last round of appearances in the U.S., someone in the audience asked him what he had learned about love. In his charming style, he proceeded to tell about his first real making-out experience when he was just a youth about fifteen years old. At least, that was the impression that was conveyed to me from what he said.

His paramour in love-making was an older, more experienced lady. With sighs of remembered pleasure, he attempted to describe his love feelings related to his initial, sex encounter, before a national, television audience. And I suppose, because he was old and famous and a master showman, he managed to pull it off--somehow.

If there was an easy way to get out of writing this chapter, I almost think I would skip it. For in dealing with abstract subjects like love, hate and sex, I realize that I, too, am in danger of letting my ignorance hang out for all to see.

But I am also concerned in another way that seems to override my apprehensions. I feel that we Homo sapiens are greatly in the dark about the existence, the essence, the meaning and power of love, just as much as we have all been screwed up in our outlandish acceptance of basic, inherent imperfection as the innate nature of ourselves and this world.

Observing the amount of hostility exuding openly in nearly every home and community, (with of course, some exceptions), it is obvious to me that many of us have lost touch with the fullness and benefits of love in our regard for ourselves and one another. Rather, we have become experts at pooping on each other and rubbing it in for good measure.

In participating in this imperfection-oriented madness, we contaminate ourselves, as well as our victims in the fecal process. The sorry imperfection appraisement we hold, even for our own personal worth, is a serious problem in the world, which can only be resolved in our individual minds and hearts before we can ever expect to realize improved, happier, love relations with our contemporaries.

A better understanding of the reality of love, its function and potential value would seem essential, if you and I are ever going to establish a satisfactory love attitude toward our own being and toward our fellow humans throughout the world.

I have no intention here to disparage the love factor involved in sexual intercourse. Because loving and copulating surely go well together. And as long as humanoids are having togetherness naturally with one another, there will always be some understanding of love; even though it might be only an incomplete and inadequate one.

There is a lot more included in the love category than a compelling gut desire that often brings two bodies together to satisfy a temporary horny urge.

Earlier, in relating my mystical soul-awareness experience, I refrained from expounding on one aspect of that most unusual occurrence. But I did mention that, in addition to the intense joy and utter happiness that appears to be the inherent and constant make-up of my soul-God existence, there was a startling recognition of cosmic love, that is incomparable--at least in degrees--with that which we usually think and feel is love in our normal experiences.

The love factor I encountered in that direct-knowing incident was as real, as knowable and fundamental to that non-physical, soul-God reality as mother earth and father sun are to the physical reality we all know so well. It was this unmistakable, overwhelming presence of absolute love, existing everywhere and in everything, that confirmed my initial, intuitive concept of unqualified perfection for all existence.

Since that mystical episode at Santa Monica in the fall of 1960, I have had sixteen years under a variety of circumstances to ponder many of the mysteries of existence. And for me, most of the imperfection-oriented perplexities have vanished. I have found most of the vital answers and solutions that I was searching for.

But in attempting to explain what I have discovered for myself (especially in the love category), I find that words alone are somewhat inadequate to relate completely the meaning I am trying to express. I suppose the reason for this is that our general understanding of verbal symbols is thoroughly geared up to imperfection based misconceptions.

I am convinced that I have been privileged to communicate directly with the one, moving God force in the cosmos. Yet my nonreligious conclusions, based partly on that mystical experience--that is, the guttural composition of impressions I received--are reported here in my words. Love and hate, good and evil, damnation and salvation, imperfection and perfection-now, God, soul and devil--in fact all words are merely man's secondary verbal creations concocted to represent, vaguely, certain perceptive impressions. <u>For sure, such verbose utterances are never God's words.</u> Judging from what I experienced, I cannot accept that the Universal Intelligence communicates to Homo sapiens in verbiage that can be easily rationalized beyond all common sense. It stands to reason that the vast Cosmic Love Force and knowledge which turns this earth, space vehicle around on its axis every twenty-four hours, would never proclaim for publication a miasma of questionable statements (represented as the sacred words of God) that are unacceptable and repulsive to the essence of intuitive

Rather, Cosmic Love seems to be the universal language of our Soul-God-Mind relationship. Whatever instinctual or mystical information humans or animals become aware of, arrives in their intuitive thinking in wordless concepts. You and I supply the precise words later (sixteen years later--as I am doing now) to fit the impressions we receive. And if we are somewhat honest (someone said no writer can be completely honest) and free from delusions, we may come close to relating our conclusions correctly.

But for the most reliable information on the subject matter of this chapter, you will have to depend on your own, soul-love, intuitive awareness.

It is difficult to put love into a separate category. For, as I am beginning to understand it, love is a composite of all truth, all knowing, and in fact, of all existence. And because of my direct-knowing contact with this Cosmic Love Force, I have sought through the years to gain some understanding of love, in all its lesser, but not less perfect, manifestation.

Seeing the world and its host of living creatures from the perfection-now position makes a significant difference for just about anything worthwhile you attempt to consider seriously. And you may find, as I have, that love takes on a more satisfying meaning than was possible when imperfection assumptions were cluttering up your conclusions.

It may sound a little incongruous, but I have found it nearly impossible to consider the love factor intelligently, without also including a rational understanding of the hate aspects of love. There is a simple relationship existing between these two, seemingly opposite, motivating forces. But when you examine hate and love from the perfection-now position, it is not difficult to grasp that each word represents, in our feelings and emotions, only different aspects of the one cosmic force.

In the realm of nonphysical, soul existence, apparently, there is no requirement for the disagreeable, hate side of that universal energizer. This is fairly well established by the fact that almost all mystics have experienced a similar, love ecstasy that is almost incomprehensible to anyone who has only known the usually vacillating, physical emotions of love and hate.

Cosmic Love Energy is a great deal more than the occasional moments of reactionary, love emotion that reach our surface recognition. If love could be compared to temperature, then mystical, soul God love would always be that constant, ideal condition between hot and cold that is exactly right. But physical love runs to the top and bottom of the love-hate meter. Human emotions are capable of sampling the intense, mystical delight of rapturous, love ecstasy, as well as crashing low into the utter despair of imperfection-oriented exasperation.

Sex and love must also be considered together. It appears that all living creatures experience something related to that compelling, primordial, sexual, gut feeling.

But for man, of all the natural body functions, sexual satisfaction has suffered the greatest emasculation from our gullible, thoughtless acceptance of the joy-killing, imperfection postulate. A personal awareness of universal perfection, plus some understanding of an overriding, Cosmic Love Power, gives a new dignity and value to the basic, human, sexual compulsion.

So we can discard all the fecal misconceptions related to sex and innate imperfection that are still running amuck in our supposedly, civilized society. With some perfection-now enlightenment, perhaps you can shed your imperfection sex shackles, if you are still burdened with them. And likely, you can live the rest of your life without undue concern over sexual guilt, natural sexual desire and "lust", illegitimacy complications, homosexuality tendencies, and all the other imperfection-based, degrading conclusions about sex that have bugged the hell out of Homo sapiens for centuries.

The whole love, hate and sex package has been terribly misunderstood and misused under strong delusions of basic imperfection. But the factual nature, that is, the cosmic perfection of whatever these word symbols represent to you, has never been altered. It is only imperfection-oriented <u>ideas about sex</u> that have been so badly distorted.

KNOW YOURSELF, LOVE YOURSELF

I knew it was only a little past five in the morning, because Ron McCoy had just gone off the air a few minutes back. Of course, that was California time, but it was also our time, even though we were in New Mexico with Mountain Daylight Saving Time. Arizona had decided to not go on Daylight Saving Time and, as our television stations were all in Tucson, we elected to stay with Arizona time which turned out to be the same as California time.

Anyway, I heard Hazel stirring in the double bed next to mine. I turned over and looked around. She waved feebly to signal that she was awake and ready for coffee. I got up, went into the kitchen, poured warm water into a pan from a teakettle sitting over the pilot-light and set it on a burner to boil. I was able to manage this task from the glare of the one street light in our little community. Then I struck a kitchen match and lit the coaloil lamp, so I could see to measure coffee into the two-cup, drip pot we were using.

Through the last few years, coffee brewing has become almost a ritual with me. And lately, I have been analyzing just what it takes to make a really good cup of coffee. When you get older you discover that too much stimulant gets you to jumping inside your skin. So Hazel and I had agreed that we were better off through the day when we restricted our coffee intake. I suppose this limitation made the one cup we had in the early morning hours somewhat tastier. And it also made us more aware of the potential, peak flavor that was possible. We noticed too, when it was not as good as it could have been.

I have found you cannot just rinse the old grounds out of an unwashed coffee pot and expect to get top flavored coffee. There is nothing worse than rotten, stale coffee to mess up fresh coffee flavor. And if you don't start with a thoroughly clean container, you are wasting your effort and depriving yourself of one of the small pleasures you could have in this world. Another thing, when you go through the same procedure every day, you can experiment to see just how much coffee is required for the amount of water you use. Coffee that is too strong is bitter. If it is too weak it is insipid. Somewhere between these disagreeable amounts is the exact measure that is just right.

The proper use of heat is also important. I always pour boiling water into the cups (large ones since we are only getting one cup) so, when I deliver them to our bedside tables, the coffee is plenty hot to start with. But I am careful to heat up only the bottom half of the cup. That's so you don't scald your eager lips on the hot rim when you slurp in that first delicious sip.

Usually we have a piece of Hazel's home-made bread or doughnuts to go with the coffee. And sometimes, there is Hazel's elderberry or wild grape jelly to go with the bread. A little dab of food improves the hot coffee's taste and effect. Somehow, coffee alone is never as good as coffee with something to go with it.

Anyway, after we were both refreshed and wide awake from our morning coffee ritual, I asked Hazel if she remembered how she had lectured me on a previous morning regarding one of her main ideas. It had been weeks before, but I could easily recall the principal point she had tried to hammer into my somewhat obstinate, male chauvinist skull.

"The trouble with the world," Hazel had said, "is that people don't really know who they actually are. They are always dividing themselves and everything else up--separating love from hate, good from evil, right from wrong, God from the devil and soul from body, and then wonder why they are always so confused and in such a turmoil.

"Existence is just one thing. It is all God. There is nothing else existing but God. And when you finally realize that, when at last you know who and what you are, your big troubles seem to fade into nothingness."

"Well Bob," Hazel remarked, "it takes you a long time to catch on. I didn't think you got it before. You always say, 'Yeah Marmalade, I know what you mean,' But I could tell that you didn't really dig it."

One point in all this is that Hazel has always insisted on doing her own thinking. And of course, I must figure things out for myself, too. In matters such as we are looking into here, I think it should be that way for everyone. That is why I have tried to present the perfection-now position as simply an alternative, new way of thinking.

In fact, the unique contents of its composition actually prevents it from being an exclusive, all or nothing selection. If you reach the top of the mountain, it doesn't matter too much how you managed to get there. The trail you traveled on was likely just as good as any other. But of course, if you had decided to never go to the top--that's cool, also. For in evaluating your situation from the perfection-now position, the bottom or any place else proves out to be just as perfect as the highest place you could climb to.

But I realize that many are struggling inside their heads (just as I was sixteen years ago) to get themselves out of depressing, imperfection-oriented complications. And at the risk of playing the damn fool role, I am going to present some of my conclusions about love, hate and sex, about being in love, and some thoughts about marriage and shacking up-

-or the new morality.

You might think some of this could come under the perfection-now position for sex. But it has nothing to do with who should be on the bottom, or if it is better to do your making out from the top. For such profound sex information you will have to figure it out for yourself. But what is looked into here might help you to find a less guilty, freer and happier attitude toward the whole deplorable, love, hate and sex dilemma.

There is a miraculous, nonphysical something permeating throughout the cosmos, and love is the only word available that comes near to expressing it. This subtle love ingredient exhibits the ultimate essence of universal perfection. And you would not be mistaken if you turned it around to say that cosmic excellence is inherent in the essence of love.

From a mystical experience, love and perfection combine--making up the miracle of the x-factor God Force. And of course, your personal soul being is filled with the God Force, permeated with perfection and saturated with cosmic love. So God, love and cosmic excellence blend to form the basic make-up of your individual soul. And your own soul is the private source of your personal intuitive awareness.

Because I have harped on it so much during many years, I think Hazel has become a little sick and tired of hearing about perfection. For a long time, she had been unable to relate the usual ideas of love with the extensive animosity in the world; uncontrolled,destructive insanity, appearing to smother and negate most intuitive impulses toward goodness and compassion.

In her individual attempt to look at existence rationally, she had, occasionally, suggested that we ought to throw out such words as love and hate, good and evil and even perfection-now and imperfection. The reason,from her thinking, was that it is almost impossible to establish a consistent, understandable meaning to such words.

In my earlier thinking on the perfection-now position, and because of my nonreligious approach, I have felt that it might be better not to use the word, "God." And I still shy away from "spirit", because of its established, religious and various, cock and bull implications. One great benefit that could emerge from an extensive, perfection-now examination would be a new basis for a more rational understanding of important words. Our present imperfection-based dialectic confusion can only increase in perplexity if we continue following the absurd, intellectual irresponsibility that has already brought us too close to global genocide.

Of course, Hazel is not at all concerned with my feelings about some words and religion in general. In fact, she is continually getting after me for being too critical of religion--although she has never been able to really take on the extreme ideas in religion that I got drawn into--fecal conclusions of which I am now openly critical.

So for Hazel and her thinking, it is satisfactory to say that existence is all God and nothing else but God. And as long as I can put my nonreligious meaning on the word, "God," I thoroughly agree with Hazel. In my book, existence, nature, Creative Force, God, soul, love and perfection are all synonymous. They are all one and the same thing in my estimation.

But I recognize that each word represents certain aspects that require understanding, more than elimination. And as a diamond has many facets, there are various segments of this cosmic something that need to be isolated and examined.

Being cold and hot at the same time seems to be a physical impossibility. Although, through hypnosis, it is apparently possible to cause a person to feel quite cold or too hot, when in fact, the temperature of the room and his body is at the place where he should be very comfortable.

Something of this suggestive, switch-thinking has occurred in our imperfection conditioning to confuse us in our understanding of love.

In the clear, absolute reality of existence, love is inherent in everything and everybody. All that prevails is composed of love and is capable of knowing and responding to love. The love factor is basic to all reality. The overriding, beneficial effects of love are an irrevocable, restorative aspect of existence. The powerful, cosmic love force is incapable of deception, or being deceived, and unable to even compromise with misrepresentation.

It was this illusive, love ingredient, underlying every facet of our experiences, that I was thinking of when I told Hazel that I was considering the significance of her idea about existence being all God--one thing. Only I was thinking that it was all love. No matter which term you use, either idea is a rational concept when you look at all the implications from the perfection-now position. But if some degree of basic imperfection must be included in the overall estimation, such simplification in looking at the totality of existence would never be possible.

No doubt, many aware persons have realized that every human problem could easily be resolved by simply replacing hatred and resentment with a happier love attitude of sympathetic understanding and forgiveness. But this has been almost impossible for most of us to accomplish under traditional imperfection concepts of living, loving and hating.

I suppose that nearly everyone has experimented, to some extent, with serious love emotions. But usually, misdirected, imperfection-based aspects of physical love (and especially some of those involved in sexually-oriented togetherness) blast the very best love intentions all to hell. And we end up questioning the usefulness, and even the validity of love.

One female, astrologer, night-club entertainer jokingly

stated that apparently, every sign was sexually incompatible with every other sign. Then there was the philosopher who concluded that the whole cosmos was evil. Nevertheless, and despite imperfection-oriented difficulties, there are some who discover in the world-moving power of love alone, a simple, joyful way to live without conflict or prejudice. But most of us get our hateful asses hung up on the complicated, hostility side of love. And the false imperfection assumption is mainly responsible for this seemingly hopeless situation.

The available joy and love experienced in a physical reality is only a partial (but adequate enough) segment of the unspeakable love delight known continually by our souls which, evidently, require a trouble-free, ecstatic love atmosphere, (otherwise we couldn't take an eternity of it), while an earth adventure is only a brief, diversified excursion into a living, physical creation with the proper (you could say perfect) love, hate and sex consciousness necessary for that unique reality.

The love awareness provided for us in our space suits of flesh and blood, bones and guts is a degree of soul and God love, exactly suitable for our earth trip. However, Homo sapiens are also capable of distressful, emotional responses which seem to be the opposite of love. When provoked enough, we can all become hateful and obnoxious.

But in our soul existence, and because of the nonphysical condition, there, apparently, is no need for fear, anger or anything preventing a full, constant experience of joyful love. The hate aspects of love appear to be a special requisite of a living, physical creation. And, according to extenuating circumstances, love, or its hateful counterpart, becomes manifest in our feelings and emotions. Some amount of constructive, life sustaining love, or destructive hate prevails, according to conditions causing us to respond one way or another.

Nevertheless, in his total make-up, each individual has

a full, ample, soul-awareness storehouse of beneficial love, always ready to function the moment he provides compatible space in his mind consciousness to recognize and accept it.

But the good love motivation is always gentle, and never demanding. Love will not manifest its subtle, healing influence into any area which is not open and willing to respond, lovingly, to its presence. For love is offered without conditions. It only seeks to be united with itself, as water rises or falls to find its contemporary level.

The basic concept, <u>existence is perfection</u>, stands without qualifications or exceptions whatsoever--or it wouldn't be valid. And the disagreeable, hostile feelings of our emotions are certainly included in the perfection-now estimation--regardless of their damaging nature.

Yet it is obvious that any aspect of our physical make-up (good or bad) can be misunderstood and misused. Such irrational abuse can come about through ignorance, illness or misdirection. And still, the innate perfection of that which is abused or the person doing the damage is never altered or impaired. The excellence quality of all existence remains exactly the same in spite of hurtful contingencies. This unique state of perfection-now applies to hateful, reactionary anger and self-protective violence as much as it obviously applies to the destructive function of fire and water--the vital goodness of which, we could not live without on this planet.

In our remarkable physical and nonphysical make-up, we possess and may be provoked into using destructive emotions of anger and violence. Under extreme exasperation and fear, any rational man would (if he were capable) kill another man, or be killed himself in the attempt--in defense of his own life, his family and friends or his country.

This capacity for violence prevails as a necessary part of the nature of the human creature. And it is senseless to rationalize (as some do) that such behavior is not a part of the God forces or reality. While such brutal (although essential) abilities and emotions appear to fall into a category seemingly contrary to beneficial love emotions, it is certainly the deep, innate, soul-God love which man has for himself, his family, friends and country, which properly motivates this protective and sometimes deadly violence.

This observation seems to answer (at least to me) the question of how the goodness of love can commingle with hate and destruction when these responsive impulses are protectively employed. And I believe such a performance could take place without any diabolical intention of condemning and punishing the perpetrator. The damn fool aggressor would only be experiencing the natural reaction to his own stupidity.

But surely, you can see that imperfection rationalizing is causing a gross misuse (overacting, over-killing) of this vital and perfect, protective ability. Hate and anger naturally boils up in our emotions when we are the objects of injustice and mistreated. And following our imperfection training, we tend to go overboard in our hate and violence reactions.

Having little or no understanding of the love alternative, we are culturally stimulated to condemn and punish every son of a bitch for the unhappiness he is causing us or has caused us--whether we are fully correct in our judgment or not.

But I have found there is a welcome difference in our hate reactions when we consider adversities from the perfection-now position. We realize that wrong thinking will always be a possibility. And it becomes understandable that making mistakes is an inescapable part of any learning endeavor. Also, no one is ever excluded from the overall benefits of universal love by their wrong thinking or misbehavior.

Then, when we are aware of who we really are and what we really are--realizing that we are all perfect human creatures, existing in a reality of absolute love and excellence-

-we find it is easily within our ability to lovingly forgive the offender, although we may damn well abhor the offense.

Knowing ourselves and loving ourselves in this concept is not likely to ever develop into a narcissistic frenzy with selfish overtones for our personal benefit alone. Rather, such a process engenders a simple attitude of good intentions that include ourselves as well as all others. It's sort of what's left over when we split away from self-destructive attitudes of resentment and vengeance.

If we can easily excuse ourselves for mistakes made in our learning adventure (and we are always learning), it is not difficult to excuse others for their damn-foolishness. And in taking on a more forgiving attitude, we are apt to find that contentment quietly replaces contempt. Tolerance and understanding takes the place of impatience and frustration.

PROTECT YOURSELF AT ALL TIMES

I thought the most significant moment of the Mohammed Ali-Chuck Wepner, championship fight was actually after the match when Ali explained to Howard Cosell about his pounding Wepner on the back of the head during clinches as the referee was trying to separate them. He said that Wepner was continually using rabbit punches on him and the referee ignored his complaints. Ali claimed he deliberately made a show of the illegal punches to call attention to the abuse he was taking from Wepner. "I was only protecting myself," Mohammed Ali said.

<u>Protect yourself at all times</u>, is part of the instructions referees give fighters at the start of a match. If it is good and necessary advice for an athlete in super, physical condition, then, surely, it is good information for anyone, anywhere and in any condition. Intelligent and effective self-protection is

obviously related to the sensible love concern we should always feel for ourselves.

I am not claiming that the perfection-now position has an exclusive option to suggest sensible alternatives such as self-protection. But there is one angle about caring for yourself that is seldom realized while we are embroiled in the typical, imperfection-based hassle. When we are really raising hell (either for a seemingly valid cause, or an insignificant, fecal reason), we hardly ever consider that our vengeful, fighting-mad belligerency is usually more harmful to ourselves than it is to whomever is on the receiving end of our vindictive, punishing attitude. Of course, it's no picnic for them either.

I found this out the hard way when, at the end of my fourth fire season with the Forest Service, I was abruptly fired from the new occupation I had become so happily involved in. This jarring event was so devastating to Hazel and me in our new adventure, that it has taken us years to recover somewhat from the unexpected treatment.

However, looking back on it now, I can realize that, despite the emotional, financial and even physical damage we went through, in some respects it became a fortunate experience for us, rather than the catastrophe we thought it was at first. In fact, several unlooked-for benefits eventually evolved as the aftermath of my getting-fired-debacle. Although, while I was ranting and roaring about the great injustice of it all, I couldn't see any good or perfection-now factors in the disgusting episode.

Actually, under the degrading pressures of the circumstances, I forgot all about my perfection-now baby ideas, (of course, at that time, they were still in a somewhat embryonic form), and for a while, I guess I reverted back to my worst imperfection, jackass state, big mouth, know it all, and belligerent as hell.

But out of the painful effects of that dilemma and its

resolution, I think I have learned a few important things about love and hate that may never have come under more tranquil circumstances. And I found the needed time to reeducate myself in what I think are the essentials and some of the essence of the perfection-now position.

Although I shall relate relative facts of the story which culminated in my getting fired, I do not intend to whitewash my own performance while damning the opposition. I am convinced now that, if we look carefully and without bias (which is hard to do), we can usually find good reasons for just about any behavior--good or bad, just or unjust. Actually, I hope I can show that, to some extent, I was responsible for part of the chaos that was laid on us.

And that brings up the vital question of responsibility. So before I get into the firing details, I think it would be good to look at some aspects of responsibility that I thought I had learned (but evidently not well enough) in that initial perfection-now period before we left California.

One important point in all this is a recognition that any philosophy for living (religious or nonreligious, including the perfection-now position) isn't going to be worth much if it is only considered intellectually. Any endeavor performed in a loveless, spiteful atmosphere is lacking in the most essential ingredient needed to assure the happy results we all instinctively desire.

And in referring to a love atmosphere, I mean that subtle, (something more than sex), universal, love factor, which, in spite of our most asinine antics, miraculously creates beauty out of ugliness, and in time fashions peace and tranquility out of turmoil and chaos.

While the perfection-now concept, <u>existence is perfection</u>, is only a statement about reality, that intangible something generally referred to as "love", is the mighty cosmic force itself, activating all material and nonphysical particles of the universe. But it is difficult to even recognize the miracle, love power for goodness, let alone take full advantage of its benefits, when false imperfection complications are screwing up our daily living experiences.

There is so much that cosmic love continually does for us on an involuntary basis--despite our degrading, imperfection-heritage habits. For instance, if we break our leg (and I did break mine the latter part of the first year we were in New Mexico), it mends our broken bones and bruised, torn flesh back together so we can walk again. Many have experienced this miraculous function of the God-love creative forces.

And all doctors are aware that some power they don't know much about, can actually cause a remission of advanced, cancerous conditions. I am inclined to believe that this latent, healing force is soul-God love, working together with human mind-love and desire. I'll admit that I don't really know any more concerning this miracle ingredient than the good doctors--except that I have had a personal, direct-knowing encounter with this universal soul-God love.

But almost anyone can see there is a facet of love that is somehow responsive to our personal, creative ability. Desiring its healing goodness for ourselves and our loved ones, it appears that it is somewhat our own responsibility to learn more about this beneficial force. And it should be obvious that we can either employ it wisely for our happiness and well-being, or misuse it stupidly to our despair.

Having a measure of responsibility in the realm of cosmic love--as well as all areas where we have the freedom and the ability to choose--is a vital segment of our human make-up of absolute perfection. This aspect is related to fulfilling the main purpose (enjoyment and appreciation) in our being here as we are. And when you have had ample time to consider it seriously, as we do in Volume 2, you wouldn't want it any other way. The whole setup is absolutely perfect as it is.

One of the most satisfying implications I have found in the perfection-now concept is the obvious realization that, if the totality of existence is perfect now--just exactly the way it all is now--<u>there is nothing basic and fundamental</u> concerning the world and its living creatures (and that includes you and me) that must be changed, converted, modified or even improved.

You and I don't have to accomplish even one little thing to make ourselves (soul and body) or anyone else, any more perfect than we already are now! Any futile effort expended along that impossible direction is wasted energy. All we have to be responsible for is to enjoy ourselves, and be grateful for the all-inclusive excellence we already have. Actually, we are not really required to do that. Because, if somehow we manage such a simple, purposeful vocation, we will discover that it has become a labor of love.

Compared to the absurd duty which most imperfection-oriented, religious doctrine places on an individual--that is, saddle him with the impossibility of saving his alleged, lost, imperfect soul--the perfection-now position immediately takes you off the ungodly, damnation-salvation hook. And in doing that, it frees you from a host of other ridiculous obligations that so many have innocently burdened themselves with.

There are two main points that must be established regarding responsibility in any situation. It is vital to know that for which we are responsible. And it is equally important to recognize that vast area <u>of which we are not responsible</u>.

There will always be a lot going on around us that is clearly out of our control, and therefore out of our responsibility. So if we can determine correctly, these two segments of the responsibility question, our personal liability in any matter should be plainly evident.

I was seriously concerned with my responsibility when the enormous significance of the perfection-now position gradually became established in my awareness. If the concept stood up under the test of time and all other qualifications for truth that I could devise, I realized I would have to adapt my new thinking to fit a vastly different world than the supposedly inadequate, imperfect one I had grown so accustomed to. And if somehow the perfection-now question ever became a serious point to consider (in education, in politics and government, in justice, crime and punishment, in business and labor, in science, psychology and religion), I had to face the prospects of being somewhat responsible for a lot of upsetting adjustments occurring as the aftermath of this shocking revelation.

And you can be sure that I thought about what my responsibility would be if the whole perfection-now idea turned out to be just another crock of fecal garbage to add to the substantial, imperfection, dung heap we have accumulated so far. That's why I was so concerned about validity for so long.

Above all, I was anxious to find what my obligation would be if the perfection-now postulate could be established as factual. If reason, logic and a lot of good, old, common sense indicated that everything and everybody existing in the universe were absolutely perfect now, I wondered if it wouldn't be almost a crime against humanity for me to do nothing about such valuable knowledge.

In addition, I also had to face the sorry fact of my limited abilities. You remember it took a long time for me to even convince Hazel that the instant perfection concept was valid. And at first, I was unable to wholly convince myself-- at least on my surface, intellectual comprehension--although intuitively, I never doubted the truth of the upsetting idea for a second, since that jolting flash of instinctual realization came to me in 1960.

But there was so much hostility and destruction fomenting in the world; so awful was man's inhumanity to man that, to claim the inherent make-up of all that existed was unconditionally perfect at the same time, seemed beyond my poor ability to even attempt to explain.

Nevertheless, I could never forget that one, clear moment of intuitive realization where I could easily see a rational explanation for every complex situation. There were satisfactory answers for every question. Practical solutions were available for every problem. Even contained in that flash of instinctual knowing was a simple way to resolve the whole question of responsibility--and especially my obligation in the developing perfection-now story.

But it was months later, after I had thought out the perfection-now position itself, <u>existence is perfection,</u> and had discovered the application theory of truth (truth applies universally and eternally), that I began to devote my attention to the seemingly complex subject of responsibility. Aspects of personal liability apparently entered into almost every segment of human existence.

I figured I should know who or what was responsible for my being here in the first place. And the answer had to go deeper than a biological urge occurring within my parents' sexual activities. I wanted to know who or what was responsible for my continued existence in a nonphysical dimension that I knew nothing about, until my mystical enlightenment happened at Santa Monica.

Was my physical, mind consciousness responsible for my nonphysical soul--a part of me of which I had no real awareness until I was forty-five years old? And who or what was basically responsible for the overwhelming distress and unhappiness in the world?

I have already told you how I put my order in for needed information. And one morning I was surprised at the simple answer that arrived in my thinking to clear up what I had previously thought was a complicated subject.

I had been scribbling down some random thoughts about responsibility when the essence of the whole question came to me in a few significant words: THE CREATOR IS RESPONSIBLE FOR THE CREATION.

If this statement were valid (and I couldn't make anything else out of it), then my responsibility in any matter existed only to the extent of my creative ability and involvement in a creation. Developments which were beyond my capability and scope of activities were clearly not my responsibility.

My first application of the responsibility statement went to answer the basic question of who was responsible for the state of being humans found themselves in. As none of us had anything to do or say with the formation of our inherent nature, it was clear enough to me that we had no obligation to do anything about that condition. It was a great relief to be relieved of a cosmic responsibility over which I had no control whatsoever.

But for a long time I overlooked another creation that I could have controlled, and in which I was very much involved. I had a big mouth and I thought I was very clever in using it. Having only the barest, initial hint of some worthwhile knowledge, I felt I knew all there was to know.

When we came to New Mexico, everything that I thought I had learned could be narrowed down to four short statements: (1) Existence is perfection; (2) truth applies universally and eternally; (3) the creator is responsible for the creation; and (4) the primary purpose of our existence is to enjoy and appreciate the excellence provided for us.

I realize now that I had only the bare-bone structure of some new, good information. And it has taken a long time to put some respectable meat on those naked bones.

As I am now able to understand, and looking at my own sorry performance, each individual has a measure of responsibility for a love, or a loveless atmosphere he creates around himself. To a large degree, he is liable for what he thinks, what he says and what he does.

But at the same time, no one is ever <u>completely responsible for his believing, his words and actions,</u> for we Homo sapiens are all somewhat the brainwashed products (or creations) of our heritage and environment. And the overall responsibility lies with the Creative Force that started us ticking and keeps us going.

But despite our unfortunate conditioning, we always have a choice in many areas open for our selection. We decide on just about everything we say and do. And the falderal coming out of our mouths determines to a big extent, a pleasing love atmosphere or a contrary belligerency that becomes a disturbing experience for ourselves and those unfortunate enough to be around us.

Anyone can see that a love atmosphere is favorable for pleasure, for good health and constructive goodness--while a hateful condition is conducive to resentment, contempt and, likely, physical and emotional disorders.

We all know that a certain amount of heat is necessary for our material well-being. And we are usually careful to regulate the temperature so that our bodies are comfortable. But often we overlook the fact that we can also regulate (at least to some degree) the kind of social atmosphere in which we must live.

From personal experiences, everyone knows that we become sick if our bodies are allowed to become too cold for too long a time. And to recover from that illness, a heat treatment is used to restore proper, blood circulation. When that is accomplished, usually the discomfort from over-exposure to the cold disappears.

But we seldom realize that we also become ill-- mentally, emotionally and even physically--when we are subjected too long to a loveless, hateful atmosphere. Adverse effects are experienced whether the tension and stress are the result of our own belligerent attitude, or the emotional contamination caused by someone else getting his ass up.

To counteract the distressful effects from too much exposure to a hate atmosphere, it should be obvious that a love treatment is needed. But useful knowledge in this area is woefully lacking. We all know how to turn up the heat when we are too cold. But in general, we don't yet know much about turning on to love when we have been subjected to too much hate.

And the reason is that, to a great extent, we have become overly dependent on exterior sources for our love atmosphere. Mostly we think that love comes gift-wrapped in someone else's affection or sexual cooperation. And when these sources fail us, we seldom feel that it is possible to manage on our own, built-in, love resources.

We have mistakenly thought that our greatest problem in the world was learning how to live lovingly and in peace with one another. But as I see it, the fundamental dilemma facing each individual is, first of all, learning how to live peacefully and lovingly with himself. If you can accomplish that problem, getting along with the rest of the world will be a breeze.

It stands to reason that no one can present a tranquil, loving attitude to those around him, when they are emotionally fighting a battle of fear, guilt and resentment within themselves. At best, our relationship with others (even a wife, husband or a shacking-up-with friend) is only a part-time involvement. But we are intimately wrapped up with our own feelings and emotions (whether they are gentle and loving, or mean and contemptible) every moment of our lives.

So it makes sense to establish (for our own well-being and self-protection) a love attitude in our own minds and hearts--if that is possible, and I think it is. For certain, we cannot always depend on a pleasing love atmosphere in someone else's attitude. That is something beyond our ability to create and control, and therefore, it is not our responsibility. In difficult circumstances, we can only rely on whatever love atmosphere we are able to manage for ourselves.

I suppose I should explain just exactly what I believe a love atmosphere for yourself is--or could be. I have already said that this universal love factor is something more than feelings involved in sexual desire or fulfillment. But just how do we think love, feel love or express love? How, in this screwed-up, imperfection environment, can we ever manage to love ourselves or God or another person? These are some of the questions that concerned me when I first thought of writing this chapter.

I think some of the answers have come, but I am not too sure I can record them so that you can grasp completely, what I mean. Nevertheless, I feel confident that your own soul-God-love, intuitive knowing will help you understand the essence of this intangible love subject--despite my somewhat inadequate, literary endeavors. And you are really going to have to want to know for yourself if you ever expect to comprehend what the total love deal is all about.

Perhaps I can relate what I think a satisfactory love atmosphere, is in a roundabout way. We are all plenty familiar with the usual hate and resentment binge so prevalent in much of our experiences. Nearly everyone has had someone or something to hate. Actors vent their wrathful feelings in hysterical rages, hoping they might get the Academy Award for their paranoid performances.

But love is something else. I thought Cloris Leachman expressed the sorry situation rather well on the Merve Griffin Show when she said, "Well, I don't really know about love. Love seems to be something you can get hold of..." And she reached out with her arms, grasping the air as if she were hugging someone affectionately.

I think I am fortunate in having some direct-knowing experience about cosmic love--the almost unspeakable love factor encountered in my mystical episode. But that ecstatic degree of love, apparently, is suitable only for the nonmaterial realms of soul-God existence. I feel that the proper love atmosphere needed for most of our physical adventure is the great expanse of ordinary, natural feelings and emotions we all know very well.

But we have never thought of this common, untroubled state of mind and heart as something related directly to love. In other words, love is the totality of all our normal attitudes that <u>are not</u> hateful, not mean and contemptible, not vindictive and angry. This almost-nothing state of mind that is always there--in back of, below, above and surrounding all other nonloving feelings--is the subtle, sustaining, love atmosphere required for our general well-being and happiness.

So in order to love someone, or something, or God or the world, we only need to stop hating and the love is automatically there. But thinking that nothing's perfect, we have underrated and devalued this unspectacular, ordinary state of mental activity. At first, you may find it difficult to consider this built-in state of mind to be a beneficial love atmosphere. But if you look for it, that is where you will find the subtle miracle of cosmic love that we all are endowed with for this earth trip.

No matter what thrilling episodes we might occasionally encounter, we always come back to that normal, steady, love mentality that seems to be nothing special. Compared to a mystical happening with soul-God love, it may appear somewhat drab and insufficient. Nevertheless, from the perfection-now position, you can discover that the simple feelings contained in our undisturbed emotions is the proper amount of physical love that we can stand twenty-four hours a day, year in and year out.

Yet, in the whole love package, there may be peaks of happiness, special moments of intense delight, and even extended periods when we feel we are riding the clouds. Still, there is no reason that these extra joyful incidents should diminish our appreciation of the perfection inherent in the greater part of our cosmic love existence that is ordinary and commonplace.

Hazel and I particularly enjoy the many trips made into the forest each year to get our wood for the next winter. We think the best time for this occupation is in the early springtime when the woods are dry, and we are a little fed up with a long winter's confinement. It is one thing to mentally observe the wonder and beauty of nature, but there is something additional that comes when you are working in close contact with the earth and with the natural products of the sun, rain and soil.

Mostly, we search for and find dead juniper wood and dead oak brush, just as people before us have evidently done for thousands of years all over the world. Of course, we will use pinyon pine or any kind of wood that is available if we have to. But we prefer oak and juniper if they can be found, because they burn cleaner, last longer and don't clog up the chimney so badly.

Usually, we start out early in the morning so we can load the truck before it gets too hot in the middle of the day. We have found a sort of love magic in the forest that seems to be evident almost the moment we arrive and begin to explore the area for our winter fuel supply.

Before gasoline became so expensive, we would travel quite a ways to remote areas where there were plenty of dead juniper trees standing. After I cut the trees into blocks and split them, Hazel would load the chunks into the truck. Like everyone else, we didn't bother with the many smaller branches, getting only the larger ones that were easy to cut with a chain saw.

But now that inflation is a problem, we go into places closer to home and collect the smaller limbs that have accumulated through many years. We pile our truck high with them after knocking off the surplus twigs and very small branches. In our yard, I have made a rack which holds about a third of a truck load. When the rack is full, I can easily cut through hundreds of branches at one time, as they are securely held together in the rack.

Although Hazel and I both enjoy the hard work involved, the best time seems to be when we stop to rest after we are a little hot and tired. We sit on our heavy work gloves placed on the ground and have time to just look and listen and become aware of where we are, who we are and what we are.

The whole creation around us is fragrant, warm and vibrant with the subtle love force we have learned to recognize and appreciate. In any direction we care to look, the beauty of the forest is free and available to us. In such a situation the troubles of the world seem remote and far away. In fact, it hardly ever occurs to us to think of irksome things when we are working in the woods. Our job is simply to find the wood and load it into the truck. Then we take it home, cut it up and stack it in a large pile. And it's always a good feeling to know that we will have an ample supply of wood to burn when the snow and freezing weather comes in the late fall.

When we are resting from our labors and sitting close to the good earth, I seldom fail to notice some subtle indication of the cosmic, love force emanating from the ground itself, the rocks and trees, and even the rubble of weeds, twigs and dead leaves scattered about.

It is hard to describe, but there is a comforting communication of some sort manifesting between the God intellect in the physical world itself, and my God-mind, perceptive awareness. And during such magic moments, I realize that nothing special is required of me. Just my pleased recognition and gratitude is enough on my part.

I don't have to love, think or believe any certain way in return. And of course, I don't have to do or say anything. But I realize that I am not in conflict with anything or anybody. Because if I were, I doubt if I would be able to notice and enjoy the love magic of the forest.

For sure, I am accomplishing something worthwhile that must be done if I expect to keep warm throughout the coming winter. But my mental activity in all this is nothing special--just my ordinary attitude. I don't have to consider that it is all perfection-now, or that it is all love--or like Hazel said that it is all God and nothing else but God. I think the verbal correctness is unimportant in such contemplation.

Still, in the depths of my awareness, I am not concerned any more that there might be some basic, imperfection flaw in me or in the world. And no matter what you want to call it, I have become very much aware of this miracle, love force for goodness and pleasure that is available to us constantly--and not only in the forest. This recognition comes easily now in my normal, surface consciousness. And a lot more of it is noticeable since I have lost some of my obdurate, obnoxious ways.

Because there is no better word, I am calling it cosmic love. And though I become involved in other thoughts and receptive feelings, its comfort and health-giving goodness are always there for me. Although I don't think about it all the time, I know the Grand Canyon of Arizona is there, because I saw and experienced it for myself. I have a direct-knowing experience to establish that phenomenon as a fact.

And in Santa Monica, I had a direct-knowing, mystical experience with the very source of this cosmic, love force. I enjoyed that ecstatic dimension of love's motivating power for myself, too. And therefore, I know it is real. I know it is good and beneficial. I know it is constantly available for anyone and everyone. And I know, too, there are no conditions of becoming anything basically different than that which you are now, that must be accomplished to qualify you for the benefits of this universal love force.

But the full goodness of cosmic love (joy, peace of mind and well-being) is never forced upon us. We have some creative ability to choose and accept. And, therefore, we have some responsibility that determines to a great measure, our daily love, or love-lacking condition on our earth-trip adventure.

Surely, you can see that, by dwelling too long in hate, we block out or prevent the love benefits from reaching us-- just as we can prevent the sun's rays from shining directly on us. But the moment we clear away the obstruction of contempt and vindictiveness, the love force floods in, just as the sunlight falls on us the moment we have taken away the interfering shade.

Because it is so commonplace, we take the goodness (its light and heat) of the sun for granted. And due to its abundance of ordinary services, we take the vast, cosmic, love force too much for granted, also. In looking at existence from the perfection-now position, we begin to see <u>all things and everybody</u> in a very different light than was ever possible when we were perplexed with the deplorable idea that "Nothing's perfect. Everybody knows we are living in an imperfect world."

Some of the satisfaction that people get from camping out and from fishing and hunting, is a measure of this refreshing love force, apparently more noticeable when there is close contact with the earth and water in its natural and undisturbed state. And evidently, there will always be that same satisfactory love feeling in these activities that Hazel and I now enjoy in our wood-gathering occupation.

In my work with the Forest Service (on the tower and elsewhere), I suppose I have had thousands of love-magic awareness moments, such as I have mentioned, that come so easily to Hazel and me every time we go for a load of wood. Compared to my previous, upholstering shop work, my forest occupation was so delightful that I was almost constantly pleased with my good fortune.

So, when I was abruptly fired, I experienced a sickening, reactionary feeling of potential disaster--a fear that somehow, Hazel and I would lose everything of value in our new life that had become so enjoyable to us.

And in the extended hassle that followed, I realized that I had been like the proverbial, babe in the woods, when it came to survival and self-protection.

LOVE ANYWAY

The whole time of our first fire season with the Forest Service was like one long, exciting fishing trip to me--although I had only managed to go fishing one time during the first four months we were stationed on that isolated mountain top. There was a beautiful trout stream only a mile away--but it was almost straight down from the tower. The distance by trail was about four miles.

Hazel enjoyed the experience just as much as I did. She eagerly took up her close, love relationship with all the natural things of the forest that had been her friends when she was a child. She was thrilled to become acquainted again with the trees, rocks, flowers and clear blue sky of New Mexico that circumstances had separated her from, for thirty-four frustrating years.

There was a family of chipmunks living in a large pile of rocks at the base of the tower. And soon, Hazel had them all eating out of her hand and crawling all over her. She named one Frank Sinatra, because he apparently liked spaghetti. Hazel was able to coax a large porcupine out of the tack room with some salt. I had tried to push him out with a broom, but he had spread his sharp, pointed quills out, digging them into the floor so that it was impossible to move him.

We also had a herd of deer that visited us every afternoon for their salt. And wild turkeys would walk through the tower grounds. About sundown, they would take off for their roosting area down the canyon. It was unbelievable the speed those big birds managed on their flight. They looked like great, black cannon balls flying through the air.

Altogether, there was a lot of miracle, love magic emanating from that park-like mountaintop. I was especially pleased to discover that it was not a bleak, barren place that I thought it might be. My idea of tall peaks were evidently formed from many visits to the California, Sierra Nevada range, where the mountain tops are mostly above timber line and barren as hell.

But as Tom Mason, our first helicopter pilot, circled us around the tower area, I could see that the forest of tall spruce trees extended clear up to the top of the mountain. And I had no idea then, that those beautiful trees would be somewhat responsible for getting me fired. However, I did notice that a big swath of timber had been cut on the north side to provide a proper helicopter, landing approach.

The lookout tower was located on the highest part of a slightly rounded knoll which was elevated a little above the main part of the mountaintop area. Alongside the tower was a sturdy, well-constructed log cabin. And about fifty feet north of the cabin and among some young trees, were the corrals for pack mules and horses.

The rest of the mountaintop area consisted of a gently sloping, rounded ridge extending about a quarter of a mile toward the east. Directly to the south was Lookout Canyon which dropped off abruptly about one-hundred feet from the tower. This steep, rugged canyon was almost barren of trees and brush. An extensive, project fire had consumed most of the vegetation in the early fifties. The conflagration which burned thousands of acres started from a lightning-caused fire, a short distance from the tower.

The lookout was sent to man the small blaze while his wife took over the tower duties. In his haste to get to the fire, he neglected to take along any food. After thinking he had the fire fairly well controlled, he returned to the tower for something to eat. But before he could get back, a strong wind blew up and spread the unattended fire into a raging inferno.

Mr. Rainwater told me that lookout made the one unforgivable mistake a forest fire-fighter could make, and that was leaving a fire before it was out, dead and cold. And I was informed that the hungry smoke-chaser paid for his mistake by being fired.

I was so happy with the prospects of my new occupation that I determined never to make that mistake or any others listed in the Fireman's Manual that would jeopardize my new position. It never occurred to me to think there might be other, less obvious ways (not listed in the manual) that could get me into trouble, and even get me fired.

I suppose it was something Mr. Rainwater said at the end of the first fire season that made me over-confident and perhaps a little too cock-sure of keeping that forest job. After looking around at the way we had cleaned up the area, repaired the corrals and fences, made new gates, oiled the cabin logs, dug a garbage pit (the first one on Mogollon Baldy) and had everything in good order, he told us we had done a good job, and that he and the supervisors at Silver City were very pleased with our work.

Also, he informed us that he was quitting the Forest Service so he could go into the cattle business with his brother-in-law. He told us that, soon, a new ranger would be in charge, but he would do all he could to see that we could have that lookout job as long as we wanted it. It all sounded very good to me, although we were sorry to lose our first ranger boss.

Hazel had some of her paintings hanging in the village restaurant near the Ranger Station. She told Mr. Rainwater that, if he and his wife would like to have a painting, he could take his pick of any that were there. He said he would be proud to have one. And we figured that, as long as he was leaving, the gift could hardly be considered anything other than a good will friendship token--which it was as far as we were concerned.

We also got along well with Fred Galley, the new district ranger who came to replace Mr. Rainwater. And a couple of years later when the Galleys left, Hazel gave them a going-away present of a painting, too. I mention these painting gifts here because, indirectly, they enter into our feelings and reactions to developments which followed, after we were fired by our third ranger boss.

At the beginning of our third fire season, Dick Johnson, who was the top-dog official over the whole Gila Forest, and was the boss over all the district rangers, visited our tower on an inspection trip. And this was the innocent beginning of events which led to my unexpected termination hassle.

"Your trees are all getting too tall," he said. "You have too many blind areas. Don't you see that a forty-five foot tower and eighty foot trees just don't go well together in the lookout business?"

I could easily see that he was right, and I told Mr. Johnson I would inform the ranger about his complaint. And I said that, if they could provide me with a chain saw, I would do what I could to cut the offending trees down during my spare time.

But I didn't get a power saw that summer. So when the next fire season arrived, I again asked for a chain saw to do the timber felling the Forest Supervisor had suggested should be done. And this time I was given permission by our third ranger to take a chain saw with me. Also, I understood I could have it for the entire season.

I should explain that our tower location was within the wilderness area of the forest. No roads are permitted in the restricted zone, and no motor vehicles or motorized equipment are allowed. But for a long time, power saws, helicopters and airplanes have been considered as exceptions when used in the fire prevention business.

Every year, when they were not working on fires, smoke-chaser crews were cutting down trees in the Wilderness with chain saws to make helicopter landing spots on ridges so that fire fighters could be let off near a small fire and control it, before it had time to develop into a large project fire.

Before helicopters and parachute jumpers took over, it usually required six to eight hours, or more, to get to a fire on horseback and pack mules. But smoke jumpers and helitack crews could often be on a fire within thirty minutes to an hour after it had been reported. Also, smoke jumpers usually would cut a helicopter landing spot with their chain saw, after they had put out their fire, so they and their gear could be picked up easily and taken back to their headquarters at the Silver City Airport.

So, when at last I had a chain saw, I began cutting down the obstructing trees during whatever free time I could manage away from my tower duties--usually, in the very early morning and late evenings.

Hazel didn't go to the tower with me that year. She has always been a frustrated farmer and has a passion for growing things. That year she asked for one summer off, so she could stay home and raise a garden.

After three years, Hazel just wasn't as enthused about the lookout work as I was. There were good reasons for this. With two of us there, we felt one person should be in the tower at all times. And, as I had to do all the heavy work below, Hazel was stuck in the tower most of the morning when the weather was usually good.

In the afternoons, thunderstorms were often threatening and the wind velocity was increased. Consequently, when I could be in the tower and Hazel was free to go below, the lightning danger and stormy weather often prevented her from going out. Once in a while I would go to a small fire. But Hazel was confined to the tower nearly all summer. And too much of a good thing can get tiresome.

That particular fire season started out a little earlier than usual (about May 1) because of a large, man-caused project fire in the Mogollon Baldy area. I had only been there a few days when our third ranger (and I'll call him Mark Edwards, which is not his real name) flew in on the helicopter and spent several hours with me, looking around. He had only been there once before, shortly after he replaced Fred Galley the previous summer.

During his visit, I explained to Mark exactly what I had in mind about cutting the trees that were causing our blind areas. Later that summer, when the fire season was over, and I was called into the ranger's office and was informed I was fired for actually doing this work, the shock of the bastardly thing apparently caused a memory blackout for me of the visit Mark had made to the tower, and therefore, he knew damn well what I intended to do regarding those trees. The cock and bull reason given on my termination papers stated that: "Although I had been an 'outstanding lookout,' I had undertaken a dangerous, timber felling operation without the knowledge or consent of the ranger."

Putting it mildly, I was hurt, bewildered and angry at this revolting turn of events. Without the forest work, which was about the only employment in the area, I didn't see any way that Hazel and I could stay in New Mexico. And the thoughts of having to go back to California and the commercial, upholstering, rat-race again, were sickening for me to even consider.

If I had only been able to recall that helicopter trip

Mark had made to the tower earlier that summer, I think I would have raised a lot more hell than I did. Nevertheless, I managed to stir things up quite a bit anyway.

The following day, after I had cooled down some, I went to Silver City and appealed to Mr. Johnson, who had suggested that the trees be cut down in the first place. His initial reaction was somewhat encouraging.

"I think I know what the problem must be," he explained. "Quite recently we had a regional meeting, attended by all the officials and rangers in the southwest area. There was an agreement established that, from now on, power saws would not be used in wilderness areas, except for emergencies directly related to a going fire. You see, it has been difficult for us to enforce the law against using motorized equipment, such as motorcycles, when we were actually breaking the letter of the law ourselves by using chain saws in wilderness forest work."

Mr. Johnson said he would put a hold on my termination papers until he could talk to Mark to see if he would reconsider his decision.

After a few days had passed and I had heard nothing further, I went back to Dick Johnson's office. He told me he had talked to Mark, but the ranger had remained adamant and would not alter his position in the matter. Mr. Johnson also said it was the policy of his office to allow each ranger to run his district (that is, hire and fire) according to his best judgment. And therefore, despite the unusual circumstances and his own involvement, there was nothing more he could do. He also mentioned that, if he insisted on Mark changing his decision, my position would be untenable under such circumstances.

I asked if there was some government appeal board beyond his authority where I could present my case. Mr. Johnson said there was for full-time people working under a civil service appointment. But there was nowhere for a part-time employee to go beyond his (Mr. Johnson's) office.

So damn it all, that was that. There was nothing more I could do. I had worked my hind end off trying to do a good job, and got kicked in the ass for my effort. I felt like a second class citizen. For once in my life, I experienced what actual injustice was-- the hard way.

Evidently, something like this (only no doubt a lot worse) was what the black people, the Jews and other minorities have endured for centuries. It is really disheartening to have your established way of providing for yourself and your family jerked out from under you. And all because a little man with a little authority to throw around was somewhat fearful of his own involvement--and took such a fecal course to establish a supposedly protective position for himself.

Later, when I applied for unemployment compensation, I was told benefits were not given when someone was discharged for misconduct. And the wording in my termination paper was considered misconduct.

But in this case I found that I could appeal. And the hearing which followed at the unemployment office was electronically recorded. I had prepared a written statement and was given permission to read it into the record to establish my position carefully.

Mark, who was obliged to defend the Forest Service side of the hassle, also had (I think) something prepared. At least he had a briefcase with him, and he placed a folder on the table at his side.

But when his turn came, he ignored the folder and decided to speak extemporaneously. He casually mentioned a few points, such as I had destroyed the aesthetic value of the area in cutting down the trees. Also, I had made a big mess. I had cut the trees so that the remaining stumps were too high. And I had not trimmed off the limbs as was required in the manual. He said also, that I had not rolled up some old fence wire that I had been instructed to do.

The examining officer questioned me about each of these points. I replied that I had been instructed to cut trees off at a comfortable, standing height. The stumps could be easily trimmed off close to the ground later, during the clean-up operation when you also cut the limbs and restored order to the mess that had been created. I had not had time to do any more than cut the trees down. And I thought that was the most important job to complete first. Rolling up the fence wire could have come later, too.

After some general discussion, Mark concluded his remarks by saying <u>he remembered discussing the matter with me</u>, but he didn't tell me to cut the trees or not cut them. When that statement was made, it was the first time I recalled the trip Mark had made to the tower at the beginning of the summer. Now, that sworn statement was a part of government records. And the words clearly contradicted the reason given for my termination--that is, that I undertook this dangerous, timber-felling operation without the knowledge or consent of the ranger.

In summing up, the attending official said he could understand my position. I had been given an order to cut the trees by the Chief Supervisor. And as long as that order had not been countermanded by the ranger, I could rightly assume that he had consented to the work by his silence--especially after I had discussed the matter with him and told him what I had intended to do.

Anyway, the unemployment people reversed their decision and I was paid the compensation I was entitled to. Later, I wrote to the board and asked for a transcript of the hearing. Instead of sending the transcript they referred my request to their counsel.

He suggested that I had their decision which was favorable to me, and that should be enough. So I didn't insist. But later, in talking with some other officials from the Silver

City office, I was told that, despite the unemployment decision, Mark had been considering issuing a timber trespass against me for cutting the trees, and making me pay for the damages. Someone in the Regional office had advised him that "legally" he could make it stick.

I thought this was adding insult to injury, and told my informer that if he tried such a thing, I would spend every dollar that Hazel and I had saved to sue him and the government for the damage we had already suffered. And I mentioned this contradictory evidence which was now available and on file in government records.

I have no way of knowing whether my counter-threat of a civil suit was responsible or not--but it wasn't long until I learned that Mark was being transferred to a different ranger job in Flagstaff, Arizona. I learned also, that because of the very high altitude, it is one of the least desirable ranger jobs of all.

The talk was, that he didn't want to make this change--because he was acting as a foster parent in caring for three small children who were wards of the State of New Mexico. It seemed there were complications in moving them to another state, and perhaps he couldn't take them at all.

When I heard this, I called on Mr. Johnson again. He assured me that I would be rehired when the next fire season came along and a new ranger would be in charge.

With these somewhat favorable new developments, Hazel and I figured the big crisis was over for us. And under the circumstances, I suppose we got a little soft hearted, and sometimes I think we became a little soft in the head. Still, Hazel decided that, despite the raw deal we had been through, she would give a small painting to Mark's wife anyway, before they moved away.

We both realized that we couldn't continue living with the whipped-up resentment we had engendered. Forgiveness on our part was in order, and our gift of the painting was a symbol (at least to us) of our giving up any hard feelings from the fecal firing episode. Mrs. Edwards almost cried when we gave her the painting, but Mark didn't express his feelings one way or the other. I don't think he was too pleased in having to undertake the move he was about to make.

Hazel and I thought that, at last this was the end to a miserable period and that everything would be back to normal soon. But when I applied for work that next spring, the new ranger (and I'll call this one Jim Clark which is not his real name) said that he didn't feel right about hiring someone who the previous ranger had fired.

I told him there were certain aspects about my being fired that he was evidently unaware of, and he agreed to talk with Mr. Johnson before making a final judgment. This was the first indication I encountered that there were other adverse influences working against me beside the tree cutting episode. Of course, the main reason was obviously a move by the ranger to protect his own neck if complications ever developed from using "illegal" power saws in cutting those trees.

Most of the helispots throughout the forest were located so they could not be seen easily from any of the forest trails. But my tree-cutting operation was wide open for anyone to see. Mogollon Baldy was the goal for a lot of nature-lover hikers. And several other groups arrived on horseback with the tower area being a natural, interesting place to stop and rest.

So, once again I took my troubles to Dick Johnson. He said he would speak to Jim Clark, and for me to not worry, as he felt the new ranger would be agreeable when he became aware of the true situation. And in a few days I received a letter saying I had been accepted for employment. Also, I would be advised later when to report for work. But the rest of the crew had been working about a month before I was allowed to start.

This new difficulty had been the last straw for Hazel as far as the Forest Service was concerned. Most of her life she had carried the delusion that there must be something very special about forest rangers and people who worked close to nature. It was a great disappointment for her to realize that they were all just ordinary Homo sapiens, some good and some, obviously, malicious, gossipy stinkers.

I could have gone to work at the regular time in another district, as I had more than one offer from other rangers. But it seemed vital to me to go back to work in the district where I had been fired--even though I felt there might have been some of my fellow workers who were gleeful when I got the shaft. I could imagine that if they had some influence with the ranger in getting me fired, no doubt, they were not too thrilled to see me coming back.

Even so, the Silver City officials apparently did whatever they could to make up for the injustice I had experienced. The new job that was (I believe) concocted for me was a combination patrol, lookout duty, with incidental work such as collecting trash at the camp grounds, and cleaning out the public rest rooms.

Other changes were also made that year. They had decided to eliminate Grouse Mountain lookout tower and none of the high-country line cabins would be manned. The cowboy smoke chasers were all stationed at the Sacaton Helitack Base. And from now on, they would all go to fires by helicopter instead of horseback.

My new work was to pick up the garbage at the camp grounds every morning and patrol the length of the valley, watching for any smokes that could be seen from the highway. In the afternoon my patrol took me through Silver Creek and on up to the nine-thousand foot elevation.

We had established a tent camp on top of Spring Mountain which was about three miles from the highway. And if there had been a heavy lightning storm, the ranger or his assistant might order me to hike in to Spring Mountain and camp there a few days. From there, and even without a tower, I could observe most of the area that was no longer covered by the now unmanned, Grouse Lookout.

Despite the restroom and trash aspects, which didn't bother me at all, the patrol work was new and different. And I could eat at home and sleep in my own bed most of the time. Every morning I had to gas up the Forest Service patrol truck at one of the village service stations. And it was some satisfaction for me to let everybody see that I was back working, while the ranger who fired me was gone from the area. But my smug satisfaction didn't last long.

Although I did my work well, when the fire season was over, I was again given my termination papers while the rest of the part-time workers were kept on to do other work. I asked Jim Clark why he was doing this to me. He said he had been irked because I had gone over his head, and he had been pressured into making concessions for me. He resented this interference from the main office, and when, at the end of the fire season, the fire money was cut off, he terminated me for "lack of funds" which was the standard reason for termination for all part-time workers.

I believe they terminate everyone when funds run out. But under ordinary circumstances, I would have been immediately rehired under a different funding classification and kept on with the rest of the crew to do the non-fire work that had to be done each year.

For instance, there was a large crew going to Mogollon Baldy to clean up, that is, cut up and burn the trees I had felled during the previous summer. They would have to do all this hard work with axes and hand saws--now that power saws could no longer be used. And knowing these guys as I did, I realized that none of them were too happy with that particular assignment.

So I could see that I wouldn't be too popular in their

minds, while they were sawing up all those trees I had cut down. And while they were confined to the remote helitack base and working on fires all summer, I was traveling in comfort in a Forest Service truck and visiting the campgrounds every day.

Still, I couldn't see where any of this would be cause enough where they wouldn't want to work with me. Looking back now on the years we had worked together, I hardly think I was any worse in the obnoxious department than anyone else. There was a sort of a mutual putting-up-with.

Of course, I was the intruder, the greenhorn, city dude from the outside. And I suppose that my eager-beaver attitude to make a showing actually worked against me. In their minds, likely it appeared that I was attempting to discredit their efforts.

Thinking it over, now, I am sure that I conducted my relations with my fellow workers in a somewhat contemptible, loveless manner. And the consequences of that slightly belligerent attitude were almost disastrous to Hazel and me.

This second "firing" because a ranger was a little irked, and after trying to do a good job, was almost too much. I could see that any more protesting would be like beating on a dead horse. I figured my Forest Service ride was over.

Somewhat in desperation, I took a job at the sawmill in Reserve, which was about fifty miles away from our home in Silver Creek. I think Dick Johnson was still pulling for me, because I received a letter sent from Jim Clark's office telling me they were accepting applications for some construction work at a new helitack base.

This was a few weeks after I had been terminated. And, as I was then employed at the saw mill, Hazel and I figured they could take their belated offering and shove it up some irked ranger's ass. By this time, we had come to our senses and realized we would manage somehow in the world, without having to kiss anybody's behind.

NOBODY'S IMPERFECT

Actually, much of the part-time employment in the Forest Service is considered to be almost chain-gang, slave labor. It's right at the bottom of the scale. Of course, lookout work is a breeze if you can stand the isolation. But, usually, it lasts only about three months and then you have four or five months of trail work or fence building--all really hard labor and a lot of sleeping on the ground.

A few nights ago, someone on a radio talk show suggested it would be a good idea to put drunks to doing forestry work, like clearing fire breaks, instead of throwing them in a drunk tank. I doubt that anyone ever enjoyed the difficult work in the forest as much as I did. And to be fired, twice, from such a nothing type job, was somewhat humiliating. However, I never considered the last termination a real firing. I was satisfied that I had come back and worked after the first firing experience.

After about five months at the saw mill, bad weather shut it down for a while, and Hazel and I enjoyed not working again, so much that we decided to quit the struggle. The meager wages earned at the saw mill or the forest work, would never equal what it would cost to pay someone else to fix up our dilapidated old building in Silver Creek.

So we thought, to hell with working any more for other people. I figured that, from now on, all of my efforts would be directed only at projects that would be directly useful to Hazel and me. We thought back to when we first came to New Mexico. At that time, we figured we could manage at least a few years without any outside income. And now it looked as if the time had come to take those years off from work, and see what good we could accomplish for ourselves.

So a new program of restoration for our old building was started. In addition, with so much free time available, I figured to start out in the writing business in order to eventually introduce my perfection-now ideas.

Looking back now, it is amazing to me, how, out of the deepest dregs of discouragement, sometimes we discover a completely new direction to explore that leads us into experiences of pleasure and adventure that we had never thought was possible. For instance, I doubt if this book (for whatever it's worth) would ever have been written if I hadn't managed to get myself fired twice from a slave-labor job.

And I am sure that Hazel and I wouldn't have the very good place to live in that we have now, if I had continued to work as I did those first five years of our New Mexico Adventure. But I consider the most rewarding part of the whole firing episode is that I have had the best part of eight years to develop and synthesize the ideas that make up the main subject matter of the perfection-now story.

Evidently, the evolution of new thinking had to come for me as it did. But I sometimes wish that my present concept of love had emerged sooner. I speculate that, if my attitude toward others had been influenced more by a love motivation, I could have saved myself and Hazel a lot of needless trouble and heartache.

Still, there is no guarantee that performing in a love atmosphere of your own creation will shield you completely from all the cantankerous behavior of your associates. Yet, I am convinced now that the emotional and physical damage occurring in a lifetime would be much less with a working, love motivation, than when your own belligerency is provoking a continuing, fecal conflict, where nobody emerges with a clean victory.

During the time I have been working on this chapter, I have been hoping to come up with a concise statement on the essence of love that will, in a few words, express the most significant facts that would help us to live happier and less troubled lives. But I must admit that I am not satisfied with any combination of words emerging so far.

Turn off hate to turn on love, is one that says

something. Yet it is almost meaningless without a fair understanding of the full value of love. Love is illusive and subtle. Its effectiveness is geared up to an equally vague factor, our desires, intentions and thinking habits--in fact, to our overall attitude and behavior.

Perhaps there is a clue here as to why we know so little about love. Our imperfection conditioning has encased us within a socially accepted barrier of vindictive thinking and contemptible behavior, where love is mostly thought to be limited to moments of affection and making love.

I believe that most young people instinctively form a more useful and deeper meaning to love. But in time, adverse encounters with the established hypocrisy and imperfection, rip-off complications, knocks the natural intuitive awareness of love, and its benefits, all to hell.

It is becoming more evident to me all the time that the worldwide acceptance of imperfection in the human make-up is the primary reason for much of our irrationality and hostility. The disastrous consequences of so much hateful living, occurring as the result of our invalid, imperfection-oriented culture, is not at all compatible with the constructive goodness of love and universal perfection.

Human existence is a combination of many factors, miraculously blended together. But each segment is somewhat dependent on a harmonious relationship with all the other facets. Cosmic love is the primordial, integrating intelligence and power source for all aspects of material existence. And when we shut ourselves off from this universal love, wisdom and energy, we are somewhat like a sun and heat-loving house plant, struggling for life in the dark and cold. Such neglected plant creatures live poorly, if they manage to survive at all.

In simply turning off our usually contemptuous and punishing state of mind, the ever-ready, love factor is always there to fill the vacancy. It isn't really necessary to learn how to love, any more than it is essential to learn how to get warm after you have built a fire in your heater.

All that seems to be required is for us as individuals, as groups and nations, to stop our imperfection-trained condemning and punishing habits. This will allow others the freedom to live without having to put up with a lot of imperfection complications thrown at them from our position. That is something that you and I can do immediately in the love department. Nonetheless, if you don't quite dig all this, yet--love anyway--if only for your own benefit.

COMMON SENSE SEX

I am thoroughly convinced that the only sensible, basic purpose of our eternal prevailing in unconditional perfection, is for us to find enjoyment and appreciate the cosmic excellence available for us. And it should be obvious that sexual pleasure and satisfaction could be one activity to help us fulfill this vital purpose. However, emotional and intellectual rip-offs we get suckered into by taking on the false imperfection postulate, tend to create in our minds an ugly, repulsive, sex-maniac monster out of the cosmic excellence, beauty and wonder that is the factual nature of all natural and normal sexual feelings and responses.

You and I and every living creature owe our present physical existence to the miraculous working of sex. None of us would even be here at all if our parents hadn't responded to the persistent, sex-call of nature. And no one will be here a hundred years from now if young people don't answer the urging of their natural, mating tendencies. But, I am not too concerned over that sort of development. There always seems to be a lot of "making love", regardless of anything and everything.

Nonetheless, a lot of distressful problems related to

the natural sexual compulsion emerge from the mistaken, imperfection contention that much of sexual activity is sinful, worldly, immoral, indecent, carnal, illegal, and even criminal--which in some cases of abuse, it certainly is.

At first, no one can avoid thinking about sexual involvement from a strictly humanistic viewpoint. Sexual urges come just as naturally as hunger or thirst.

For some there is a religious approach. And often, these complications become a real pain for those who try to live up to their convictions.

For many though, the new social and cultural attitude toward sex is proclaimed loud and clear throughout the land. It is not shocking any more to hear a young lady say she thinks it makes sense to live with someone for a while, to see if they are compatible before getting married.

To make love or not, is hardly the question any more. To keep from getting a terrible disease or pregnant is the big problem. And, as long as parents get married before the kids graduate from high-school, is jokingly considered to be OK.

But the legal aspects of sex have not caught up to the new, sex morality finding acceptance in our troubled society of the seventies. It seems incredible that, when many children and old people are not getting enough to eat, that millions of dollars are wasted by officials sneaking around monitoring someone's sexual involvements.

Some day there may be a sensible, thorough, perfection-now consideration of sexual problems and sex-related questions. The most I can attempt here is, perhaps, show that new, liberating thinking is needed, and is possible in all approaches to sex from the perfection-now position.

I think the ecclesiastical attitude about sex has been the most bothersome obstacle for many to put up with, although religious-oriented, sex absurdities are at last, in general, being recognized for the poppycock, fecal matter they are. It still seems necessary, though, to resolve the religious quandary regarding sex, before looking at it from the basic universal perfection viewpoint.

In the first place, most religious doctrine looks with grave suspicion on any activity that could be classified as "worldly enjoyment." Sex is certainly worldly and, in most experiences, it is surely enjoyable.

From the perfection-now position, you can establish for yourself that there never was and never will be a religious hell to go to. And no matter how much worldly pleasure you get from sexual involvement, it's never going to jeopardize your future soul position in the absolute perfection of eternity. One female entertainer said she didn't think God is any more concerned about our sexual enjoyment than He is about how we blow our noses. I surely agree with her conclusion.

As I see it, imperfection-based nonsense, falsely palmed off as the authentic words of God, is actually responsible for much of the sexual and marital distress many young people (and older ones too) encounter during their "in love" experiences, a beautiful time that could and should be more enjoyable and enduring, if certain incorrect religious assumptions were not wrapped around them like pampers taped around a baby's behind.

Most children are endowed with a full, natural awareness of love. Their instinctual purpose is to seek enjoyment and experience the fascination of the marvelous creation which unfolds before them. However, with imperfection training, they gradually tend to lose some of their intuitive love feelings. Still, at the right time, nature provides an extra powerful shot of love. The love and sex combination is increased when young people fall "in love."

For a period, even the most revolting factors of imperfection conditioning are unable to conceal the factual reality and beautiful truth of existence. Love and perfection appear blended into a somewhat mystical light of understanding. The whole world and all its people are seen in their unconditional perfection and goodness.

No problem is too complicated for resolution. Providing answers to all questions, love forgives everything and everybody. (Taking on the perfection-now position is a little like falling in love and staying in love with the totality of existence.)

But having accomplished its essential, procreative purpose, the mystical, in-love experience diminishes like any mystical encounter, and the lovers come back down out of the clouds to contend with the ordinary, love consciousness needed for everyday living.

Not understanding the subtle mysteries of love, lovers might feel cheated thinking that nature has played a trick on them. Instead of more romance and dream castles, there is often hard work, some disappointments, and maybe swabbing off baby butts. Looking with an imperfection-oriented perspective, our normal consciousness seems inadequate and joyless, compared to our thrilling, mystical, in-love happiness.

Factually, the lovers have not lost anything. Only the peak, delightful experience of something beautiful has come and gone as it should. But too often, with imperfection suggestions that we live in an imperfect world where nothing and nobody's perfect, we might react with anger, thinking we should condemn and punish those who seem to be offending us.

With a perfection-now understanding of love, believing that <u>existence is perfection</u>, the same situation could occur with less disturbance. And though the in-love awareness has run its pleasant, mystical course, I believe a deeper, more lasting, though less intense, love-condition can be realized from within our own intuitive nature.

I remember one special day last fall when Hazel and I were sitting on our front veranda in the warm sun and looking at the mountain scenery which has never become boring for us. The wind was blowing a little and, occasionally, there were stronger gusts. Some leaves were falling, but the things that caught our attention that day were the novel, winged seeds from the box elder trees.

Instead of falling directly to the ground, these seeds would start whirling around like the rotor blades on a helicopter. When a strong gust of wind caused an upward air current, they would soar up into the blue like a toy flying machine.

A few of them landed on the porch boards at our feet, and I examined these fascinating products of nature carefully. The small seed itself was incased in a flat envelope which was attached to a perfectly designed airfoil about an inch and a half long. I could see that, if you glued two of them together, you would have a suitable propeller for a tiny model airplane.

Box elders become large trees requiring lots of growing room. And here in my hand I was holding one of nature's (or I could say one of God's or love's) miracles of propagation. Performing perfectly as they were meant to, these seeds were scattered far and wide, up and down Silver Creek canyon.

I have no explanation to account for this particular aspect of nature, or various other seed designs which are just as remarkable. One seed actually performs like an augur, effectively screwing itself into small openings in the soil.

I cannot accept that a man-like, cosmic magician just spoke the entire physical creation into existence six-thousand years ago as the Biblical story would have us believe. Neither can I take on the absurd account of an accidental emergence of the miracle of life over a period of many millions of years, according to Darwin's scientifically, sacrosanct theory of evolution.

It is far easier (at least from the perfection-now position) for me to speculate that the countless miracles that exist now, making up the living physical creation, have always existed somewhere in the vastness of the universe.

Why must we assume there had to be a beginning for a rose? It makes as much sense for me to think there has always been roses, as to think there has always been an x-factor, Creative Force or God, or the sun or sixteen-billion suns commingling together. But this is getting into a different subject which will be considered more thoroughly, later.

What I had in mind when I started this seed story is that no one can explain the everyday miracle of reproduction in either plants, animals or Homo sapiens. And while the mystical essence of falling in love and sexual ecstasy is practically incomprehensible when you attempt to account for its origin, out of either nothing at all or a molten mass of cosmic debris, there is no problem in recognizing that sex is here now, and has evidently prevailed in much the same form on this planet for more millions of years than anyone really knows.

For sure, our ancestors in the eternity of past ages managed their sexual activities a long time before the comparatively recent time of recorded history--secular or religious. The point I am getting at, is that it should be clear that mankind doesn't require a pseudo-religious, "word of God" manual on who, when, what and how you should control your sexual feelings and desires.

Almost everyone knows from personal experiences that a large measure of freedom is necessary for sexual satisfaction--as it is for nearly every other worthwhile, creative endeavor. But unnecessary religious meddling in sexual involvement has removed the essential freedom, and replaced it with degrading fear. Natural forces tend to bring two persons of the opposite sex together, while imperfection-based, religious fear and guilt complexities work insidiously to keep them apart.

Of course, fear has its perfection factor, too. But while a certain amount is necessary and therefore beneficial, more than is needed becomes toxic and destructive.

If you can establish to your own satisfaction (as I have) that there is no factual, basic imperfection existing in the universe, you can easily take on the corresponding fact that there is nothing imperfect prevailing about sex and sexual experiences. All sexual taboos concerning carnal lust, impure desires, adultery, illegitimacy, holy matrimony, prostitution and homosexuality, are manmade commandments and regulations. Certainly, <u>they are not God-made</u>.

I think it is important on this earth trip that the actual source of all regulations on human conduct be firmly established. But just because you may agree that sexual taboos are not made in heaven, <u>does not give anyone a sexual hunting privilege to abuse the delicate experience of male and female sexual togetherness</u>.

Even though the authentic source of laws (sexual and others) has been misrepresented as coming directly from God--your freedom in such areas does not imply that you are at liberty to fornicate promiscuously. God didn't write the ten commandments on tablets of stone with his fingernail (I'll attempt to establish that later in Volume II), so it is believable that the cosmic forces are not too concerned with stealing or fornicating on a soul-eternity, security basis.

But that does not make it all right to steal--no more than it makes it right to drive on the wrong side of the road--just because the nonphysical forces don't enter into such determinations. Like we said before, if you rob a bank, you might get shot or thrown in jail--no matter who makes the laws. And you might get into serious trouble engaging in questionable, sexual activities, when common sense should tell you to lay off.

I could be a little mistaken, but I believe that one aspect of sex actually may have saved my behind, or my life--or at least was a factor in helping me avoid serious trouble.

This episode happened on one of our ten-four, camp-out, work trips (ten days work and four days off). The Forest

Service was building a barb-wire, cattle fence on the New Mexico-Arizona border in the Warm Creek area. Fence construction is hard work on flat ground. In rough mountain country, it is very difficult.

On this trip, there was the usual arguing and bickering over a lot of things, such as how to keep a straight line going over hills and down into deep gullies. But you get accustomed to such hassles, and nearly everyone becomes too exhausted to worry over the many minor squabbles that take place.

On this project, there were four young fellows. And for a couple of them it was their first encounter with the serious business of making a living. Three older men, two of them about my age, plus myself made a crew of eight.

Frank, (I am using fictitious names for all these characters) who was the only real cook of the bunch, did the cooking, and I sort of helped him with breakfast. That meal was always the same; pancakes, bacon and eggs--as long as the bacon lasted--then it was just pancakes and eggs. You needed a good bed of coals to cook on a campfire, so someone had to get up early and get a substantial fire going so there would be plenty of coals available.

With the first light of dawn, I would usually be glad to crawl out of my hard pad on the ground and get on with this initial chore. I didn't mind doing it at all, and, as I said before, despite the discomforts and the tough labor, I really enjoyed the whole experience.

Knowing that I would have to have a good supply of fuel for the morning fire, every evening before it got dark, I would gather up a large pile of wood. It took quite a lot for our evening campfire, too. This work came at the end of the day. I was just as tired as the others, and as long as I went ahead with this chore, the young fellows would just sit around and talk, while I did the extra work.

Our first ten-four period wasn't too tough for getting wood because we camped in an oak brush area and there was an abundance of dry oak wood all around the camp. But on our second work period, we had to move camp, and the wood was not so available at the new location.

I finally got a little fed up with these lazy kids, and one morning after breakfast, I reminded them that they were not youngsters living at home any more, but were equal adults out in the big wide world--and how about a little help with the wood gathering? I said it didn't bother me to get up first, start the fire and make coffee for them, but getting all the wood in the evening was too much. I also added that it wouldn't hurt for one of them to get up early and start the fire, as well.

Mike, who was a little more tolerant of me than the others, said, "Hell Bob, I thought you really enjoyed doing what you do." The others didn't say anything, but I could see they were a little irked and embarrassed by my lecture. Nevertheless, they did cooperate better afterwards.

I can realize now, that it would have been more considerate of me to have casually asked one of them privately to get the others to do their share of the work.

Later, I learned there was some adverse reaction to my confronting them as I did. Mike and I had been cutting juniper fence post and packing them over to the fence right-of-way. We were sitting down under a big juniper tree for a rest, when Mike told me that Oliver was really upset with me. He had suggested that they all tie old Bob up, have a little fun with him and then roll him down the mountain a little.

My response to this seemed a little strange to me after I said it. I guess my mouth was still running ahead of my brain. Anyway, I said to Mike, "You tell Oliver and the rest of them, that I am a lot older than you guys are, and I have learned some things that you don't know anything about.

"And because of what I know, I am not afraid of the devil, of Jesus Christ, or even God Almighty, himself. I am not a bit worried about death or dying or being killed. And for damn sure, I am not afraid of any one of you young fellows, or all of you put together. What's more, I will coldcock anyone who is foolish enough to mess around with me. And I am enough of a mechanic to do it.

"What I mean by coldcocking is this. There is a sensitive nerve running from your brain that regulates the blood pressure going to your penis. I have made it my business to know where that nerve area is, and I'll give anyone that fools around with me a concussion on his head that will damage that nerve. So tell your friends they had better figure on doing a thorough job, because otherwise, I'll fix them so they will never get a hard-on again as long as they live."

I knew that those fellows were always talking about girls and making out. But it never occurred to me until many years later that those kids might have been conspiring to use my behind for a homosexual rape. At the time, I was more concerned about being rolled down the mountain like a rock. Actually, I didn't think too much about it. And I was quite surprised at myself for putting up such a bravado story.

I really don't know what I would have done under such circumstances. I doubt if anyone could ever know. Surely, those boys eventually figured I must have been conning them. Nevertheless, nothing of any consequence ever developed.

However, a couple of days later, I was working with Oliver installing steel posts. I had just placed one in position and Oliver had placed the heavy post-driver hammer over the top end. But before I had released my grip on the post, he let the driver come slamming down. Fortunately, my heavy work gloves protected my hand from the blow and, somehow, didn't get hung up on the rough stobs of the post.

There was a little verbal explosion on my part for his carelessness (if that's what it was). And Oliver bristled up some hard looks, but that's all that ever happened. No real harm was done. In a short time, I think the whole episode was forgotten by all concerned.

I don't suppose there is much difference in irritations occurring with men working on a difficult job in the forest, and men and women engaged in the complex business of holy matrimony. In either situation, it seems as though most of us flub our way through with little thought of another's feelings, or the consequences of our belligerent attitude. And most of us are fortunate we haven't ended up killing one another.

Of course, in the usual marriage debacle, the antagonists started out in the joint venture as happy lovers. But just what goes wrong when lovers soon turn into haters--while tranquility and sexual pleasure is exchanged for bitching and ass kicking?

When young people get married, it is almost inevitable that they will take on several, false assertions, accepted by our imperfection culture as being almost self-evident facts. The most tragic aspect is the antagonism emerging between men and women who once loved each other. The distressful situation of men and women blaming each other for their unhappiness is a common occurrence--sort of expected with two, allegedly imperfect people striving, without success in an assumed, imperfect world, to be everything that is desirable and good for each other.

Eventually, both partners attribute the complications they encounter to the almost expected male or female imperfections becoming evident in the cantankerous nature of their contentious mates. Finally, the original, in-love desire to please and serve each other has been replaced by an <u>obnoxious demand</u> that the inadequate mate fulfill his marital obligations--or else.... Under such threatening atmosphere, love has seemingly disappeared.

Believing the offending spouse should be corrected, minor deprivations are managed. Ultimately, a full-fledged program of condemning and punishing is put into operation.

The previous, tranquil pleasure of sex is reversed. No more sex for the imperfect, son of a bitch. Without love, making love turns into a pain in the ass.

And invariably, the only alternative is to start looking for another partner who will hopefully have less imperfections--especially in the love and sex departments.

The perfection-now concept, in itself, cannot make us happy. I have said before that we cannot depend on circumstances in order to have a sense of well-being, a satisfied feeling about ourselves and the world. I have made it clear that we can only find peace of mind and a good feeling about who and what we are from within our own being. And this is easier to accomplish if we can observe ourselves and the world--with all its complications--from the perfection-now position.

BUT HAPPINESS IS SOMETHING ELSE.

There is something missing in Homo sapiens--a sort-of incompleteness in either male or female makeup. This inherent, built-in lack can only be made complete when there is a joyful, coming together under favorable circumstances.

It is possible that the world-wide condoning of innate imperfection (nobody's perfect) is understandable when, in our aloneness--in our unhappiness--we feel this factual incompleteness. Though we may have found a mate, perhaps even experienced an "in love" adventure for a while, we still may have this incompleteness feeling--a definite knowing that we are not happy. In fact, we sometimes realize that life is hardly worth the effort to keep on living, because we are unhappy as hell!

Happiness between a man and a woman can hardly be forthcoming when there is an imbalance in many factors that is the source of daily irritations and conflict. The best philosophy is worthless, if someone is hurting you--perhaps punishing you--either physically or emotionally--because it is impossible to regulate your emotions and ideals according to their estimations of what is right or wrong, good or bad, correct or incorrect.

In such situations, there is certainly an incompleteness in our aloneness, because loving and togetherness cannot function properly, regardless of how devoted we are. <u>This factual, unhappy incompleteness could easily be thought of as an imperfection flaw in humanity.</u>

<u>BUT THERE IS NOTHING IMPERFECT ABOUT THE WHOLE UNHAPPINESS SYNDROME.</u>

There is a good reason in back of every irritation and uncomfortable feeling we endure. And unhappiness is no exception to that principle. The discomfort from any adversity is there to turn us away from whatever is causing the trouble.

Improper circumstances, continuing beyond endurance, are the causes of unhappiness. Happiness is just not there and, likely, will never be there, unless the conditions causing the incompleteness changes--allowing the imbalance to be reversed, where love can once again be given and returned.

Sex alone can never be enough to provide happiness. We are all capable of loving. But love cannot function unless it is accepted and given back, thus completing the love-happiness circuit.

If we are involved in one of these loveless, inadequate, togetherness dilemmas, and we are being abused in various ways, it is natural that we sometimes wonder if we are somehow responsible for the trouble that seems impossible to resolve. It is easy to blame ourselves, thinking we haven't loved enough, haven't tried hard enough or haven't been good enough.

But finally, you realize that you cannot love when the goodness and love on your part is not even recognized or returned. You cannot love someone if you cannot admire them. If their performance continually falls below what you have a right to expect, they have put themselves outside of your capacity to love.

Ultimate physical happiness can only be realized when you are giving out your love, and having it given back to you in equal measure. There is no question but that a full measure of love awareness between two persons creates a joyful atmosphere of exceptional delight. And it is equally true that such a happy condition can never be ordered into manifestation, or held on to by contrivance or manipulation.

Love and sex can only be experienced satisfactorily on love and sex's own terms--which are in essence, no terms or conditions that can be directed unlovingly by us. We can only go with love. We cannot insist that love should function according to some erroneous concept of an imperfect existence.

Adding to the love-sex, marital debacle, is the ridiculous assumption of the superior and dominate position of the human male. This also implies a somewhat less imperfect nature for the man of the family. Easily seeing through this male-contrived delusion, women have put up with, but never condoned, this asinine presumption of the typical, male chauvinistic attitude.

But the gullible men need not be condemned because of their credulous acceptance of this particular, superior, head-of-the-house attitude. Getting hooked on to this supposition is understandable when you consider the myths and fables that have been part of our imperfection culture for thousands of years.

For instance, in Western religionism, God is pictured as a heavenly Father, having, and coexisting eternally with a heavenly Son. In addition, there is a third member of the Godhead--the Holy Ghost, also claimed to be of the male gender. In the early records, no mention is ever made of a heavenly Mother or Daughter.

It was as late as the fifth century that the Mother of Christ was given the title of Holy Mother of God. And I think this clever introduction of a female into the deified hierarchy has been one of the principal reasons for the phenomenal development and expansion of the Roman Catholic Church ever since.

In the Biblical fabrication of the story of creation, the first woman was, allegedly, created as an afterthought. God had created the animals, birds and fish, and established a man in the Garden of Eden. Adam was living there all by himself and had given names to all the birds and animals. The contrived record makes it clear that Eve was created especially to be a helper for the man. And as she was formed from Adam's rib, the implication was that the man was to rule over her.

The first female also bears the stigma of eating the forbidden fruit, and then nagging her husband so that he ate the fruit, too. And this alleged, cock and bull episode is supposed to be the cause of the fall of man, and the damnation of the whole physical creation. Such an indictment inflicted upon the women by the men of the world, is hardly a proper foundation for loving togetherness.

Under the Mosaic Law, women's position was not too secure, and certainly not one to insure a happy, continued life of marital bliss. If God had communicated with a man, he was respected as a prophet. But when a woman claimed that she had intimate contact with the powers above, she was often thought to be a witch, a servant of the devil, and condemned to a horrible death.

And even today, women in some ways are still looked upon as second class citizens. Their partial emancipation has only lately been managed during this tumultuous twentieth century. In some countries, women are still sold as servants and slaves. A man buys a wife for so many cows, and thinks of her as something he bought at the supermarket.

In our modern marriage ceremony, the father symbolically hands over the custody of his daughter to the bridegroom. And to some extent, she becomes his legal property. Her former name is relinquished, and the female creature is sort of branded with the name of her new master.

But women have always responded to the unjust, deified deceit with some equalizing, feminine intrigue of their own devising. Ancient and contemporary man, flubbing through the imperfection, love and sex game, has always found woman's intuitive thinking incomprehensible to their own, distorted understanding of reality--and, especially, feminine reality. And when the humble females can't take any more of their master's superior attitude, they invariably tell him to go to hell, and what to do when he gets there.

Attempting to win a victory for one side or the other in the male-female battle is utterly futile. For neither the man nor the woman will ever be liberated from the asinine complications of imperfection-oriented, sexual incompatibility, until, as individuals, they discover the beautiful truth of absolute cosmic equality for all existence.

And I firmly believe the perfection-now position will be helpful for all lovers in their search for meaningful understanding in the exciting love, hate and sex package.

THE END